EASTERN GERMANY
with Berlin

by Charles A. Leocha

WORLD-LEISURE CORPORATION
Hampstead, NH   Boston, MA

Send mail to:
World-Leisure Corporation
P.O. Box 160
Hampstead, NH 03841

Cover design by Jutta Gork,
R&R Communications, GmbH, Leimen, Germany.
Cover photos: upper row left to right—Meißen, student, Moritzburg all
courtesy Saxony State Tourist Board, lower row left to right—Rathaus,
Eisenach by Greg Ballinger; view of Elbe from Königstein and
Cecilienhof in Potsdam by Charles Leocha.
Maps in history section are modified from *Germany: A Short History* by
Donald S. Detwiler, Southern Illinois University Press.

Printed in the United States of America
by BookCrafters, Fredericksburg, VA tel. (703) 371-3800

Distributed to the trade in USA and Canada by
The Talman Company, 131 Spring Street, Suite 201E-N,
New York, NY 10012 tel. (212) 431-7175 or (800) 537-8894.

Distributed to the trade in Europe by Roger Lascelles,
47 York Road, Brentford, Middlesex TW8 0QP Tel. 081-847 0935.

Distributed to U.S. Military, Stars & Stripes Bookstores,
Mail Order and Special Sales by
World Leisure Corporation, 177 Paris Street, Boston, MA 02128
Tel. (617) 569-1966, fax (617) 561-7654

ISBN: 0-915009-20-X

EASTERN GERMANY

with Berlin

Rügen

• Binz

Stralsund
• Rostock
Greifswald •

•Güstrow

• Schwerin

Western
Germany

• Gransee

Poland

Brandenburg •

• Berlin

• Magdeburg   Potsdam

•Spreewald

• Wernigerode Wittenburg •

• Quedlinburg

• Leipzig

Meißen

Eisenach Erfurt

•   •   • Weimar

• Gotha

• Dresden •

• Meiningen

Czechoslovakia

Contents

Thanks to James Thompson whose esoteric knowledge and excellent editing made this guidebook as understandable as possible and whose researching and writing efforts can be seen in the history and personality sections of this book. Thank you to KLM Royal Dutch Airlines for helping to get me across the Atlantic to Eastern Germany and Auto Europe for providing an automobile during my research efforts.

I also owe deep gratitude to my Mom and Dad, Sam and Adelaide Leocha, who always encouraged my travels and who always provide shelter from the storms of a freelance Zorbaesque life.   CL

Preface

Welcome to my guide to Eastern Germany. I say "my guide" because it is personal. I've filled these pages with my observations about travels through Eastern Germany, my conversations with locals trying to deal with the radical changes in their lives, an overview of German history, and city-by-city descriptions of the best sights to see in Eastern Germany, their stories and legends. In short, after nearly three decades of travelling through Europe and much of the world, this is the type of guidebook I wish I'd had for every country.

Planning this trip to Eastern Germany was an adventure—I was astounded at the lack of information about travel through this section of Germany, which for so many years was nothing to me but a blank, with an island called West Berlin, on a map of Germany.

The German National Tourist Office in New York has helped me gather information in the past . . . they confessed to knowing very little about their "new states." I grilled my friends in Western Germany about what it was like in the "East" . . . they also shrugged their shoulders and only could repeat rumors such as, "They have 100 mile-an-hour cars and 50 mile-an-hour roads. Be careful." Or "Don't take anything valuable—the Easterners will steal it." Or, "It's a disaster, no one has an indoor toilet."

Once I had ventured across the formerly forbidden border, traveling through the countryside was even more of an adventure. Every rumor I had heard was untrue. Every day I was on a frontier. I was amazed at the wealth of culture, at the monumental palaces. Every day I heard from locals about the changes being foisted upon them and heard a rekindling of "Eastern pride." Every day someone told me that I was the first American they had ever met. Every night I slept with an East German family and heard about how they used to live, how they hope to live, and how they are coming to grips with the reality of capitalism and the realization that they may have done much wrong in the past but that they had also created much that was good.

For those of you who have a working knowledge of German, a trip through these new Federal states will be a joy and an experience that can never be quite repeated: Eastern Germany is changing too rapidly. A trip this summer will be much different from my trip in late 1992. This is a part of the world where history is unfolding, not in its normal pattern of decades and centuries, but in a fast forward mode where today's reality will be tomorrow's past. Here, The Times They Are A-Changin' at 78 rpm, even though they were recorded on a 45.

Without some command of German, you will find getting around somewhat more difficult than in Western Germany, where everyone speaks English more or less. But you will be able to enjoy a world of architecture, art, history and nature that was closed for four decades. Eastern Germany is the real treasure vault of German history and art. It forms a true cultural core of Germany.

How to approach Eastern Germany

Don't let little inconveniences such as few English speakers, changing street names, traffic jams, relatively few hotels and restaurants, limited gas stations, or tricky telephones put you off. Travel here is as rewarding as anyone can find in Europe.

This book is organized in the order that major cities might be reached on a trip generally winding from Frankfurt through Weimar, Leipzig, Dresden, Berlin, and then north to the Baltic through the Mecklenburg Lakes District.

I feel the best way to explore Eastern Germany is by car. Once you find a place and room you enjoy, you can stay there and take day trips to nearby towns and villages. My favorite towns in the southern part of Eastern Germany for use as hubs were Weimar and Dresden.

Weimar can serve as a hub for visiting Erfurt, Eisenach, the Wartburg, and the entire Thüringerwald (Thuringia Forest) area with its majestic castles. Dresden is the perfect base for visiting the land of the Sorbs, the Elbe Valley with its fascinating natural formations and fortifications, and Meißen and surrounding palaces.

Berlin is a must, but try to stay, as I did, just outside the city. You'll appreciate the contrast of the modern city with the relatively rural suburbs, once patrolled 24 hours a day. And in the north take your time and wander along the Baltic coast.

Naturally, if you plan in advance, you can visit this region of Germany, stay in modern hotels and take tours to visit the "sights." My own taste would find this a bit sterile—I hope you dive into Eastern Germany and experience the thrill of upheaval and get a feeling for the failures of the past and the people's hope for the future.

How to use this book

I have taken the liberty of interspersing my own observations throughout. There are passages about my discussions with people along every stage of my trip. I recount stories they told me about living under the Communist regime and their problems with the current government.

Together with what amounts to my personal journal, I have included basics needed to make one's way through Eastern Germany—driving, finding rooms, meeting locals, testing family-run *Gaststätten*, enjoying regional beer, buying gas—basics that are sufficiently different from Western Germany to warrant special mention.

The Tourist Office List at the end of the book, with phone numbers and many fax numbers of local tourist offices and room reservation agencies (*Zimmer-vermittlungen*), is invaluable as you travel through this country and plan your journey.

I have also included detailed descriptions of Eastern Germany's major cities, art treasures and historic sights. There are maps of downtown areas. For many of the major palaces and museums, I have attempted to mention the most important pieces of art to search out, and where possible I have included room-by-room walks where the guides only speak German.

As background, you will also find a synopsis of German history designed to bring these monuments and museums into some historical perspective, and a chapter with capsule biographies of some of the Germans whose names you will encounter most often.

Getting To
Eastern Germany

If you are planning your own vacation, your first step is to get across the Atlantic. This is simple enough, but transatlantic air travel is where the clever traveller can save money and an unwary sojourner can end up spending more than necessary.

A travel agent can help out with the specifics, but if you are a do-it-yourselfer, remember that there are tradeoffs between cost and convenience while doing your homework for the best deal.

The main airport in Eastern Germany, served by virtually every major airline, is Berlin. Several American carriers fly directly to Berlin from U.S. cities. Almost every European airline can get you there as well, with a change of plane in their hub. For example KLM, though not touting direct USA-Berlin service, connects more than a dozen North American cities with Berlin, requiring only one stop in Amsterdam, one of the friendliest and easiest-to-transfer airports in the world. Other carriers provide the same convenient service.

If you aren't planning on flying directly to Berlin, there are plenty of other options, both in the air and on the ground. Airports at Leipzig and Dresden have limited international connections. You can also drive across the former border on the Autobahn without even noticing that it was there. Or take the small back roads and look carefully for the remains of the fortifications. Trains zip between the German cities, lacing the country together, and ferries connect former East Germany with Denmark and Sweden. (The next chapter details getting around Eastern Germany once you are on the ground.)

There are no special visas required and no border checks other than the initial control when you enter the European Community. NOTE: If you are entering Germany from Poland or Czechoslovakia be prepared for a long wait—delays at border crossings from these countries can take hours.

Getting across the Atlantic

Transatlantic airfares have been at all-time lows for several years. There is more capacity and more service from almost every area of the U. S., which makes getting to Europe more convenient and less expensive than ever.

A travel agent can be extremely helpful during this phase, but supplement this information by doing some investigating on your own. Airline fare structures are complicated and seemingly change daily—even with scheduled airlines. And when charters and group tour flights are included, the options can become phenomenally complex.

Tell the travel agent exactly what you are looking for and explain what you think you should have to pay, based on ads in papers, magazines and brochures you have read. The agent will either confirm your opinions or let you know what changed since your last information. Try to find an agent who will guarantee the lowest possible fare.

These agents often will let you know exactly what is available and you can then make a decision, even if it's to take a more expensive flight based on convenience or better connections. There is no additional cost for using a travel agent; you can only save both time and money by working through a good one.

You have several choices for transatlantic air travel:

Scheduled airlines — There are many advantages in taking a regularly scheduled airline. One is that it must adhere to its schedule: if there is a problem with the aircraft, passengers are normally transferred to a flight on another airline. In emergencies, a scheduled airline offers flexibility with additional flights and interline connections.

Another aspect of the flexibility offered by scheduled airlines is the option of landing in one city and leaving from another. Called "Open Jaw" in travel jargon, this

type of ticket might allow you to land in Munich or Frankfurt, travel through Eastern Germany, and then fly home from Hamburg or Berlin. You can arrange limited stopovers for an additional charge, depending on your ticket, making it easy to squeeze in a few days in Amsterdam, Paris or London either on your way to Germany or on the return trip.

It helps to plan your trip as far in advance as possible. You may have to book—and pay—in advance by as much as a month to get special fares that approach the lowest charter prices. Arrival and departure dates must be set in advance and any changes may result in added charges.

Ticket Consolidators — You may have heard of these money-saving sales offices. They sell discounted tickets, normally about the same as advance purchase fares. It is almost the best of all possible worlds and can be fine if everything goes exactly according to plan.

*But . . .*these tickets have restrictions you won't have with tickets bought through regular travel agents or the airlines. Unlike normal tickets, consolidator tickets may not be switched to another carrier in the event of a delay, cancellation, or mechanical problem. Plus, if you cancel your trip or have to buy a different ticket, the airline is not responsible for refunds—you must go back to the consolidator to get your money refunded.

Many agents work closely with these operators. For another source, check in your library for recent issues of *Consumer Reports Travel Newsletter*, which may have ratings and listings of reputable consolidators.

Charter flights — These flights are money-savers and in some cases offer excellent connections to Germany. There are some problems with charters, though. Even when everything goes perfectly, you are virtually guaranteed being on a packed and uncomfortable flight . . . forget dreams of an empty seat next to you. Often you are only guaranteed the *flight date* rather than a time. The charters also reserve the right to reschedule your flight, cancel it, and add fuel charges. These possibilities all have happened to me in my decades of traveling. Fly with a charter airline that has been in business for some time, one with which your travel agent is familiar.

Try to get some form of flight cancellation insurance, in case you don't leave on the date requested, and get additional medical insurance to cover the cost of an emergency trip home in case of an accident.

With so many competition-driven deals and the development of good-quality consolidators, I suggest you stick to scheduled airlines in one form or another.

Courier Flights — If you are more interested in transatlantic travel on the cheap than in exploring Europe, courier flights can be a bargain. But for serious travelers these aren't a great deal. You can only travel with carry-on luggage; you are only allowed to stay for a few days in Europe; and most flights begin and end in New York, which significantly reduces your flexibility. The money you save isn't worth the restrictions and hassles. If you are curious about this way to get to Europe, you can pick up a copy of *The Air Courier's Handbook*, which includes a list of reputable courier companies, or pick up a copy of

Let's Go, which also mentions several. Another book recommended by the *Consumer Reports Travel Letter* is *The Insiders Guide to Air Courier Bargains,* by Kelly Monaghan, Inwood Training Publications, NY, $14.95.

Dealing with jet lag

The most unwelcome travelling companion on an overseas vacation is jet lag. While there are no cures, following these time-tested suggestions may help ease you into the European time zone.

• Go to bed early and wake up early for three or four days before your flight. This will allow your body to get a gradual head start in adjusting to European time. At 9 p.m. on the U.S. East Coast, it is 3 a.m. in Western Europe—if you can go to bed around 9 or 10 p.m. for a few days before your trip, you will only have to overcome about three hours of jet lag rather than six.

• Try to sleep as much as possible on the plane. Many people take sleep aids and ask flight attendants not to disturb them for meals or drinks. If you have a sleep mask, use it, and cover up with the blanket stowed in the overhead: this helps conserve your body heat and energy.

• Drink as little alcohol and eat as little as possible during the flight; drink plenty of water or non-alcoholic beverages, however, because the cabin air is very dry.

• When you arrive in Europe, take about a two-hour nap in the afternoon or early evening. Make sure to get yourself up, then go out and explore the town, returning to sleep at about 11 p.m. or midnight.

Visas and Customs

North American passport holders do not need a visa for visits of three months or less. There is no limit on the amount of foreign currency one may take into Germany. You may take in no more than 400 cigarettes (200 cigarillos or 100 cigars or 500 grams of tobacco); one liter of spirits; and 2.5 ounces of perfume.

Getting Around Eastern Germany

There are many ways to plan your travel through Eastern Germany. I recommend touring by car, which normally means renting. The costs, especially with two or more sharing, work out about the same as taking the train, and you have much greater freedom for exploration. A car also frees you from the hassles and limitations of scheduled transport, making your trip even more of an experience of unfettered discovery.

Forget those horror stories about cobblestone-paved highways and miserable roads in Eastern Germany. The rebuilding of the road system has been one of the first success stories of reunification. Nearly every road in Eastern Germany has been repaved, widened, or otherwise improved in the past year and a half. Even the Autobahns, which once were limited to speeds of 100 kph (62 mph) have been resurfaced and now have no speed limits, just as in Western Germany.

You will still find plenty of construction and many delays, but for the most part the older roads have been sufficiently repaired to make motoring a pleasure rather than a penance. Two of the most important signs you will encounter are the "Road Closed" sign, a simple red circle around a white center, and the "Priority Road" sign, a yellow diamond with black border (this means you are on the main road and have the right of way). Attention to these will help get you through the improvements, especially in city centers.

For those of you who would rather take the train or ride a bicycle through the countryside, see below.

The German Autobahn

Avid drivers will probably agree with the Germans that there's an untamed beauty to the last driving frontier; however, initiation can be challenging. That the Autobahn is slightly different from any other highway you've ever driven becomes obvious when just about everyone passes you at speeds best described as breathtaking.

If you are not being passed, it's a good idea to check the rear-view mirror to see if someone is glued to your rear bumper, flashing his lights and working his blinker. This is Autobahn code for "Get out of the way, I'm coming through."

Germans take driving seriously. It's not surprising that having no speed limits on the main highways also fosters production of such motoring standards as Mercedes, BMW, Porsche, Audi and Volkswagen. The whole country seems to be a test track.

Coping at 100-plus mph

Stay in the right lane and use the left only for passing. Blinkers are *always* used for lane changes; things happen fast at 100-plus mph, and there is no room for surprises and no time for second chances. Seat belts are required in Germany and failure to use them normally results in forfeiture of any insurance claim in the event of an accident.

Autobahn signs

Entrances to Autobahns are marked *Einfahrt*; exits, *Ausfahrt*. It is important to know the major cities along the route to your destination, as these are shown on signs along with the number or letter designation of the Autobahn. Autobahn signs are blue.

Automobile clubs

These organizations offer emergency road repair service regardless of whether you are a member, though you will have to pay for parts or gas if you are stranded on the road. Germany's ADAC (Allgemeiner Deutscher Automobil Club) patrols the major highways from 8 a.m. to 7 p.m., or you can call from roadside phones at any hour for assistance (*Strassenwachthilfe*). From a pay phone call 110 (police and emergency service).

The address of the ADAC is 70 Am Westpark 8, W-8000 Munich (tel. 089-76760). The AvD (Automobil Club von Deutschland) is in a Frankfurt suburb at Lyonerstrasse 16, D-6000 Frankfurt-Neiderrad (tel. 069-660306).

Right of way

American drivers seem to have more problems with questions of right of way than any other road situation in Germany. If you are ever unsure, remember that on a non-priority road you must always yield to the vehicle coming from your right (priority roads are marked by yellow diamond signs), and that pedestrians have right of way. Also, keep in mind that on any road in any country, *common sense* dictates yielding to a streetcar—or indeed to any vehicle much larger than yours.

Buying gas

We are used to finding a gas station, it seems, on every other corner . . . not so in Eastern Germany. Gas stations are few and far between. They are so limited that many of the older maps created during the Communist regime had gas stations marked in the city. For instance, Dresden, with a population of half a million, has only about a dozen gas stations.

The rule here is to plan ahead. Don't wait until you are almost empty to start looking for a station. Keep that gauge hovering between full and half-full.

One other note: Few if any gas stations in Eastern Germany, as of Autumn '92, accepted credit cards, so keep a little extra cash handy. Figure a gallon at about DM4.

Car rental

For the independent traveller who wants to get the most out of his trip to Eastern Germany, a rental car offers the most flexibility and is a bargain—especially when you share expenses. Rental cars can be picked up directly at the airport upon arrival in Europe. A rental car gives you the freedom to explore the surrounding area or take side trips.

When you pick up your car in Germany, check to see whether there are restrictions on taking it into Poland, Czechoslovakia or Romania. Many rental companies restrict their cars from these countries at present, owing to problems with massive theft and insurance fraud.

What license do you need?

The driver of the car usually must be at least 21 years old and must have a valid driver's license that has been in effect for at least one year. It is not necessary to have an International Driving Permit when driving in Europe—your home state license is acceptable—but it is a good idea. The AAA issues them, and they are good for a year. Fill out an application and give them two passport-type portrait snapshots. By mail, start the process a month before your departure. If you live near an AAA office, you can accomplish the entire process, including photos, there in less than an hour. International Driving Permits cost $20 ($17 if you are a member). Call AAA for details and the location for the nearest office issuing International Permits at (800) AAA-HELP. Remember, even with the International Permit you will *still* need your U.S. state license as well. Canadians can call (800) 336-HELP for information on the nearest location to pick up an international license.

NOTE: In Germany you need to have what is called a Green Card (*carte verte*) for insurance. This is provided by rental companies, but it is best to make a quick check of the documents when you pick up your car.

Getting the best rates

If you make reservations two to seven days in advance of your arrival with any of the major car rental companies, you will qualify for special European vacation rates. These rates normally run about $200-$250 a week, excluding taxes.

(If you're comparing car rentals to possible train travel, this will mean that each person will pay about $400 for a full month's automobile use—plus gasoline, which even in an extreme case shouldn't run more than an $200 apiece.)

The only requirement for this rate is that you keep the car for at least five days. If you return it before that, you will be charged at the daily rate, which often can cost more than keeping the car the entire week.

While all car rental companies may offer reasonable rates throughout the year for tourism, only Auto Europe (800-223-5555) guarantees that they will find the lowest rate. Auto Europe also can organize camper van rentals, handicap vehicles and chauffeur services in Germany.

Value added taxes (VAT)

Depending on where you pick up the car, you will have to pay an additional value-added tax (VAT), which is significant. Current VAT in Germany is 14 percent

Many travelers compare VATs when deciding where to rent their automobile. If you are searching for the best bargain, remember that different cars are less expensive in different countries. For example, while a Ford Escort is less expensive in Germany than in Switzerland by $40 including taxes and insurance, a VW Minibus will cost you $46 more if you rent it in Germany instead of Switzerland. The best bargains on rental cars in Europe can normally be found in Germany, even after all taxes.

Drop-off charges

Generally, there are no drop-off charges if a rental car is returned in the country where it was picked up. Some rental companies will allow rental cars to be dropped off in other countries for no drop-off charge if the rental is for at least 21 days. There are some companies that will allow one-way rentals, but only to a limited group of cities. Your best bet is to ask whether your case falls into one of these special categories and if not, pick up and drop off in the same country.

Collision damage waiver/insurance

If you rent your car with a credit card which provides collision damage waiver (CDW) you have adequate protection. American Express, MasterCard Gold and Business, and VISA Gold and Business all provide this coverage automatically as long as you decline the CDW option on the rental contract.

This credit card coverage only covers the card holder and not additional drivers. Read the fine print. Some credit card companies do not cover your car if you were driving on a dirt road or in the case of hit and run accidents, etc. Check also to see whether this is primary or secondary coverage. Primary coverages is what you want. Secondary coverage only comes into play after your own insurance company pays for damages . . . then the credit card company pays the difference.

In the US, most insurance collision coverage applies to rental cars as well to your own automobile, however in Europe most American coverage is not valid. You should have some form of collision damage insurance. According to Auto Europe the normal rental contract deductibles in Europe range from $2,000 to $5,000. Even with your credit card coverage, your rental car company may demand a security deposit to cover the deductible until everything is settled. You must, in most cases, settle with your credit card company and then reimburse the rental company.

Rental car operators highly recommend the purchase of CDW. It makes your life easier in the event of an accident for an average cost of about $11 a day. If you can handle the hassles of handling some of your own accident paperwork during the settlement, credit card companies allow you to save money.

Special airline car rental deals

Airlines often offer reduced price cars or "free" cars with many promotions to Europe. You may be able to take advantage of them.

• You normally must travel with another for the deal.

• Your deal is only for one week, or three days in most cases, and then you begin paying the regular rates—either weekly or daily. These may be high enough to wipe out the original savings if you remain in Europe for a week or two.

• You will have to pay the insurance, taxes, gasoline, and any drop-off charges in most cases.

Current rental car prices (as of June '92)

We called Auto Europe, which has locations throughout Europe. Prices for a two-door Ford Escort for one week, including taxes and full CDW in Germany, was $276. If you wanted to rent without CDW and use one of the credit cards which includes collision coverage, or use your own insurance, the cost would have been $169 plus 14 percent value added tax, bringing the total to about $193.

A larger car such as a four-door VW Passat would cost $355 a week with full collision coverage and taxes, or $196 plus 14 percent VAT. A VW Minibus would cost $692 with full insurance and taxes, or $467 plus 14 percent VAT, about $533 a week without insurance.

Renting a camper or motorhome

This is one of the best ways to discover a country, and Eastern Germany has plenty of campsites through the countryside. These campsites are not as luxurious as those found in the Western section of Germany, but they do provide the bare basics, normally with cold water and occasionally with electricity, but you'd better come prepared to do without outside electric power.

There are so many facets to camping and motorhoming through this area that it is best to just recommend another book, *Europe by Van and Motorhome*, by David Shore and Patty Campbell, $13.95 in U.S.; $15.95 in Canada. It lists a dozen rental agents as well as more than a score of national offices. The book also provides tips on buying motorhomes, plus plenty of suggestions on making your trip easier and the basics of camping in Europe.

Wen you arrive in Europe pick up a copy of the current camping guide, *Europa Camping*, which lists virtually every campsite in Europe and a short description of the facilities and their phone numbers. *Europa Camping* can be easily found in Europe or may be purchased in the U.S. from Recreational Equipment Inc. (REI), PO Box C-88126, Seattle, WA 98188 (tel. 800-426-4840). *AA Camping and Caravaning Guide*, published by the British Automobile Association, can be found in many AAA bookstores here.

Taking the train

You may have heard that Germany's railway system (*Deutsche Bundesbahn* or DB) is one of the best in the world. This is only half true: while Western Germany has rail transport second to none, the much more primitive Eastern system is still saddled with slower trains, a smaller track network and limited computer reservations. These shortcomings are being worked on by the Bundesbahn, with much of the computerization scheduled for completion in 1993.

InterCity trains, the main fast trains between major cities, now connect all of Germany, and this is a relatively seamless network.

The other types of trains in the German system have letter designations, shown on the train schedules. These are very important for travelers: here they are in order, from the slowest trains to the fastest. Commuter trains are marked CB (*City-Bahn*) or N (*Nahverkehrszug*). The S-Bahn, found in many large German cities, is part of this local network, but offers fast, efficient transportation within major metropolitan areas. Local trains are designated by D (*Direct*). E designates *Eilzug*, or fast train. The InterCity trains require an additional fare called a

Zuschlag , which must be purchased at the station for DM6 or on board for DM7.

When looking at the train schedules in stations, note that *Abfahrt* (normally on yellow paper) means departures, *Ankunft* (normally on white paper) is arrivals, and *Gleis* means track. When making seat or couchette reservations note that *Raucher* means Smoking and *Nichtraucher* Non-smoking.

Rail Passes

If your trip is taking you beyond Germany, look into buying a Eurailpass before striking out on your journey. These passes are good on the rail systems of 17 European countries. They can be used in Germany, France, Holland, Belgium, Luxembourg, Ireland, Italy, Switzerland, Liechtenstein, Spain, Portugal, Denmark, Sweden, Norway, Austria, Greece and Hungary. You can, contrary to popular belief, buy a Eurailpass at many large stations in Europe, but it is much easier to handle the purchase before you travel.

The Eurailpass is good for discounts on many ferry lines, and lets you ride the S-Bahn in German cities as well as the DB buses. *Eurailpasses are not good on the U-Bahn—if you get caught on the U-Bahn without a ticket it can mean a DM50+ fine levied immediately on the spot, no questions asked, no amount of whining tolerated.*

As soon as you validate your ticket detach the stub and stash it away with your travelers cheque numbers. If you lose your Eurailpass this stub will allow you to get a replacement pass for only a $5 fee.

The 1992 rates for Eurailpasses: $430 for 15 days; $550 for 21 days; $680 for one month; $920 for two months; and $1,150 for three months.

Eurailpass also offers many variations. If you are planning to travel with a companion between October 1, 1992 and March 31, 1993 a Saverpass is available for 15 days of travel for $340. Those under 26 years of age qualify for a second-class Eurail Youthpass good for one month ($470) or two months ($640) of second-class rail travel. The Eurail Flexipass allows unlimited first-class travel for five non-consecutive days during a 15-day period ($280), nine days out of a 21-day period ($450) or 14 days out of a month ($610). Children under 12 pay half-fare. Other reductions are available for groups of three or more traveling together. Ask for all the options when you have decided how many will be in your entourage.

Eurailpass has also teamed up with car rentals and offers a EurailDrive Pass which combines the Flexipass (4 of 21 days of unlimited train travel) with three days of unlimited mileage car rental. Prices vary with different classes of auto and numbers of travelers sharing the car. Prices, for example, range from $538 for two sharing an economy car to $618 for two sharing a medium car.

German Railpass

Germany has its own railpass, similar to Eurailpass but limited to travel within Germany's borders. Five days costs $240 first class, $160 second class; ten days, $360 first class, $240 second class; 15 days, $450 first class, $300 second class.

If you are traveling with a partner the additional companion fare is: Five days $184 first class, $128 second class; ten days, $288 first class, $192 second class; 15 days, $360 first class, $240 second class.

Travelers under 26 can purchase a Junior Pass good only in second class costing $110 for 5 days; $145 for ten days; or $180 for 15 days.

If you are under 23, or a student under 27, you may purchase a Trampers-Monats Ticket for one month of unlimited second-class travel on the German Rail network and on the DB buses.

Children under 4 travel free, those 4-12 pay half fare.

A Junior Pass (DM110) is available for those 18 to 22 as well as students under 27. A Senior-Pass for travelers over 60 is also available for DM110. Both these passes are good for an entire year and provide a 50 percent discount on all rail tickets. (Seniors can purchase a less expensive pass for DM75, good for 50-percent fares only Monday through Thursday and on Saturday.) Younger children 12 to 17 get the same deal with a Taschengeld-Pass for DM40, and families (parents, up to three children—17 and under—and married couples) traveling together can get similar discounts with the Familien-Pass for DM130. These are good deals and can be purchased in Germany at any train station; they require a small ID photo.

GermanRail authorized travel companies in the U.S. and Canada sell some German Railpasses and Eurailpasses in person and by mail. Their services vary. Headquarters is in New York at 122 e. 42nd St., Suite 1904, New York, NY 10168 (tel. 212-922-1616, 800-421-2929, fax 212-922-1868). Other offices are Atlanta, 3400 Peachtree Rd. NE, Atlanta, GA 30326 (tel. 404-266-9555, fax 404-264-0424); Boston, 20 Park Plaza, Boston, MA 02116 (tel. 617-542-0577, fax 617-451-0828); Dallas, 222 W. Las Colinas, Irving, TX 75039 (tel. 214-402-8004, fax 214-402-8007); Chicago, 9575 Higgins Road, Rosemont, IL 60018 (tel. 709-692-4209, fax 709-692-4506); Los Angeles, 11933 Wilshire Blvd. Los Angeles, CA 90025 (tel. 310-479-2772, fax 310-479-2239); Toronto, 904 The East Mall, Etobicoke, Ontario M9B 6K2 (tel. 416-695-1211).

Sleeping on the train

Within Germany, it is hard to imagine anyone needing to spend the night on the train unless they were going from Munich to Warnemünde overnight, but you may be heading elsewhere and be making a decision about whether to sleep on the train. Normally, German trains offer pull-out seats which can be used to sleep (more or less). But try to reserve a couchette. These bunkbed four- to six-person sleeping compartments have their own sheets, and on overnight trips the conductor takes care of ticket control and so forth, leaving you to a good night's sleep. Couchettes are amazingly inexpensive, providing a restful night for only about $22.

NOTE: Germany doesn't have the theft problems encountered in many southern European countries, but to be on the safe side make sure to lock your compartment door when you nod off.

Basic Train Phrases

Auskunft - (sometimes Information or just "I") travel information

Fundbüro - (sometimes written as **Fundamt**) lost and found office

Geldwechsel - Currency exchange

Gepäck-Aufbewahrung - baggage storage or deposit
Schliessfächer - coin operated baggage lockers
Toiletten (sometimes **WC**) - bathrooms. "**H**" stands for
   Herren: Men. "**D**" stands for Damen: **Women**.
Wartesaal or **Warteraum** - waiting room

Traveling by bike

More and more folk are choosing bicycles as an alternative means of transport through Europe. If you are planning a European trip of this kind, pick up a copy of *Europe By Bike*, by Karen and Terry Whitehill, published by The Mountaineers, Seattle, WA ($10.95). This book does not cover travel in Eastern Germany, but its introduction on preparing for your trip is important.

• Buy panniers (bags that strap to your bike). Fastening a backpack to a bike is a sure path to trouble.

• No matter what the sales material claims, panniers probably won't prove waterproof in a downpour, so line them with plastic bags.

• Follow all traffic rules. In Germany you must stop for lights, at crosswalks . . . bike as if you were driving a car. You have all the same right-of-way rules and must obey traffic rules. NOTE: Police here give out tickets to bicyclists as often as they do to motorists.

• Airlines in most cases will consider a bike a second piece of luggage. Box your bike to get across the Atlantic. (Some airlines charge $50 or so for bikes. Check before getting to the airport to eliminate surprises.)

• You can combine bikes with train travel. Bikes may be brought on trains with *Gepäckwagen* (noted by a small bike on the schedule). If there is no such baggage car, ship your bike two days in advance for a small fee. Pick up a copy of a GermanRail brochure, *Fahrrad am Bahnhof*, where you can get local bike trails and a list of stations which rents bikes. GermanRail also has special bike/train discount programs.

Accommodations

Overall, Germany has one of the highest standards for hotels, pensions, *Gasthäuser*, bed & breakfasts, and private rooms in the world. Eastern Germany, however, has one of the most limited lodging systems in Europe.

The shortage of hotels

Other guidebooks may list a selection of a half-dozen or so hotels in a city such as Dresden, much as they do for cities in the West such as Stuttgart, Munich or Hamburg. What they don't tell you is that the hotels they list are the *only* hotels in town . . . not their carefully researched personal selection. Hotels which reach normal European standards for first class are very limited. Most available rooms are what we would call tourist class at first class prices thanks to their rarity.

For example: In October 1992, a year after German unity, Dresden, a city of a half million residents, had a total of eight hotels in and around the center of town. We all know that new hotels will be built as quickly as someone can get construction crews together, but in the meantime, don't even dream about cruising into an East German city and finding empty rooms . . . at any time of the year. Now I'm not saying that it can't be done—just that you must be mighty lucky.

Traveling in Eastern Germany needs new habits

If you travel as I do, wandering through the country and making plans on the spur of the moment, you'll have to change your normal travel routine. My travel operations usually have me searching for a room wherever I happen to be in the early evening, then settling in and heading out for dinner and later enjoying a night with the natives. This is not the way to do it here.

Plan your accommodations much earlier than normal. In Eastern Germany you should make your overnight arrangements no later than 2 p.m. Once you have your room reservation, in a hotel, pension or a local family's extra room, head out and spend the afternoon sightseeing then go to your overnight spot in the early evening.

This room reservation network also means that you should plan on staying where you are, or taking day trips, over weekends since many of the tourist information offices are closed on Sundays and close early (around 2 p.m.) on Saturdays.

Getting private rooms

The mainstay accommodations in Eastern Germany are with families in private rooms. Many local families, contacted by the tourist boards, have set aside extra bedrooms, or their living rooms with sofa beds etc., for foreign guests. These rooms are clean and most families offer an excellent breakfast along with the accommodations for an additional few DMs. There is no better way to get to know a country than by staying with its people. During my tour through Eastern Germany I stayed with former policemen, with tram drivers, with lumberjacks, teachers, widows, and unemployed university graduates. Everyone has a different story and a different point of view . . . and for many I was one of the few Americans (if not the first) they had met.

German is normally the only language they speak, but many can make themselves understood in English and other European languages. They learn fast from visitors.

Cost for these private rooms range from DM30 to DM45 with an excellent breakfast (*Frühstück*—normally coffee or tea with rolls, butter and jelly, cheese and cold cuts, and an occasional medium-boiled egg). Translated into US dollars that reads $18 to $28 per night including breakfast: a bargain in any currency. Normally you'll share a bath with the family and other guests and in most cases you'll be given your own set of towels.

Making arrangements

To make arrangements for a private room, or to try to get a hotel or pension, go to the tourist office in town. Every tourist office has a *Zimmervermittler* (room agent) or can direct you to one. These agents can let you know if there are any rooms in hotels or pensions, though in many cases they can't make the reservations, but can send you there and will call to make sure there is still a room.

Private rooms, in most cases, are kept on file cards. The tourist office personnel will flip through their supply of rooms and announce that they have the perfect spot for you. How they determine the "perfect spot" is a mystery, but has to do with quietness, quaintness, language and whether or not you are traveling with a family.

If you are travelling with a family, let the agent know and she or he will set you up with a shared room or adjoining rooms. (This system is really quite well organized).

If you are a single traveller you can even request the type of family with which you might like to stay. Say for instance, you are a professor back home in Iowa . . . you might like to stay with a professor in Leipzig, or an American journalist might like to speak with a local journalist. There are no guarantees that you will get your request, but the local folk at the tourist information offices and the private room agents know their room suppliers quite well and will be pleased to help if they can.

Reservations by phone and fax

This private room reservation system can also be used long-distance and to make reservations in advance. The limitations, naturally, are mainly language. If you speak good German there are no problems—in Eastern Germany, few tourist office personnel speak English. The list at the back of the book gives most of the major tourist offices and phone numbers, with fax numbers when available.

Another problem besides language is room availability. The large cities limit the number of their rooms that may be pre-assigned or reserved. I ran into this problem in Dresden, but the tourist office agent told me they had plenty of rooms, and to just be there around noon on Saturday to be sure to get one.

Hostels

Germany is the home of the hostel and boasts more hostels than any other country on earth. Eastern Germany has an excellent system of youth hostels. However, if you are not a "youth," check to make sure you are eligible to stay. Unlike most hostels in the West, these places cater to a much younger crowd.

If you are planning on staying in a hostel, stop first in the tourist information office of the town before setting out for a hostel listed in *any* guide, unless you have already discussed that hostel with a fellow traveler and are sure it is still in operation. It seems that many youth hostels were established in large manor-like houses once "liberated" for the people. Quite a few of these buildings have been reclaimed by their prewar owner families since reunification, and the hostels have been forced to shut down or move. In other cases where hostels have prized locations with beautiful views, they have fallen victim to capitalist instinct and have been made into luxury hotels.

If you are planning to stay in a hostel, the normal restrictions apply. You will have to deal with early curfew, a midday lockout, and the need for a sleeping sheet sack. But you meet fantastic and interesting people sitting around the tables in these places. To be eligible to stay in a youth hostel you must purchase a membership. The International Youth Hostel Federation has offices in most major cities throughout the U.S. and Canada.

Pensions

Pensions are usually smaller, family-run affairs that cost significantly less than hotels. As with hotels, you can get information at the local tourist offices. In Eastern Germany as in all of Germany, the rooms are kept scrupulously clean. The pension guest in many cases feels a part of the family during his stay.

Some lodgings have a bath and toilet in the room, others have the bath and toilet down the hall or just next door. In Eastern Germany, virtually every pension has a shared bath.

Helpful Hints

Shopping and business hours

One major difference between America and Germany is the shopping hours. We in the U.S. seem to try to make shopping as easy and as convenient as possible. In Germany shop opening hours are strictly limited, which makes shopping, especially for such groups as working parents, rather difficult. (I mention this to alert you to major shopping crowds between 5 and 6:30 p.m.). Even the name of the law which controls the opening hours of stores is phrased in the negative, *Ladenschlussgesetz*, which means store closing laws.

Store hours are Monday through Friday from 8 a.m. to 6:30 p.m., Saturday from 7 a.m. to 2 p.m., with some stores remaining open on Thursday nights until 8:30 p.m. and all stores allowed to remain open the first Saturday each month until 6:30 p.m.

Banking hours are not any more convenient, running from 9 a.m. to 12:30 p.m. and from 2:30 p.m. to 4 p.m. Monday to Wednesday and on Friday. On Thursday the afternoon hours are extended until 5:30 p.m. Banks are closed on Saturday and Sunday, but you can exchange money at train stations or in hotels.

Post Office hours are Monday to Friday from 8 a.m. to 6 p.m. and on Saturday from 8 a.m. to noon.

Climate

If you are planning a trip to Germany, don't do it for the weather. This is not a country where you'll find long warm sunny stretches, even during summer. In the winter you'll be lucky to find any sunshine at all. When I lived in Germany, we used to joke that when the sun disappeared in September, you wouldn't see it again before April.

Weather in Germany is comparable to southern New England's, but less extreme. You won't find too many unbearably hot summer days, nor will you experience much bone-chilling cold. The north coast of Germany gets more rain than the middle and southern areas, and snow is pretty much restricted to the mountains.

	July	October	January	April
Berlin	58-76°	43-56°	27-36°	40-56°
Dresden	56-76°	41-56°	25-36°	40-58°
Magdeburg	56-76°	43-58°	27-36°	40-58°
Rostock	56-72°	43-54°	29-36°	38-52°

Rain is also a reality. You will make great use of your *Regenschirm* (umbrella). The rainiest months in Berlin are June, July and August; in Frankfurt, November, December and January; and in Munich, May and June.

Changing money
Changing money is simple throughout Germany. Banks have opened throughout Eastern Germany and money changing centers are open in most train stations.

You can also get cash advances in DMs through MasterCard or Visa at many train station banks in Germany, including those in Eastern Germany.

The exchange rate for the past few years has been fluctuating around DM1.6 to $1. This makes one Deutschmark worth about 60¢, so DM10 is worth $6.00 more or less. This rule of thumb will give you a feel for how much you are spending. You'll find that many items in Germany cost about the same as in the U.S. and many cost much more. Needless to say, Germany is not a great bargain for American travelers.

Credit cards
I have already mentioned that you can get cash advances from your credit cards at banks in train stations. This service is available from many other banks as well. Though you pay a service charge (which you pay to change money anyway) you will be getting the best interbank exchange rate with the credit card. I've found using a credit card for advances an advantage when playing the ex-

change rate game. In fact, if you use your credit card in preference to travelers checques whenever possible, you save money on exchange fees and get better exchange rates.

Credit cards are accepted virtually everywhere in Western Germany and they are also becoming more and more acceptable in Eastern Germany, but they can be used in only a small fraction of Eastern stores, restaurants and gas stations. Don't count on using credit cards anywhere outside of major cities, business centers, or such resort areas as Binz on Rügen Island.

Visa is also called Visa in Germany. American Express and Diners Club are clearly recognizable. The only major credit card with a different name is MasterCard (called EuroCard), but the symbol, orange and yellow circles, is universal and your MasterCard is accepted. Discover Cards and bank cash cards can be left at home.

Using the telephone

Get ready for an experience if you are planning to do any phone calling outside of Eastern Germany. Within the former DDR calling is relatively easy as long as your phone terminal has a current list of area codes, such as in a post office. Don't assume that the area code to call Dresden from Weimar will be the same area code to call Dresden from Berlin or from Rostock. Except for the area code problem, the calls are relatively straightforward. If you need to get a number, Directory Assistance in Eastern Germany is less than helpful. It is normally easier to look up the number on your own with the help of a local. They're helpful: they have the same problem.

When you are trying to call internationally, or even to Western Germany from Eastern Germany, you will encounter more problems. The country code for Western Germany varies depending on which city you are calling from. For example, to call the west from Dresden requires a country code of 07; if you call from Leipzig you'll have to dial 0649. I have no idea, nor does the German government, when the telephone systems will be seamlessly interconnected. In the meantime the rule is to ask about how to make phone calls in each city.

Try to call from a post office. You have someone who can help you out when you get stuck, and you pay after the call is completed. When you call from a phone box only deposit the least possible amount of change—these Eastern German phones are notoriously hungry critters and will swallow money without a thought. If you must use a phone box, look for the newer pay phones recently installed. Wait patiently.

If you are planning to call back to the USA there is no simple way to make a collect call from public phones nor from post offices. It can be done, but there is paperwork needed and then you'll have to wait in line. Theoretically, you can make collect calls from Eastern Germany by calling 00114 which rings an operator in Berlin. You'll listen to a recording for 15 minutes to a half hour and then either get an operator or get cut off. From major hotels, the rates are horrific, but worth the cost in an emergency.

My suggestion is to wait until you are in Western Berlin or dash across the old border to a city in the former West to call back to the U.S. Here the phones are among the best in the world and you can access AT&T's USA Direct as well as MCI's and Sprint's similar services from any phone. It's like a dream after dealing with Eastern phones.

Within Berlin making a phone call can also be difficult. East and West still have different systems within the city. The basic city code for Western Berlin is 030. The prefix for Eastern Berlin is 0372. If you are calling from Western Berlin to Eastern Berlin use the prefix 9. If you are calling from Eastern Berlin to Western Berlin use the prefix 849. Once again the rule is ask.

Throughout this book few prefixes are included because of their variations within Eastern Germany. For numbers in Berlin, those with no prefix are in Western Berlin and those preceded by (9) are Eastern Berlin.

If you are planning to call from outside of Germany to Eastern Germany, ask the operator for assistance. The country code for the eastern part of Germany is in a state of flux. The old country code, 037, works to reach most areas, but the system is being integrated into the overall German system and now some areas and some select phone numbers even in remote areas can be reached by calling the country code for Western Germany, 049, and then adding a 3 before the city code.

Change is coming fast enough that in some cases even international operators will have to make last minute queries to get the latest prefixes.

Tipping

Eastern Germany has accepted the Western German custom of including the tip in the cost of a meal when eating at a restaurant. It is customary to leave the small change when settling the bill, such as rounding the bill up to the next DM or leaving at most a couple of Marks.

In hotels tip porters DM1-2 per bag. Leave about 50 pfennigs for washroom attendants. Round up taxi fares to the next DM.

Entertainment and nightlife

Other than in Berlin, nightlife such as cabarets, night clubs and discos will be limited. Cities in Eastern Germany, however, do have an exceptional program of cultural events, classical concerts and theater.

I suggest that you make sure to take a walk through the town after dark and wander into small *Gaststätte* or *Kneipen*, until you find a spot that feels comfortable. Take a seat at a table and order up one of the local beers and watch the action. If all the tables are taken, you can always just grab a seat at a table along with another group. This is common in Germany where the folk are not as territorial about their table as we are here.

There is a protocol, however. Don't just sit down at a table already occupied—ask first if you may. Try (phonetically speaking) DARF ICK EIN PLATZ NAY-MAN. That should elicit a response such as YA or NATURLICH, which loosely translateds into "sure" or "naturally." Or you can ask whether the seat is free (unoccupied): IS DIS PLATZ FRY.

Unlike in the U.S. where waiters and waitresses are urged to "turn the tables," in Eastern Germany as in the rest of Europe you will practically have to tackle your waiter (or at least catch his or her eye) to get your bill. You can make a gesture that looks like writing on an imaginary blackboard, which translates to "My check please, " or mumble TSAH-LEN BIT-TER which means the same thing. If you are with a group you'll be asked, SOO-SA-MEN or GAY-TRENT, which translates to together or separate checks. Unlike the U.S., separate checks are normal here so that everyone can easily pay his share.

Beer and wine

This seems as good a spot as any to mention beer and wine in Germany. In Eastern Germany beer seems to be the libation of choice except in the southern reaches near Meißen, which has a wine tradition.

Each Eastern German town, it seems, has its own local brew. My favorite was Apoldaer from a town near Weimar, and Rostocker from, you guessed it, Rostock. Beer here is brewed according to the *Reinheitsgebot*, the old purity law decreed in 1516 by a Bavarian duke, which rules that pure beer may only contain water, hops and barley. Other countries get a lot of rice and other grains in their beer.

German beer comes in more than 6000 varieties. The normal beer is about 4% alcohol, Export is about 5% and Bockbier is just over 6%. If you want the beer on tap ask for *Bier von Faß* (BEER fon-FASS).

To order one beer hold up your thumb which means "one" in German bar hand language. Your thumb and forefinger translates to "two" in this sign language and "three" is designated by holding up your thumb, forefinger and middle finger. (Incidentally, holding your forefinger up means "wait" or "hold on" in German sign language.

If you are drinking beer outside it will probably be in a *Biergarten* (no need to translate) and if you are inside it will probably be called a *Bierkeller*.

If you decide to have wine, be advised that most German wines are relatively sweet compared to those of France, Italy or California. White wine is *Weisse Wein* and red wine is *Rot Wein*. There are three basic classes of wine in Germany: *Tafelwein* is ordinary table wine; *Qualitätswein* is quality wine; and the best wine is *Qualitätswein mit Prädikat* (quality wine with distinction). If you want the drier version of white wine, which I suggest, ask for *trockener Weiss Wein*.

A Little German History

The part of Germany we're visiting, with the Oder River on the right, the Baltic Sea on top, and a zig-zag line around the rest—making a vertical oblong the size and shape of a slightly melted Indiana—stood outside Germany for a long time, about half its known history. The eastern border with Poland used to be quite different, too: for most of the last four centuries, it was much further to the east. Along the Baltic shore, it once ran all the way across the top of Poland to Lithuania, and as late as 1939 it extended down the back of Czechoslovakia to include most of the upper Oder Valley (this arm of land is Silesia, for which Frederick the Great fought his first campaigns).

Most of this eastern territory is now part of Poland, the Baltic States, and Russia, but its inhabitants made great contributions to Germany and her culture; two examples just from the city of Königsberg (now Kaliningrad) are the philosopher Immanuel Kant and the critic Johann Gottfried Herder. And indeed Prussia, under whose leadership all Germany was united, was once part of today's Poland.

The new German states

The states that now make up eastern Germany have their old names again and occupy, more or less, their old positions on the German map. Starting just east of the Danish peninsula and proceeding clockwise, they are Mecklenburg-Pomerania, Brandenburg (with Berlin an island in it), Saxony, Thuringia, and Saxony-Anhalt.

These lands only began to be colonized shortly before 1000 A.D. At that time, there had *already* been a historical

Germany in some form or other for about a thousand years. It was this nucleus of German civilization that spread to the eastern territories.

Flashback: Rome

It is just a few years B.C. Having established Roman rule over Gaul, which corresponds roughly to present-day France, Rome now concerned herself with setting up some kind of stable frontier to the north and east. For a few decades there were campaigns across the Rhine, raids by German tribes on Roman settlements, and punitive expeditions by the Romans.

These Germans included the tribes of the Goths, Franks, and Vandals. They were the descendants of settlers who had come down from Scandinavia a few hundred years before to occupy the area from which the Celts had begun their extensive migrations about 1000 B.C. These immigrants brought with them their own culture, and strong loyalty to the clan—everyone who shared your ancestry—was all-important. The network of family allegiances, combined with the warrior's adherence to his leader, would later be refined and expanded to become the feudal system of Europe in the Middle Ages. These Germans farmed and tended their livestock on the land surrounding small settlements and villages, where the clan lived communally.

The names of the ancient gods of these Germanic tribes still appear in the names of the days of the week. Sonntag (Sunday) is the day of the sun; Montag (Monday) is the day of the Moon; Donnerstag (Thursday) is the day of Donner, the god of thunder; and Freitag (Friday) is the day of Freia. Wednesday is named for the god Wotan.

The Germanization of the frontier

After a short period—about twenty years—of inconclusive military action, the imperial Roman government began early in the first century to come to a series of arrangements with the German tribes that worked well for almost four hundred years. The border was strongly fortified, with forces on permanent duty. Veterans of these legions retired and made settlements here, and the German tribes along the Rhine basin began to be assimilated in various ways, eventually becoming the guardians of the frontier themselves (finally, as barbarian invasions from the East broke up the Roman Empire, much of the Roman army and its leadership would be German).

Cologne, Bonn, Trier and other Rhine cities were founded in this period, and there was trade with the lands to the east through this Roman province of *Germania*. But this Romanized Germany was never more than a strip of land perhaps 200 miles wide at most, straddling the Rhine from its mouth in present-day Belgium and the Netherlands, cutting down through the northeast corner of France, and ending in Bavaria at the Alps. The rule of the Roman Empire never extended into our part of Germany.

Invasion of the Huns

In 370 the Huns, nomadic herdsmen who fought with bow and arrow from horseback, arrived in Europe; they had come bursting out of Central Asia in all directions but north, and before they were done they would disturb the empires of China and Persia and destroy those of Gupta India and Rome. As the Huns advanced westward they exerted a pressure that the German tribes could not withstand, and many tribes began massive migrations far into western Europe. The Visigoths, for example, kept on the move until they reached Spain, and it was a Visigoth king who was ruling there when the Moslems invaded across the Straits of Gibraltar in the early 700s. This influx of Germanic tribes broke down imperial control of a Roman Empire already weakened by other forces.

The Huns, defeated in battle in Roman Gaul, pulled back into German territory, and after their leader Attila died in 453, retreated to the east.

The rise of Christianity and Charlemagne

After the retreat of the Hun armies, a half dozen Germanic kingdoms maintained some aspects of Roman government and administration. The conversion of the Frankish king Clovis to Christianity in 497 was a landmark, though many areas of the former Roman empire had already been Christian for some time. Religious conversions continued for the next few centuries, together with the growth of the Frankish Empire under Clovis's successors. Eventually, when they were not fighting each other these kings managed to expand their territories past the Pyrenees, halfway down the Italian peninsula, and just into the western edge of today's eastern Germany.

The Moslem invasion of Spain in 711 was followed by a brilliantly successful sweep through the Iberian peninsula and across the Pyrenees into France. In 732, outside of Tours, they were defeated by Charles Martel—Charles the Hammer. They retreated to Spain, never to invade Europe from that direction again.

Charles Martel's son later seized royal power (with the approval of the pope, setting an important precedent for succession), and *his* son, Charles Martel's grandson, was crowned in 768. This was the legendary Charlemagne, Karl der Grosse, ancient hero and father of both France and Germany.

Europe under Charlemagne

Charlemagne is one of those figures about whose great achievements we know, as well as certain details of his aspect and bearing, but who remains a fabulous character. He had great physical size and strength, his military campaigns doubled the size of the Frankish Empire, and he was also a skilled student of foreign languages and able to speak with great eloquence. He imported some of the most learned men in Europe and the best teachers, pushing education for his court and not neglecting it himself, being a keen student of astronomy among other things. (Legend suggests that the measurement of a foot, Charlemagne's foot, became the standard measurement.)

He had wide-ranging friendships, including a long-standing correspondence and many exchanges of gifts with the caliph of Baghdad, Haroun-al-Raschid, who sent him an elephant (one story claims that he sent Haroun a Narwhal's tusk, believing it to be a Unicorn's horn). Of all the projects he set in motion at his court at Aachen, the one that may most deserve our gratitude is the searching out, collecting, and copying of ancient manuscripts: some classical texts that we now possess might have been lost to us without his efforts.

Behind Charlemagne's military conquests and diplomatic maneuvering was his dream of a united Europe; others were to try to accomplish this by various means in the twelve centuries since his time, and today it looks as if it may come true in the very near future, this time with the consent of those being united.

Above all, Charlemagne began a formal association with Rome that would grow into the Holy Roman Empire, the framework of German-speaking states whose members would colonize eastern Germany.

Creation of the Holy Roman Empire

At the end of the 8th century, Pope Leo III, a genuinely religious man of humble background, was abducted by the family of the pope he had succeeded. By good fortune, representatives of Charlemagne's were able to free him and let him rest in safety at the court in Aachen while the rebellion against him was fought out in Rome.

Leo returned to Rome with a bodyguard of troops provided by Charlemagne , who followed in the summer of the year 800. He assisted at the trial of the conspirators, who had been condemned to death, and intervened to have the sentence reduced to exile. (Out of this trial, conducted by eminent theologians, came the principle that no earthly court might try the pope.)

The Eastern Roman Empire at this time was still in existence while the Western Empire had crumbled when the last emperor had abdicated in 476. During Leo's stay at at Charlemagne's court, the idea of reviving the Western Roman Empire had been discussed at length. And on Christmas morning, Charlemagne, dressed in the same type of tunic and cloak worn by the Caesars, was crowned Charles Augustus, Emperor of the Romans, by Pope Leo III. He ruled for 14 years more and died at 71 from a chill he caught while out hunting.

For all the brilliance of his statecraft and all the innovations he made in the administration of his realms, Charlemagne could not pass along his personal authority

The core of Germany after Charlemagne in 814

to his successors. His empire was divided, then divided again, and the next few centuries are a seemingly endless and repetitive story of alliances, intrigues, and wrangles between popes, disgruntled heirs, and ambitious nobles. Nonetheless the idea of Emperor as protector of Pope and Roman Church survived, and after the successes of Otto I against the invading Magyars it was formalized, Otto being crowned Holy Roman Emperor.

The Holy Roman Empire centers in Germany

In principle, the head of the Holy Roman Empire held a position in the matters of this world parallel to that of the pope in matters spiritual—he was God's vicar on earth and political leader of Christendom. In reality the power of the Holy Roman Emperor was limited to an area with the rough boundaries of today's Germany, Austria, Czechoslovakia, Belgium, Netherlands, Switzerland, and northern Italy. However, France, Poland, and Bohemia were outside this empire almost from the start, and England and Spain were only nominally under it.

The origins of the Electors

Imperial control was loose at best, and often challenged by ambitious princes. The method of succession was regularized in 1356 to a form the Empire kept for the rest of its thousand-year history: seven powerful lords (the archbishops of Mainz, Trier, and Cologne, the duke of Saxony, the count palatine of the Rhine, the king of Bohemia, and the margrave of Brandenburg) would meet at Frankfurt to elect the Emperor.

These nobles and church leaders were the Electors, and the allocation of votes shows the importance of the towns that had grown from the Roman settlements. Three of them were represented on an equal footing with entire countries, partly because of their wealth and influence, and partly because these archbishops were papal appointees who provided a counterbalance to the more independent and often difficult nobles.

CITIES AND RHINE-LAND ELECTORATES
- ▨ Cologne
- Mainz
- ▦ Trier
- Palatinate

1. Cologne 6. Heidelberg
2. Bonn 7. Speyer
3. Mainz 8. Esslingen
4. Frankfurt 9. Rothenburg
5. Worms 10. Nuremberg

Holy Roman Empire in 1250 with hundreds of independent kingdoms and the seven electors—Mainz, Cologne, Trier, Palatinate Rhineland, Bohemia, Saxony and Brandenburg.

In practice, the Holy Roman Emperor was usually an Austrian Habsburg. Though these Emperors remained strong in their own right as heads of their Austrian lands, their power as Holy Roman Emperors became less real with events and the Empire more a show of outward form. Finally, with the abdication of the last Holy Roman Emperor in 1806, even the ceremonial aspect of the Empire was ended.

The Empire, in one form or other, had lasted a millennium. Its temporary unification of Germany and Italy had fallen prey to geography, and its ideal of a universal temporal leader protecting his spiritual counterpart the pope, and ruling with his blessing, was never really achieved.

The drive to the east

Back in the earliest days of the Holy Roman Empire when Christianity was losing ground to the Hun invasions from the East and the Moslems pushing north from Spain, Christian missionaries were being sent on successful expeditions into Thuringia, a frontier region. Many of the pagans were converted to Christianity, monasteries were founded, and Anglo-Saxon missionaries began the organization of a German church closely allied to Rome. These missionary efforts east of the Rhine, then east of the Elbe, would continue in parallel with the desire of the princes of the Holy Roman Empire to expand their domains.

The tribes in this territory were the Wends, a Slavic people some of whose descendants still preserve a folklore of their own in Lusatia, the southeastern corner of Saxony. They speak a language with elements of both Czech and Polish, and today are called Sorbs—a tribal name allied to that of the Serbs.

The power of the Teutonic Knights

Beyond the Oder to the east, in the lands that have now reverted to Poland, Russia, and the Baltic States, these efforts fell increasingly to the Order of Teutonic Knights— the *Deutscher Orden*, or *Deutsche Ritter*. During the Crusades in the late 1100s, this group of merchants from Lübeck had the original purpose of providing a hospital, but was soon made a military order under Pope Innocent

III and in the 13th century transferred its activities from the Holy Land to the North of Germany.

Their task was the conversion of the heathen, and by 1236 they had completed the conquest of the Prussian tribes, who fought hard to keep their ways and ended by being more exterminated than converted. With Marienburg (now Malbork, Poland) as its principal seat, the Order continued to expand the faith and its territory eastward, and in another hundred years had captured Lithuania. German settlers had followed and founded towns that soon prospered, among them Danzig (Gdansk) and Königsberg (Kaliningrad).

The decline of the Teutonic Order and the rise of a strong Poland

Though their domain expanded, the Order began to lose its grip on political power. The rise of a powerful Polish state began the real decline of the Order, whose forces were defeated by the Poles in 1410 at Tannenberg (where there would be an even more famous battle in 1914). Continuing conflict with the Poles in the next few years resulted in the loss of western Prussia, but East Prussia, with its capital Königsberg, remained German. It continued to operate under the Teutonic Order until the Reformation, when in 1525 its last Grand Master declared himself a Protestant and duke of Prussia.

Prussia, a century later, would play an important part in the history of the people who had originally colonized it. At this point in history, one thing was certain: the political center of gravity in Germany had shifted eastward from its traditional position near the Rhine.

People of all classes headed east from the older Germany—and from other countries too: there were for example many farmers from Holland. Nobles, burghers, and peasants migrated here to build new estates, enrich themselves by trade and by their crafts, and clear new land. The towns they built were modeled on the towns they had left, and this was not surprising because the old towns worked: they were going concerns. Walled and fortified, they had spent enough of their wealth on defense so that they could be safe, and inside their walls the arts, learning, and commerce flourished.

Even though their lands were nominally governed by the Holy Roman Empire, the towns were peaceful enclaves in a countryside where the norm was large or small wars, feuds, and brigandage, and no security of person or property was reasonably to be expected. As common interest was recognized, towns along the Rhine formed associations to protect themselves and their trade along the river.

The Hanseatic League

In the mid-1200s Lübeck, Stralsund, Rostock, Wismar and other towns trading on the Baltic joined in a trade agreement, the Code of Lübeck. From this association the Hanseatic League grew. (*Hansa*, in medieval Latin, means "group" or "company.") Although the Hanseatic League was centered in the Baltic ports of North Germany, it eventually included over 100 inland towns, and reached as far as Holland to the west and Poland in the east. The concerns of the merchants' guilds in the towns were much the same everywhere: piracy, exorbitant customs duties, and various trade barriers (not unknown even in our day). The League worked to reduce these threats and inconveniences, and also to secure monopolies of trade for its members when it could.

They had quite a variety of goods to trade in: grain, salt, timber, naval stores (pitch, tar, and turpentine), amber, horses, wool, cloth, hides, and the products of their fishery, especially herring. Although the League had no central treasury or officials of its own, it was quite effective in gaining advantages. A successful war between the Hanseatic League and Denmark in the 14th century resulted in a virtual monopoly of Baltic trade for the League and veto power over the succession to the throne of Denmark if the monopoly was not renewed. The League had especially good relations with England, having made loans to the Crown during the Hundred Years War. Although there was some competition when England began to trade in the Baltic, League trading privileges in England continued until the reign of Elizabeth.

The League declined in overall influence in the late 1400s, partly from internal rivalries, and partly because such south German towns as Leipzig commenced east-west trade themselves, bypassed the Baltic ports, and began to have their own trade fairs. Also, as the principalities, such as Brandenburg under the Hohenzollerns, became more powerful and increased their centralized control, they reduced the independence of the towns.

Farmers in revolt (woodcut by Hans Burgkmair, 1525)

The first peasant rebellions

This period, however—the 1200s to the end of the 1400s—was a time of growth and increasing riches for eastern Germany; even the Black Death, the bubonic plague that swept across Europe from the Black Sea in the 1340s and 1350s, had a relatively mild effect here while killing as many as a third of the population elsewhere.

There was less improvement in eastern Germany for those who worked the land. Where peasants in the western and southern parts of Germany had often freed themselves of feudal duties and even developed some economic independence, those in the east were forced to return to serfdom on the enormous estates that the knightly settlers had built up. But even with comparatively better living conditions and less serfdom, the peasants to the west and south faced severe taxation and increased military obligations, sufficient to drive them to revolt. These revolts were widespread and frequent. Their emblem became the peasant shoe—the *Bundschuh.*

Luther and The Reformation

Today some historians suggest that Martin Luther didn't actually nail his 95 theses to the church door at Wittenberg on October 31, 1517, but placed them there in some other fashion. It doesn't really matter how he did it— the man and the moment met, and Luther set in motion one of the great events of world history. We can still see its continuing effects surrounding us, and many of the questions he raised are still unresolved.

Prince Albrecht of Brandenburg, who was bishop of Magdeburg, wished also to be Archbishop of Mainz and thereby an Elector of the Holy Roman Empire. The price charged by the pope for the Mainz position was steep—to pay it Albrecht was given the papal privilege of selling indulgences in his lands. With the purchase of an indulgence, one could be forgiven all one's sins—it was necessary only to confess them to be returned to a state of childhood innocence.

Luther's 95 Theses included a call for the end of selling indulgences, but the practice was nothing new— indulgences had been used to raise money for hundreds of years.

Nor was there anything new in a plea to reform the church. Pope Innocent III had called a world council to discuss this question as early as the year 1215, and since then there had been eight more such conclaves, all of which agreed that the problems remained and that nothing had been effective in fixing them.

The sale of indulgences had been recognized as only one source of abuse. Another included the bad moral example set by many of the clergy, such as their failure to live up to their vows of celibacy (priests could in some places buy releases from these vows, and their superiors made a good thing of selling them). These and other faults had often been attacked, often in the most violent terms, from within the church.

The legitimacy of the Roman church had been vigorously questioned from outside as well: from the time of the crusade against the Albigensian heresy in southern France (also in the reign of Innocent III), there had been frequent uprisings by heretical sects of varying beliefs, but usually with the rejection of the Roman church as a necessary pathway for salvation.

Calls for change in the Church before the Reformation were nothing new

Less than a century before, Jan Hus, who became a martyr and a Czech national hero, had been tried as a heretic and burned at the stake in Prague—in violation of a safe conduct given him—for preaching against papal infallibility and for the final authority of Scripture over the word of the church. The Hussite wars which followed, and which were to continue less as religious conflicts than political ones, had gone on for much of the 15th century and had extended into Germany on occasion.

There were other forces at work as well. The authority of the church had been weakened by the Great Schism, with rival popes at Rome and Avignon; by the very wealth of the church itself, which owned perhaps a quarter of the land in Europe and yet claimed to be free of taxes; by a growing national spirit in many parts of Europe; by the repressive measures of the Inquisition; and by the rapid spread of learning, not least attributable to the invention of the printing press some 60 years before.

Luther takes on the papacy

Luther's questions were seen as an attack on the papacy itself, and the more he was called to present himself before the local church authorities to explain, the more obvious his differences with church doctrine became. In public debate he admitted believing that not all the positions of the Hussites had been wrong, and this helped bring about the excommunication that followed. His preachings and publications made him enormously popular, and made his proposals for church reform the most important political question in Germany.

Luther in his writings claimed that he never intended his 95 Theses to receive such wide circulation. But the printing press churning out thousands of copies of

Luther's Thesis brought him into formal conflict with the authority of the church almost by accident. Copies of the theses were printed in Latin and German and had such a wide circulation that the sale of indulgences was actually hurt in the marketplace.

It's interesting to imagine what might have happened at any time during this process if the central figure had been anyone but Luther, someone less learned, less skilled in debate, less passionate in his beliefs, or above all less willing to live his convictions without apparent fear.

The new Holy Roman Emperor Charles V agreed to hear Luther, at the first Diet of his reign, in Worms, if the newly excommunicate monk wished to defend himself before having the ban of the Empire placed on him. Luther went to defend himself, and 2000 people came out to meet him. Before the Emperor and the princes of the realm, asked if he would retract his publications, he stood by his earlier statements, notably those that disagreed with the infallibility of church councils, and said that he would not recant this position unless it could be proved wrong by the Scriptures.

The next day, January 19, 1521 the Emperor read his reply: a steadfast adherence to the doctrines of the church, its infallibility, and its temporal authority. Charles V pledged all he possessed on earth, and his very soul, to defend them, and he called on the assembled princes to join in this crusade, at which many of them "turned paler than death." They had heard Luther; they had heard Charles; there was no compromise. And it was not at all clear, with Luther's books being sold in great numbers through their lands, which way things would go.

Luther's time at the Wartburg and the spread of Protestantism

With his safe conduct to expire shortly, Luther left Worms and was met by a troop of horsemen in the forest of Thuringia. This had been arranged with the Elector of Saxony, Frederick the Wise, whose protection Luther now enjoyed in the Wartburg, Frederick's hilltop stronghold near Eisenach. Here Luther began his most important literary work.

There had been earlier translations of the Bible into the German vernacular, but these had been limited, expensive editions. Luther's was a brilliant translation of the New Testament from the Greek to Middle High German, setting the standard for the German language. He also continued to write pamphlets on the current controversy. These, and all Luther's other writings had been banned by Charles V in the Edict of Worms after Luther's departure.

The ban, however, was unenforceable—Lutheranism had spread too rapidly in the Empire, and would soon be a major religion outside it. All Scandinavia and most of the Baltic states were Lutheran by 1540; Zwingli had led Zürich and the rest of German-speaking Switzerland into his form of Protestantism even before the Diet of Worms; Calvinism had converted much of France and all of Scotland by 1560, and was strong in eastern Europe.

Germany's uneasy separation of church and state

The eventual European separation of church and state was made possible by a series of diplomatic maneuvering overseen by Luther's right-hand man Philipp Melanchthon, at such diets as Augsburg (1525, 1530, and 1555), Speyer (1526), Nürnberg (1532), and Frankfurt (1539). It was also helped by Charles V's preoccupation with foreign wars, and by the attitude of the papacy itself, which hesitated to give the Holy Roman Emperor total support for fear that the Empire would become too strong to control. (This was frequently the situation.)

Even so, there were numerous armed conflicts on the religious question throughout the century. For Germany, the matter was settled temporarily with the agreement in 1555 to abide by the principle of *cuius regio, eius religio* : each prince might choose Catholicism or Protestantism, and his subjects could abide by the choice or emigrate to more sympathetic lands if they wished.

Through the rest of the 16th century Rome attempted to regain the control of all Christendom—the Counter-Reformation would be targeted against Germany in particular, but succeeded best in Bavaria and along the Rhine. Eastern Germany remained preponderantly Lutheran.

During this same time, the Age of Discovery affected Europe as profoundly as the Reformation had done. While Luther was speaking at the Diet of Worms and writing in the Wartburg, Magellan was crossing the Pacific; his crew was on the first circumnavigation of the earth. In 1524 Verrazzano was following our Atlantic coast from Florida to Nova Scotia. Europe was turning in a new direction—the Mediterranean was no longer to be the center of their world. Northern Europe took on a greater importance, and during the next century while the French, English, and Spanish colonies were being settled in North America, Germany would be suffering her greatest tribulation.

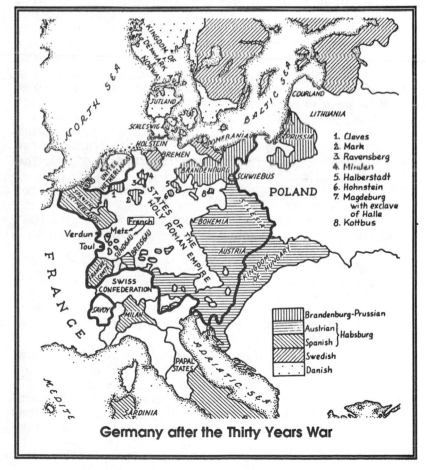

1. Claves
2. Mark
3. Ravensberg
4. Minden
5. Halberstadt
6. Hohnstein
7. Magdeburg with exclave of Halle
8. Kottbus

Brandenburg-Prussian
Austrian } Habsburg
Spanish }
Swedish
Danish

Germany after the Thirty Years War

The Thirty Years War, 1618-1648

This was the last of the religious wars on the European continent, and it brought the Counter-Reformation to an end. It also ended the Holy Roman Empire as a political force. This was double irony—it all began because Emperor Ferdinand II wished to reimpose Catholicism throughout the Holy Roman Empire.

One of the prime incidents that set off hostilities had a certain charm, except for the victims. Two representatives of the Emperor were receiving a delegation of Protestants in the castle in Prague. They were so unresponsive to the grievances of their visitors that they were thrown from the windows and fell 70 to 80 feet, landing unhurt in a pile of manure. This was the Defenestration of Prague (for the very pedantic, the Second Defenestration of Prague, since the Hussite leader Jan Zizka had done the same thing with the burgomeister and councillors a century before). The locals' merriment, at the expense of the Emperor's representatives who were mired in manure, was the last good laugh anyone had for a while.

A general revolt in Bohemia followed and was defeated by the Imperialist Catholic League, which caused the alliance of some north German states, England, and Denmark against the Emperor and the Catholic League. The war spread into Germany, where it was fought for the rest of its 30 years.

The Imperial forces' destruction of Magdeburg in 1631 and the killing of almost all its population provided an impetus to allow the Swedish forces into Germany. Saxony had been neutral but joined the force of Gustavus Adolphus to defeat the Imperial general Tilly at the battle of Breitenfeld.

Spain now came in on the Imperial side, and France eventually declared war on Spain. The war had by now become political, not religious.

The Peace of Westphalia restored the religious situation to something very close to what it had been before the war began. Some lands changed ownership for a time—Sweden, for example, received Pomerania and the island of Rügen, and France gained territory on its eastern frontier. The Netherlands got its independence. Switzerland's freedom was recognized. Germany and Austria recognized each other as separate countries.

But the most important effect of the war was the near destruction of Germany. Nearly half the population was killed or died of starvation and disease; agriculture, trade, and industry were ruined; and the suffering of the people would not be forgotten.

Germany's pre-unification patchwork of kingdoms

The Thirty Years War had another result. The Holy Roman Empire's power over its member states was virtually eliminated, as was the influence of the papacy. This gave individual German princes more freedom to conduct their own affairs. In a Europe where most national states had already jelled into something like their present boundaries, this independence would have the long-term effect of delaying the unification of Germany for another two centuries.

Other forces were also at work. If we look at any historical map of Germany or the Holy Roman Empire from the beginning of the 15th century to the end of the 18th, we see the same general picture: in eastern Germany, three or four large patches of territory—Mecklenburg, Brandenburg, Saxony, and perhaps Pomerania. Their outlines shift over time, but their size and number remain about the same.

West of the Elbe, however, it looks like a piece of very busy wallpaper. In the late 17th century, Germany comprised some 300 independent duchies, landgravates, bishoprics, counties, free cities, and other principalities. Later, when Napoleon went to work on them in the very early 19th century, there were still well over 200. They were bound by numerous treaties, family alliances, associations, and other understandings. The term "patchwork" is frequently used, and it is inescapable. And many of the states were under the influence of foreign countries who had no desire to see these pieces assembled into one Germany. How was this unification brought about by a relatively poor eastern backwater, colonized only a few hundred years before?

The Hohenzollerns
The Great Elector

In 1648, at the time of the Peace of Westphalia, the Hohenzollern family were well established as rulers of Brandenburg. They had been here since the early 1400s and in 1618 had extended their domains by marriage to include the duchy of Prussia (now northeastern Poland), which brought with it other possessions further to the west.

Friedrich Wilhelm, who would eventually be called the Great Elector, became the Elector of Brandenburg in 1640. Even before the end of the Thirty Years War he signed a treaty with Sweden that would allow him to gain additional lands after the Peace of Westphalia.

Though Friedrich Wilhelm's kingdom had increased in size, it was still poor. Trade had been cut to almost nothing, what was once farmland was now wasteland, and the population had been reduced by half. Friedrich Wilhelm, who grew up abroad, had observed the successes of a centralized government in the France of Louis XIV. He began working toward the same end.

Reduction of internal barriers to commerce, a postal system, and a standing army were some of his contributions. Almost as important was his principle of religious toleration, which was vital if he was to get immigrants from other parts of Germany and the rest of Europe to build up the population again. Dutch farmers and French Huguenot artisans—the latter by the thousands—came and made an all-important contribution to the land's rebirth.

The Great Elector, now free like his fellow princes to carry out his own policies, sided first with Sweden, then with Poland in the next war. There was then no further question of his title to Prussia.

All the while, agriculture and the economy continued to revive: with growing demand for grain in western Europe, the great estates cleared more farmland and added this source of revenue to their trade in timber, naval stores, and other raw materials. For all his desire to centralize power, the Great Elector had less trouble with the nobles in his lands than other European monarchs; as long as they were loyal to him in foreign policy and gave him military support when he needed it, they had a pretty free hand in their own domains.

Friedrich III

Friedrich III, the son of the Great Elector, inherited in 1688 a Brandenburg-Prussia with its situation in the world much improved, thanks to his father's decades of hard work. It was now second only to Austria, of all the states in the Holy Roman Empire, and was the leader of the German Protestant states. Its army was one of the best in Europe, though far from the biggest, and it had replaced Sweden as the greatest power on the Baltic. It also owned land—Prussia—outside the Holy Roman Empire, a circumstance the new elector would use to fulfill his ambition for a royal title.

The Holy Roman Empire, though it was not all it had been, still had the authority to approve the titles the heads of its member states might assume. In return for Brandenburg's military assistance in the War of the Spanish Succession, the Empire agreed that Frederick III might be a king. He could not be king of Brandenburg, since it was part of the Empire, but he could be "King In Prussia," and was so crowned in Königsberg in 1701. Thus the lands of the Hohenzollerns would be known as Prussia rather than Brandenburg, and the name would eventually denote a huge area.

Where his father had tried to emulate France's system of central government direction, Frederick III admired the more superficial aspects of French greatness: the court at Versailles was his ideal, and he did his best to approximate it in Berlin, building the Schloß Charlottenburg, making French not only the language of fashion but also the language of correspondence, and importing instructors in French etiquette and similar skills. To his credit, his interest in matters of the intellect led him to found the Prussian Academy of Sciences and the Academy of Arts, but the extravagances of the court at Berlin did little to continue the Great Elector's excellent beginning.

The Sergeant King and Frederick the Great

We now enter a time full of extraordinary, larger-than-life figures, whose lives are so full of rich anecdote that it's almost painful to try to describe them briefly. We know a great deal about this group of Hohenzollerns thanks to the correspondence and diaries of their contemporaries—families, diplomats at court, visitors, friends and enemies. They are the ones who will change things even more than the Great Elector and make Prussia a major player in Europe.

When Friedrich Wilhelm I succeeded to the throne in 1713, the country was in debt. He got rid of the dancing-masters, sold the decorations and jewelry, moved his family into five rooms of the palace, and then set about extending his economies to the rest of Prussia. He had enjoyed saving money since childhood, and his frugal philosophy, extended and refined, would eventually be felt everywhere—If it can't make a profit, why are you doing it?

To put his ideas into practice, Friedrich Wilhelm needed an administrative system that could follow orders and give him information. He drew up a plan of training and examinations for the civil authorities, written records of official meetings, and a system of weekly reports. There were similar examinations for judges and the rest of the legal system.

Much has been made of the gross personal attributes and boorish manners of the "Sergeant-King," but these were only an aspect of his single-minded and complete devotion to Prussia; he felt himself to be the principal servant of the state.

Perhaps he felt that if *he* didn't deal with *this* problem here and now—often by belaboring the supposed offender with his stick—he couldn't expect anything else to get accomplished. And he was consistent about his bullying: a stranger on the street (people would go indoors when they saw him coming) was in just as much jeopardy as the poor court official who, summoned to the royal presence, is said to have died of fright before the king could even speak to him. (And if anything, life was worse for his family.)

As his grandfather the Great Elector had done, Friedrich Wilhelm encouraged the immigration of the skilled and industrious, and made regulations that would increase revenues from trade and industry. Tax officials were given broad powers, and exercised them.

The money he amassed went to the enlarging his army, which grew from about 30,000 to more than 80,000 and had its efficiency improved all the while. Friedrich Wilhelm's right-hand man in these efforts was Prince Leopold of Anhalt-Dessau, the "Old Dessauer," a tough campaigner who could match crudities with his monarch. Together they introduced the steel rifle ramrod to speed up the reloading process, and started the armies marching in step; this had been practiced by the Romans but only recently rediscovered.

Here we must speak of the Potsdam Giant Guard, the king's passion, a regiment of very tall infantrymen who had been gathered from all Europe, seemingly from the ends of the earth, and almost invariably kidnapped. Friedrich Wilhelm called this his only vice (he was forgetting the thirty or so pipes of tobacco he would smoke at his *Tabakscollegium*, a nightly gathering of cronies, mostly generals and foreign diplomats). His recruiters ranged widely, with plenty of cash ready, and no very tall man in Europe was safe, whatever his civil status had been. Friedrich Wilhelm affectionately called these guardsmen his "Long Fellows."

(In his will, Friedrich Wilhelm reportedly claimed that his keenness for collecting tall soldiers was all a deception, something notorious to decoy the attention of Austria away from his more hidden agenda: to build up Prussia's regular army. This, if true, may suggest that Friedrich Wilhelm, like Huey Long and other politicians, was not so simple as he pretended to be.)

Frederick the Great

In 1740 Frederick II took command of Prussia and quickly demonstrated to members of the court, beginning with the Old Dessauer, that he was no fool. He had been through much already—a rigorous education prescribed from earliest childhood, with military training to match.

Frederick's friendship with Voltaire and other modern thinkers and writers resulted in steps toward a more enlightened government for the Prussians. Frederick had always been interested in the philosophy of government, and he could now, in the first weeks of his reign, put some of his ideas into practice.

Torture as a means of examining trial witnesses—standard in Europe even into the 18th century—was immediately abolished, along with specific cruel and unusual punishments, and the worst army recruiting abuses. The press was made relatively free, and indeed Frederick helped new periodicals in French and German get started in Berlin (he said he would be pleased to write for the French one). Religious toleration was likewise made formal policy. Finally, Frederick began efforts to bring the Berlin Academy, founded by his grandfather but lying dormant through the last regime, back to life.

With a good deal of fanfare, he disbanded the 4000-strong Giant Guard regiment. More quietly, he used the saving, which was enough to pay the upkeep of four times that number of regular troops, to further increase the size of the army. Despite Friedrich Wilhelm's possible subterfuges, Austria had been unhappily watching the Prussian military buildup, and Frederick had had a covetous eye on Austria's rich duchy of Silesia, to which Prussia had a semi-persuasive historical claim.

War with Austria

Frederick the Great attacked and occupied Silesia before the year was out. The operation was swift and smooth thanks to Frederick's careful planning with his staff. The political preparations were as detailed as the military ones, especially as they concerned administration of the new lands and relations with the civilian population. This resulted in a fairly warm welcome in an area where Austria's troops had not always behaved so well as the new Prussian garrisons. The welcome from the Lutheran minority, prevented from practicing their religion and kept out of office since the Thirty Years War, was vigorous. As an old tale recounts, one heavily taxed Silesian looked at the Prussian eagle being raised victoriously over his town and speculated that it might eat less than the Habsburg (two-headed) eagle just hauled down.

Austria, by way of contrast, responded with an army that came across the Bohemian mountain barrier in the winter, and the battles in Silesia and Bohemia that followed showed how effective the Prussian army was. These engagements were fought with perhaps 30,000 men on a side—infantry armed with muzzle-loading flintlocks, detachments of cavalry armed with sabres, and artillerymen with muzzle-loading cannon. Typically the Austrian force would be superior in numbers, but no match for the remarkably disciplined Prussians, whose drill at marching in step had been extended to the most intricate changes of formation, executed as soon as orders could be communicated, and while taking terrible losses from enemy fire.

Frederick was there, a commander in the field, having occasional narrow personal escapes but never in a panic, even when things looked very bad. (At Soor two of his horses were killed, and his camp was overrun and looted by Austrian cavalry; before the tide of battle turned he lost everything but the clothes he had on. Writing in pencil on scrap paper he reported his victory to Berlin, and later requested replacements of money—the war chest had gone—and books, clothes, flutes, snuffboxes, and other necessaries. His pet Whippet bitch, Biche, could not be replaced, but was returned by the Austrians. He was later pleased to report that she had had "a litter of Bichelets.")

These hostilities with Austria became, after the initial occupation of Silesia, part of a larger conflict, the War of the Austrian Succession. The complexities of this war affected Austria for the most part; we need only note that Saxony was allied first with Prussia and later with Austria, and that the treaty concluding the war in 1748 ratified Prussia's claims to Silesia. Silesia would be part of Germany for the next 200 years.

The Seven Years War, 1756-1763

Well before the treaty of 1748, Maria Theresa of Austria was preparing the next war. She had begun secret plans with Russia and France. Other European states, including several German ones, were to join in an effort to defeat and dismember Prussia.

It developed into a worldwide conflict, with England and France fighting not only in Europe but also for possessions in India and North America. Even before Frederick attacked the armies massing around him, Maj. George Washington of the Virginia militia was part of a British force operating in the Ohio Valley. This was our French and Indian War, and it ended with Wolfe's victory at Quebec, leaving France with only the land that would be our Louisiana Purchase 40 years later.

For Prussia, it was a period of sustained effort, with not every battle a Prussian victory; in 1760 the Russians burned Berlin before Frederick could relieve it. At the end, little land changed hands, but Prussia was recognized as a major power in Europe and Frederick was a legend all over the continent. Much of the war had been fought in Saxony, with disastrous effects.

During the Seven Years War, Frederick's dream palace in Potsdam, Sans Souci, was being built. For the next two decades, he would retreat to it when he could and relax with such simple pleasures as the flute (he not only played but composed excellent chamber music), and carry on discussions with visiting intellectuals.

Much of the time, however, he was on the road, visiting the provinces of a greatly expanded kingdom—and it grew again with the partition of Poland in 1772, which joined old Brandenburg with East Prussia. He was still, body and soul, the first servant of the state, tireless in his inspections: marshland was being drained, canals dug, factories for new industries built, a uniform law code created. He was everywhere, until he died in 1786 a familiar figure in his ratty old cloak and three-cornered hat, a beloved character, "Old Fritz."

The French Revolution and Napoleon

It did not take the successors of Frederick the Great long to dissipate the wealth and military power he had built up. An attempt at intervention in the French Revolution in 1792 ended in defeat and France's occupation of the German states west of the Rhine. Prussia was able to stay out of the Napoleonic Wars despite French encroachments in the west until 1806, when she was quickly defeated at the battle of Jena and soon after occupied. Huge tracts of Prussian land were given up, and the rest of the kingdom settled into a long period of French occupation.

For various reasons the egalitarian beliefs idealized in the French Revolution had less tangible success in the still fragmented German states. For one thing, France was at this point a national enemy and an invader. However, this time of foreign oppression created a different type of German national consciousness based on the wish to drive the foreigner out. And with this came the desire to throw off the remnants of feudalism as well. (*see Weimar*)

Attempted Restoration: 1815

With Napoleon defeated for good and nearly a quarter century of war concluded at last, the representatives of the powers meeting at the Congress of Vienna had, along with numerous agendas of their own, the common wish for European stability. There were two principal methods of achieving it, as overseen by Austria's Prince Metternich: a redrawing of the map of Europe to assure a balance of power, and a strict censorship of ideas to forestall any further radical activity.

Prussia benefited considerably, on balance, from the redistribution of land. In return for giving up a part of Poland to Russia, it gained the northern part of Saxony, more of Pomerania, and, to counterbalance any future French threat, all of Westphalia and the Rhineland. Its population thus grew by nearly half and it was now in control of much of the oldest and richest part of Germany— Roman *Germania*. There was still no unified German state—Metternich was going to create no such thing if he could avoid it—but there was a loose German Confederation, 'whose representatives would meet at Frankfurt, but still under an Austrian overlord. (Note that Napoleon, while ruling the myriad states of Western Germany, had done some consolidating and had greatly reduced their numbers: the total of monarchies and free cities in the German Confederation was now in the low forties.)

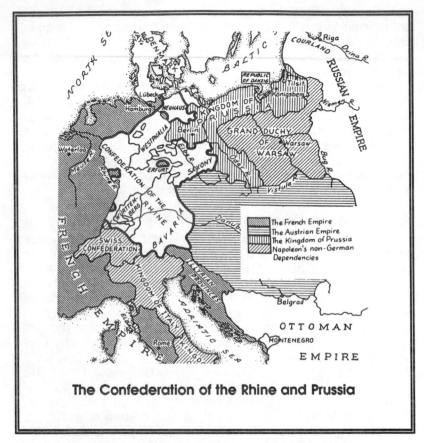

The Confederation of the Rhine and Prussia

Metternich's attempt to hold back democratic movements met with trouble everywhere. In Germany, student societies (*Burschenschaften*) were a leading force, and nowhere more than at the University of Jena. In October 1817 they invited representatives of fellow societies from all Germany to the Wartburg, where Martin Luther had enjoyed the protection of the Duke of Saxony; it was the 300th anniversary of his posting of the 95 Theses, and would also be the day of the Battle of Nations near Leipzig, where Napoleon was defeated. Several effigies were burned in a bonfire, including symbols of Metternich's repressive acts. Reaction in the form of tighter controls on the universities and more stringent censorship followed, and these efforts were formalized in the Carlsbad Decrees of 1819.

Steps Toward Unification

For the majority of the people, however, the more immediate reality was economic: the great 19th century industrialization had begun, and would eventually mushroom here as nowhere else. At the same time the *Burschenschaften* were meeting at the Wartburg, Prussia was doing away with internal customs duties and forming the *Zollverein* (Customs Union). This worked so well that most of the other German states had joined by the 1840s, and all the non-Austrian German states by 1853.

Otto von Bismarck

Descended from a very old family of landowners in Brandenburg, he grew up on their country estates there and in Pomerania. His father was a retired army captain. Bismarck, after training in the law, was briefly a civil servant but resigned to help his aging father with the management of their lands. Attending the first meetings of the Prussian parliament in 1847, he spoke in support of the king's divine right of rule, and in the Revolution of 1848 again had a strongly conservative message. He represented Prussia at the Diet of the German Confederation at Frankfurt, was ambassador to Russia and then to France, and was appointed Prime Minister and Foreign Minister by the new Prussian king, Wilhelm I.

Bismarck knew what sort of unified Germany he wanted: a Germany absorbed into Prussia rather than vice versa; and a Germany that did not include Austria. He set about building up the army.

Schleswig-Holstein

The Schleswig-Holstein Question dealt with hereditary and dynastic rights, as between Germany and Denmark, to two duchies on the Danish peninsula and was so complex that, as Lord Palmerston said, only three men had ever understood it; one had died, one had gone mad, and the third (Palmerston himself) had forgotten it.

A Danish royal proclamation on the subject in 1863 sufficiently upset the shaky state of things so that Bismarck
was able to get Austria to join Prussia in a military alliance to regain the two states. The war with Denmark was
short and successful, and Prussia and Austria adminis-
tered the two states jointly at first, then separately.

The Seven Weeks War

There was soon a pretext for war with Austria, which
took place in the summer of 1866. The American Civil War
had been studied with the greatest interest by the Prussian
General Staff, and they had learned much about how the
railroad and the telegraph might be employed. The
Prussians were also equipped with breech-loading rifles,
while the Austrians still carried muzzle-loaders. The war
was fought in much of the same area—Bohemia and
Silesia—as those between the same opponents in the previous century, but was much shorter.

Terms of the several peace treaties included the end of
the German Confederation and thus the end of Austrian
influence in Germany; the German states north of the
Main River joined a new confederation led by Prussia;
those south of the Main (Bavaria, Württemberg, and
Baden) formed military alliances with Prussia. Saxony,
which had sided with Austria again, paid a large cash indemnity and was required to join the new North German
Confederation.

Bismarck wrote the constitution for this confederation himself, and organized the representative bodies so
that Prussia might not be overridden in the matter of any
constitutional change; the individual states kept their
own governments, but the king of Prussia was comman-
der-in-chief of all military forces and the chancellor
(Bismarck) was his immediate subordinate.

There was still some reluctance in the south German
states for union with a Germany led by Prussia, but it was
thought that this might be overcome if they perceived a
threat from the direction of France.

The Franco-Prussian War

Late in 1868 a revolution in Spain deposed the queen and a new Spanish monarch was required. In the greatest diplomatic secrecy, Bismarck, with the unenthusiastic acquiescence of the Prussian king, put forth to the Spanish provisional government a Hohenzollern candidate, Prince Leopold. The proposal was well received, and King Wilhelm agreed to continue, provided there was strong enough approval by the Spanish assembly. At this point, the Hohenzollern candidacy leaked out. The response in Paris was dramatic, with threats of war unless Leopold were withdrawn. Ten days later, even though Leopold's father had stopped the candidacy (the candidate was in the Alps), France was insisting on apologies and assurances that the Hohenzollern candidacy would not be brought up again. An account of the king's rejection of the French demands (The Ems Telegram) was rewritten by Bismarck to make the rejection sound stronger, and published.

That was all it took. France declared war on July 19, 1870. After a hard-fought campaign through Lorraine, the French Emperor Napoleon III capitulated on September 1 after the Battle of Sedan. The siege of Paris lasted until the next January. By the peace treaty, Germany gained Alsace and Lorraine and an indemnity of 5 billion francs. (This was also the end of Napoleon III's empire and the beginning of the Third French Republic.)

The German Empire

The Franco-Prussian War brought the remaining German states together; Bismarck had made separate treaties with them, and now Wilhelm I was proclaimed Emperor of Germany in the Hall of Mirrors at Versailles. Unity of the German nation, the last in Europe to be brought together, had been accomplished in spite of all the forces inside and outside Germany that had worked to delay it. The tide had begun flowing eastward from the lands of Charlemagne a thousand years before, and now it had come back to reclaim the lands of its origin.

Wilhelm II

Bismarck stayed on as Chancellor for 19 years more, active in opposing the power of the Roman Catholic church in Germany, still more active in forestalling attempts at Socialism by any means, but particularly by his own social legislation. Germany's industry grew at an extraordinary pace in this last part of the 19th century, so that she was soon second or third in the world in such categories as steel production and merchant marine tonnage.

With the accession of Wilhelm II (whom we know as "The Kaiser") Bismarck was no longer welcome as chancellor. Wilhelm II was especially determined to conduct his own foreign policy, and forced Bismarck to resign in 1890. Through the rest of the 19th century and the beginning of the 20th, Germany would be on a collision course with the rest of Europe, and needlessly.

For a capsule view of the events of the 20th century, which will be more familiar, see the Berlin and Weimar chapters.

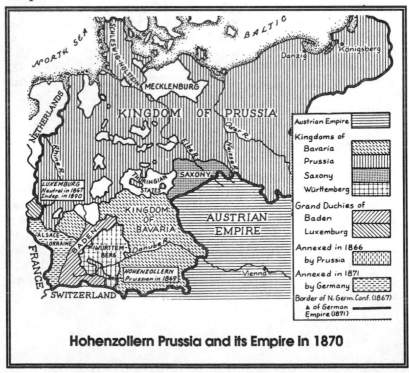

Hohenzollern Prussia and its Empire in 1870

Eastern German Personalities

As you travel through this part of Germany, certain names keep appearing on streets, squares, parks, and houses. Some of these people will already be familiar to you and others are mentioned in our historical paragraphs and city descriptions.

The following list gives thumbnail sketches of a few of the people worth knowing in Eastern Germany. It is based on geographical considerations: for example, Bach, who was born in Thuringia and spent most of his career at Weimar and Leipzig, is included; Beethoven, who came from Bonn and lived in Vienna, is not.

Political and military

Augustus II (The Strong) (1670-1733), Elector of Saxony.

At least as colorful a character as his contemporary Friedrich Wilhelm of Prussia, Augustus became Elector of Saxony in 1694, and in his nearly 40 years of rule was responsible for many of the greatest public monuments of Dresden.

To gain the crown of Poland by election, he converted to Roman Catholicism, and to pay for Poland's wars with Sweden reduced the wealth of Saxony without gaining it any long-term advantage. Always an active diplomatist and intriguer, he pursued his schemes with the aid of huge social events, fabulous feasts with extraordinary staging, courtesans and entertainment. Most of the European nobility was invited. This was in marked contrast to the plain, austere style of the Prussian court in Potsdam.

Friedrich Wilhelm of Prussia, was invited by the lusty Augustus to one of these affairs, but managed the fortitude to "resist the temptation of willing courtesans." Unfortunately he brought the future Frederick the Great who succumbed to ecstasy at the expense of piety and caught a social disease, the inept treatment of which affected him for life.

Augustus himself, in addition to physical strength and mental acuity, had notable appetites and indulged them; he is known to have had over 300 illegitimate children, one of whom became the Marshal of France: Maurice de Saxe, commander of the French victory at Fontenoy.

The Hohenzollerns (1417-1918)

Most of these monarchs are mentioned in the history chapter.

This house oversaw the growth of Brandenburg-Prussia into a strong kingdom. In 1417 **Friedrich I** formally became the Elector of Brandenburg. **Friedrich II** (1440-1470) made Berlin his capital. Later **Albrecht of Brandenburg**, grand master of the Teutonic Knights, in 1525 secularized Prussia, leading to the early religious toleration that became a mark of the dynasty.

Frederick Wilhelm (The Great Elector) (1640-1688) was the ruler who consolidated the Hohenzollern power and created the absolute monarchy. His son, **Friedrich Wilhelm I (The Soldier King)** (1699-1740), through his genius at setting up administrative organizations and developing the army built the foundation of power. **Frederick the Great** (1713-1786) would extend Hohenzollern power to Silesia and partition Poland.

The rest of the rulers were rather mediocre and eventually, just over a century after Frederick the Great, the monarchy lost all power.

Karl von Clausewitz (1780-1831)

This famous military writer was born to a poor family in Burg, a town which happens to be on the former corridor route from West Germany to Berlin.

Always a student of military history, Clausewitz had also had the opportunity to see it at first hand, from several points of view and in various situations. Clausewitz was commissioned before he was 14. Later, while a student at a junior officers' school, he was noticed by

Scharnhorst, who was reorganizing the Prussian army and given a good position. He served as chief of staff to one of Blücher's generals in the Waterloo campaign, and was soon a general himself.

His greatest work, *Vom Krieg* (On War) was published from his papers by his widow. It is still one of the classic works of military theory, and is still studied worldwide. It presents war as an extension of politics. It was also influential in its presentation of the concept of a nation totally at war—which had not always been the case—and of the importance of bringing hostilities to a swift and decisive conclusion (a view which has yet to go out of fashion).

Helmuth von Moltke (1800-1891)
The Prussian Field Marshal who made the army that carried out Bismarck's plans, and who directed the campaigns that led to Germany's unification. He continued the army reforms, such as accepting commoners as officers, begun by Scharnhorst. He took a few years' leave to serve in the Turkish army in the 1830s, and wrote a memoir which provides an interesting picture of the Ottoman Empire at that time.

He was an influential military theorist, whose policies of concentric attack and flexibility were most effectively carried out. While Chief of the Prussian General Staff during the war with Austria, he was responsible for the brilliant victory at Sadowa. In the Franco-Prussian War he was the architect of Prussia's encirclement of the French forces at Sedan.

He continued overseeing the work of the General Staff during the years of the German Empire. (His grand-nephew, Graf Helmut James von Moltke, led an anti-Hitler group and was executed by the Nazis in early 1945, a few months before the end of World War II.)

Religion
Martin Luther (1483-1546)
Creator and leader of the Protestant Reformation. Born at Eisleben, west of Leipzig and not far from the old border with West Germany, Luther went to school at Eisenach and Magdeburg, and entered an Augustinian

monastery in his early twenties, after study at the University of Erfurt. He received the degree of Doctor of Theology at Wittenberg, and his lectures as a professor there brought attention and students from other areas.

Luther married Katharina von Bora in 1525; it was an act in opposition to celibacy for the clergy, and also resulted in a happy marriage.

As noted, his greatest literary achievement is the translation of the Bible, which set a standard of written German that had lasting influence.

(*See Reformation section in History chapter for more details of Luther's influence.*)

Philipp Melanchthon (1497-1560)

A classical scholar and theologian, he was closest to Martin Luther and had the greatest influence on him. Melanchthon was professor of Greek at Wittenberg, and worked with Luther on his translation of the Bible. Luther made excellent use of his learning and lucid writing style during the Reformation—Melanchthon drafted and wrote most of the important documents of the Reformation, and frequently represented Luther at meetings with the Roman Catholic clergy and with other Protestant sects.

Born not far from Heidelberg, he went to the university there when he was only 12. His mother's uncle had taken an interest in him and given him the name Melanchthon, the Greek version of his family name Schwarzerd (Black Earth), as was frequently done in the enthusiasm for things classical during the Renaissance. (This enthusiasm was compounded in Germany by a low opinion of German as a language, among the learned at least. Ironically, this situation would be changed by the German translation of the Bible done by Melanchthon's friend Luther.)

After Heidelberg and Tübingen Universities, Melanchthon went to Wittenberg in 1519, at the invitation of the elector of Saxony, to be professor of Greek. He had been brilliant as a student; now, as a teacher and a leading spirit of the Renaissance, he was a magnet, and made Wittenberg the leading school of Germany—his lectures on Homer and others helped to inspire Luther in his studies of Greek and his translation of the Bible.

From the beginning Melanchthon was a major player in the Reformation, leading the cause at Wittenberg while Luther was in the Wartburg. As a Protestant representative in summit meetings with Roman Catholics and as Luther's spokesman with other reform factions, Melanchthon employed his diplomatic and writing skills. He was usually the one who drafted the agreements, and he could almost always put them in terms that both sides could live with. It may be said, very roughly, that he was conciliatory where Luther was a hardliner.

So many of the documents of the Reformation were done by Melanchthon's hand, so many were his refinements of Luther's ideas, that he may be called the Scribe of the Reformation. He died in 1560, and was buried next to Luther in the Schloßkirche of Wittenberg.

Music

Johann Sebastian Bach (1685-1750)

Born in Eisenach, near the Wartburg where so much has taken place, Bach moved around a good deal, but had almost all his career in our part of Germany. He is one of the major musical figures of the Western world.

The majority of his compositions are religious, including a tremendous output of choral works, numbering in the hundreds although not all have survived. His music for organ is so familiar that it hardly needs to be mentioned, as are such popular examples of his secular music as the Brandenburg Concertos.

Bach's interest in music was profound from early childhood, and he was chiefly self-taught. His pilgrimages on foot to hear such famous organists as Buxtehude at Lübeck are legendary. He was court violinist, choirmaster, organist, and music director at Weimar and Leipzig.

Bach's music brings the Baroque period in music to its perfection and conclusion; perhaps because styles were changing, his music was largely neglected in the period after his death, not to be properly rediscovered until the 19th century, when Mendelssohn and Lessing would begin to restore the reputation it now enjoys.

Felix Mendelssohn (1809-1847)

A grandson of Moses Mendelssohn, he was born in Hamburg and with his brother and two sisters baptized a Lutheran. Brought to Berlin when the French occupied Hamburg, he first played in public at nine and very soon showed himself a prodigy at composition, first for a family string ensemble and then for a general audience.

He was taken to visit Goethe at 12 and they made an immediate hit with each other (Goethe had not liked Beethoven when he visited, and Mendelssohn was able to bring Goethe around, at least partially, to his own admiration of Beethoven's music.)

He visited Paris and met the great French masters of the piano, as well as Rossini and Meyerbeer. He composed the overture to *A Midsummer Night's Dream,*one of his masterpieces and far ahead of its time in its orchestration. There were numerous visits to England and Scotland, and his performances were received with wild enthusiasm—in addition to his own compositions, he introduced several of Beethoven's piano concertos to the British public.

Stories of his amazing musical memory abound—playing a concerto from memory was practically unknown before his performances, and when the score for *A Midsummer Night's Dream* was mislaid in a taxi after its first performance in London, he simply sat down and wrote it out again.

He became the permanent musical director of the Gewandhaus concerts in Leipzig in 1835. It was considered the pinnacle of any musical career, and Mendelssohn's presence raised the reputation of the Gewandhaus still further. Six years later the King of Prussia called him to Berlin, and he accepted the title of Kappelmeister while continuing his Leipzig duties. In addition to giving us such works of his own as the Violin Concerto, the Scottish and Italian Symphonies, and the oratorios *St. Paul* and *Elijah,* Mendelssohn brought Bach's *St. Matthew Passion* out of obscurity and performed Schubert's great C Major Symphony—a single manuscript, nearly lost—for the first time. (He also presented Jinny Lind before P. T. Barnum did, although perhaps not in quite the same spirit.)

Richard Wagner (1813-1883)
   One of the great figures of 19th century music, whose
innovations in opera were often vigorously and vocally
detested in his lifetime, but whose influence was profound
and irresistible.
   Wagner was born in Leipzig and had his musical education and early work there and in Dresden. He spent much
time abroad, first in pursuit of a career and later as an exile. In his twenties he worked in London and Paris, where
he wrote his first opera, *Rienzi*. Its great success at
Dresden, where it opened, gained him the post of musical
director there. His next operas, *The Flying Dutchman*,
Tannhäuser, and *Lohengrin*, were based on semi-histori-
cal and mythic figures, with characters beginning to function as symbols as much as persons of the drama. He
aimed to have music completely integrated with the
drama on stage. "Endless melody" replaced the older oper-
atic form, with its arias and recitatives.
   For his association with the Revolution of 1848,
Wagner had to escape Dresden; Franz Liszt helped him go
to Switzerland, where he wrote the *Ring* and composed
much of its music. King Ludwig II of Bavaria made produc-
tions of *Tristan und Isolde* and *Die Meistersinger* possible,
and Wagner was later able to build his own theater at
Bayreuth, which today is a musical Mecca. At Bayreuth,
the *Ring* was first performed complete.
   A lot of very violent ink was spilled by Wagner's critics
and by his defenders during his lifetime; today an opera
season without Wagner seems rather flat, and recently the
entire *Ring* at the Metropolitan was shown on television.

Literature and the arts

Lucas Cranach the elder (1472-1553)
   He took his name from Cronach, his birthplace in
Franconia, and learned how to draw from his father. He
would pass his skills along to his own three sons, of whom
Lucas the Younger is the best known. He lived briefly in
Gotha, drawing and working in oils as well as wood and
copperplate engraving, and from 1504 was based in
Wittenberg, appointed to the court of his patron the
Elector of Saxony.

A master of religious subjects in all media, he created several altarpieces at Wittenberg, at least one in competition with his contemporary Albrecht Dürer. He was friend and early supporter of Martin Luther. After 1517 he expanded the themes of his religious pictures to reflect the ideas of the Reformation. In addition to Gospel scenes, they now included allegories of salvation by faith.

He was also noted for his mythological subjects, frequently done with a humorous touch. Most of all, however, we are indebted to Cranach for his portraits, which were the greatest part of his output and the only clue we have to the appearance of many historical figures. As court portraitist for almost fifty years, through the reigns of three Electors of Saxony, he painted not only the ducal family but also Luther and the other reformers, Emperor Maximilian and the future Charles V of the Holy Roman Empire, and several other members of the nobility. His last known work is the altarpiece in the Herderkirche at Weimar, completed after his death by Lucas the Younger.

Johann Wolfgang von Goethe (1749-1832)

The term Renaissance man applied to Goethe. He seemed to be an expert at virtually everything he touched— politics, languages, literature, architecture, design, science, music, theater, biology, zoology.

He was born in Frankfurt and went to Leipzig to study law. After his first works were published, Charles Augustus of Weimar invited him to come to become his chief minister of state. He would remain in Weimar for the rest of his life. He was responsible for bringing the best thinkers and writers and composers of his time to Weimar to work and converse together.

Goethe's desire was to live his life as an example of the full potentialities of man. He probably succeeded as no man has before or since. (See Weimar)

Jakob and Wilhelm Grimm (1785-1863, 1786-1859)

The Brothers Grimm are best known for their collection of fairy tales, but these were only a small part of their output in folklore and philology. They always worked closely together, Jakob as the more original thinker, Wilhelm as the more poetical. After several posts in the western part of Germany, they came to the Berlin Academy, where they began their great German Dictionary, a monumental and definitive work corresponding to the OED or the dictionary of the French Academy; they began it in 1852 and their successors completed the last volume in 1960.

In addition to their collections of folk tales, there were also numerous histories and grammars of the German language; their studies of the development of the Indo-European languages were the basis for Grimm's Law, which describes the ways that consonants shifted in groups from their original pronunciation in Sanskrit to their present sounds.

Ernst Theodor Amadeus Hoffmann (1776-1822)

Like Kant and Herder, Hoffmann was born in Königsberg, the principal city of what was once East Prussia and is now Kaliningrad in the former Soviet Union. He pursuing a somewhat successful career (with occasional upheavals thanks to his insubordination) as a lawyer and public official in East Prussia, Dresden, Berlin, and Poland. At the same time he was a composer, music critic, and writer of tales.

His opera *Undine* was performed with acclaim in Berlin. Using the name "Johannes Kreisler, Choir Master" he wrote a series of influential and enthusiastic criticisms of J.S. Bach—who at that time had fallen into near obscurity—and interpretations of Mozart and Beethoven.

Hoffmann is also considered one of the great novelists and storytellers of the Romantic movement in Germany. He is best remembered for his stories of the supernatural and grotesque. He is also known for his portraits of life in old-time Germany, recountings of strange happenings from European history, and his own early memories.

Offenbach's opera *Tales Of Hoffmann* has Hoffmann as the central figure and is based on three of his stories; and the Christmas season never goes by without ballet performances of *The Nutcracker*, which is based on his story *Nutcracker and Mouse-King*.

Gotthold Ephraim Lessing (1729-1781)

Born in Saxony, the son of a Protestant pastor, he attended the famous St. Afra's School in Meißen, then the

University of Leipzig, studying theology and then medicine. His real interest was in the theater at this point—his comedy *Der Junge Gelehrte* was accepted by a Leipzig company which involved him in its debts, forcing him to go to Wittenberg and Berlin to avoid prosecution.

His literary criticism, poetry, translations, and plays were collected and published in several volumes while he was still in his early twenties.

His studies of early Christianity and of Spinoza's philosophy would emerge later in his *Nathan the Wise*. His essays presenting Shakespeare as superior to the French dramatists, led to a falling out with Voltaire and consequently with Voltaire's patron Frederick the Great, who prevented Lessing from becoming royal librarian.

Lessing now produced some of his best work, including the influential *Laokoon: The Boundaries of Painting and Poetry*, which remains a milestone in aesthetics. His analyses of the poetry of Homer and Sophocles also resulted in a revival of appreciation of Greek literature.

When his public writings on Christianity were suppressed, he presented his arguments on stage in the blank verse play *Nathan the Wise*, whose characters—Nathan, Saladin, and the Knight Templar—he used to demonstrate his belief that adherents of any religion might have the same greatness of spirit.

His message was always for greater tolerance and breadth of understanding. The poets and philosophers who came immediately after Lessing were some of Germany's greatest, and they were generous in recognition of their debt to him.

Adolph Friedrich Erdmann von Menzel (1815-1905)

Menzel came from Breslau, now in Poland. He began supporting his family when he was orphaned in 1832. Menzel painted many historical events and large canvases of Hohenzollern court life—parades, festivals, balls, receptions, often immortalizing interiors of palaces that no longer stand.

Interestingly, he captured scenes that were just as full of color and movement, but of a different kind: workers in the foundries, mills, and factories that were making Germany the economic powerhouse of the continent. It has been suggested that Menzel's style, often with bright splashes of illumination reflected in shimmering colors and a light, elusive treatment of what might often have been a rather heavy subject, predicted the school of the Impressionists.

Johann Christoph Friedrich Schiller (1759-1805)

Historian, dramatist, and poet, Schiller ranks with his friend Goethe at the summit of German literature. He was born in Württemberg and was first trained, involuntarily, as an army surgeon. His plays, central to the *Sturm und Drang* movement, got him in trouble with the local authorities from the beginning, since their message was against political tyranny.

He came to Leipzig at the invitation of a small group of literary admirers, then to Weimar, where he settled into a life of great productivity. He was also professor of history at the University of Jena, and wrote, among numerous other works, a history of the Thirty Years War and studies of Kant's philosophy. At Weimar he worked closely with Goethe, editing a literary review. They amused themselves with satires of their critics, collections of poetic epigrams they divided into aggressive and "tame," all of which attacked narrow-minded attitudes.

From his studies of the Thirty Years War came his greatest tragic drama, *Wallenstein*, and this was followed by such plays on the lives of historical figures as *Mary Stuart*, *The Maid of Orleans*, and *WilliamTell*. The works of dramatic theory and criticism he produced did not receive the immediate acclaim of his plays, but had a huge influence later on. It is Schiller's *Ode to Joy* that Beethoven set to music in the last movement of his Ninth Symphony, appropriate to the nobility of spirit that Schiller celebrated.

August Wilhelm von Schlegel (1767-1845)

From a literary family, Schlegel is best remembered for his active part in promoting the Romantic movement and for his superb translations of Shakespeare's plays.

He was born in Hannover, to the west of our area. After a post as a private tutor abroad, he came to the University of Jena in 1796 and contributed to Schiller's periodical, later propounding the Romantic view in a series of lectures in Berlin. He later joined Mme. de Staël on far-ranging travels though Europe, and settled at the University of Bonn, where he turned to the study and translation of oriental languages. Schlegel's translations of Spanish, Italian, and Portuguese poetry and drama did nearly as well as his Shakespeare.

Philosophy and science

Immanuel Kant (1724-1804)

Kant was born in Königsberg, once part of Prussia. He eventually taught at the university in Königsberg. This Enlightenment philosopher believed that reason was the most fundamental human activity. Reason ultimately creates a world of space and time where all events are causally connected with each other. Reason demands respect for all persons, enables us to enjoy beauty and to appreciate the beauty of nature.

Kant believed that we can't know a thing in itself apart from our conceptualization of it. In other words, we may through our experience, perceive a situation differently from another person with different experiences working on his reason—a form of philosophical relativity.

For Kant space and time are not realities, but rather tools created by reason for organizing experience. Kant asserts that we endure a struggle between duty and desire. Kant's "categorical imperative" is to act as though everything you do will eventually become a law of nature.

His influence on subsequent world thinkers has been monumental.

Georg Wilhelm Friedrich Hegel (1770-1831)

Originally from Stuttgart, Hegel spent much of his early university life as a professor at Jena. He then moved to Nürnburg and Heidelberg before settling in Berlin.

Hegel was perhaps the most influential holistic philosopher in the western world. He saw life as a series of relationships within a whole. Our life is only a small manifestation of a larger entity—it only has meaning as part of this larger entity. We are individuals, but we exist within a larger picture.

This led to his view that just as the heavens and nature are evolving, so does man and his institutions. The relationship between man's quest for individual freedom and his necessity for interdependence leads to the need for government and that these governments continue to evolve to an absolute.

These changes come through "dialectic," a process of development where one truth or belief inevitably generates its opposite and then the interaction between these two opposing thoughts creates a new concept. This newly formed concept then goes through the same process. In other words life is a continuing and changing dynamic.

Johann Gottfried Herder (1744-1803)

A leader in the *Sturm und Drang* movement whose works included a study of German history and art as well as detailed studies of German folk poetry and song.

He was born in Königsberg (once Prussia, now in Russia) and eventually settled in Weimar where he became a close friend of Goethe. (*See Weimar chapter and Sturm und Drang below.*)

Karl Marx (1818-1883)

Marx studied law in Bonn, Berlin and then settled into philosophy while studying in Jena. His writing was always considered revolutionary since it called for more return of "profit" to the workers who create it. He was the primary writer who focused on the injustices that the ruling class was forcing upon the workers.

This great philosopher and economist created the basis of belief which eventually came to control more than a third of our modern world. His socialist influence is still felt in many ways within most governmental institutions. The moral state requires some countervailing power to the force of pure capitalism which strives only for greater profits and to exploit workers as much as possible.

His philosophy stated that a government can only rule when it effectively represented the economically productive forces in society. When it failed it would be replaced. He saw the rise of the workers as inevitable since they were the real power, and the real value behind the industrial revolution. The power of the people and a selfless distribution of profits created by their work would eventually eliminate the need for government and everyone would live in a Utopia.

He eventually became a virtual Messiah in Communist countries and was considered the devil incarnate in Capitalist countries. Even though the Communist governments failed economically and his vision of Utopia was replaced by harsh dictatorships, his thoughts have been phenomenally influential in western economies through unions, strong labor law, profit sharing, price controls and the strict control of monopolies.

Friedrich Nietzsche (1844-1900)

This monumental philosopher was born the son of a minister in Saxony. He studied in Bonn and in Leipzig and was appointed to the chair of philology at Basel at the young age of 25. Illness forced him to move from Basel ten years later and he moved from place to place trying to improve his health. He had a stroke in Turin which left him hopelessly insane and he lived his last tormented years with his manipulative sister in Weimar.

Nietzsche is one of the most important existentialists. He believed the only reality is here and now—life as we live in the present. For him the life force is the "will to power."

For Nietzsche man must eliminate the concept of God from life and define his goals and live for the here and now. The concept that "God is Dead" is the starting point for his thinking. He bluntly condemns organized religion which posits that we are on Earth only to live correctly until an afterlife of some sort. By focusing on the next life and by defining our actions today based on an imaginary afterlife we are denying life. The meaning of life is found through creativity and interaction.

He claims that the rules and traditions developed to define the good life sap Man's thinking and creative spirit and encourage a life of simple unthinking "herd instinct." He also feels that acceptance of religious and political "truths" limits creativity.

He may be seen to espouse a religion where the ultimate goal is not an undefined "life ever after" only attained by adherence to strict rules, but a full and complete life here on Earth with complete freedom of thought and expression.

Elisabeth Förster-Nietzsche (1846-1935)

Born in Saxony, Elisabeth Nietzsche eventually settled in Weimar with her husband. She took care of her brother after his stroke and took full advantage of his fame, eventually becoming what some call the "High priestess of the Nietzsche cult."

She became the main force behind her brother's works after he became an invalid. She was a Nazi sympathizer who created the impression that the Nazis were following Nietzsche's philosophy, when her brother was strongly against war and any dictatorial regime. She developed so much influence within German political circles that she was eventually nominated upon three occasions by the German government for the Nobel Prize for Literature.

Max Planck (1858-1947)

Originally from Kiel, Planck studied theoretical physics at the University of Berlin and eventually returned there as a professor. An early supporter of the theories of Einstein, he had published his radiation law in 1900, which first postulated, based on his work in blackbody radiation, that energy was radiated and absorbed in certain multiples that depended on the frequency of the electrons involved; these multiples he called "quanta" and this was the beginning of quantum physics, upon which he and many other twentieth century physicists would build. The Nobel Prize for physics was awarded to Planck in 1918, and he became one of the four permanent members of the Prussian Academy. After World War II the Kaiser-Wilhelm Institute was renamed for him; he is remembered not only for his professional contributions in physics but also as a man of wide culture and great personal integrity.

Arthur Schopenhauer (1788-1860)

This philosopher of pessimism was born in Danzig (now Gdansk in Poland) and then moved to Berlin and Jena where he pursued philosophy.

He claimed that there were two basic aspects to the world: Representation (what we see) and Will (hidden reality). Will is a blind irrational natural force. Will is metaphysical reality and each person's only can glimpse it through his individual experience. Will, not reason, is the controlling force within us. Our will to live is a cycle of want, temporary fulfillment and more want.

Lets assume that we desire something, like a new car. We work and save to get the car. Once we have it, we see another bigger and better car. So, once again, we go back to working and saving to get the next model. In Schopenhauer view are suffering while we strive for our desire. Then new desires replace any satisfied ones. So no final or lasting happiness is possible. Every time we get what we want, we will want something else. We can never be satisfied. Even our overall will to live is doomed to failure . . . we all will eventually die. There is no overall purpose of life.

This "pain and suffering" of striving for something with you which will never be satisfied, expresses the world's true nature. Suffering and pain outweigh rewards in life and are central to the riddle existence.

Artistic movements and styles

Sturm und Drang (c.1770-c.1780)

In Germany, this was a prelude to the Romantic Movement. Basically Sturm und Drang was a back-to-German-cultural-roots movement. It literally translates to Storm and Stress. This was a unique German literary movement without parallel in other European societies.

This movement loosely followed the exaltation of freedom and nature proclaimed by Rousseau and amplified by Johann Herder (see Weimar chapter) with the inclusion of folk poetry and an exploration of German history and art. Goethe wrote the movements most important works and served as the focal point for most of the thinkers connected with this movement. His friend Schiller was the last major Sturm und Drang writer.

Sturm und Drang literature celebrated nature and individual strength at the expense of contemporary social rules and regulations. It was also an intellectual assault against the stylized way of thinking demanded by the

18th-century neo-classical conventions. The movement eventually developed into the Romantic Movement.

The Romantic Movement

The worst thing about this is its name. The term "Romantic" has been used so loosely over the years, to describe so many things, that it now carries a lot of misleading baggage. It has nothing to do with stories about sappy love (and often unrequited), unrealistic dreams, and whiny self-pity.

In Germany, the movement is generally seen as a revolt against the ordered, reasoned constraints of classicism. It was an extension of the thought of the *Sturm und Drang* thinkers. German Romantic artists and writers were the first group to fully embrace Romanticism.

The movement eventually flowered in other European countries as well as in Germany in the middle of the 19th century. In France it is associated with the works of writers such as Victor Hugo and George Sand. In Britain it was associated with Shelley, Keats and Byron.

German painters who are considered romantics are landscape artists such as Friedrich and Kersting, with their mystical and pantheistic points of view.

The movement spilled over into music with an emphasis on feeling and a loosening of form constraints which resulted in the music of Liszt and Wagner who linked literature with music. (*See Goethe, Hoffmann, Lessing, Schiller, and Schlegel above.*)

The Enlightenment

This was the mainstream thought in Europe during the 18th century. It was the first more or less universal call for more power to the people. This view was based on a belief in natural law and human reason. Major champions of Enlightenment held that man is rational and should be free to live in harmony with the world. Dogmatism, authority, censorship, and intolerance were all seen as impediments to human progress.

The Age of Enlightenment changed the way the western world perceived itself. It eventually resulted in the American and French Revolutions, as well as the concept that man is a reasoning creature.

Gothic

Gothic style developed from the mid 1100s through about 1400. The style was centered in northern France but spread throughout Europe. Basically the architects found a way to make light and windows an integral part of the building by developing other weight-supporting methods such as flying buttresses, ribbed vaulting and peaked arches.

The peaked arches directed the weight outward and the buttresses countered that force by pushing inward, creating an architectural balance which allowed the churches to have massive windows and very high ceilings.

Gothic churches in Cologne, Freiburg and Ulm mirror the French Gothic style. The cathedral in Meissen also reflects many of the traditional Gothic styles. But in most of the eastern part of Germany a simplified style emerged using brick as the basic building element and vaulting became somewhat of an eastern German specialty.

They developed what became known in architectural circles as the Hall Church. There columns rose to dizzying heights and then blossomed into an array of vaulting and windows extended the full height of the buildings. There are external buttresses however they are not the light spindly type found in France.

Renaissance

This period of architecture roughly covers the period from the early 1400s through the early 1800s. Though Baroque made some inroads during the early 1670s. The center of Renaissance architecture was in northern Italy and most of the Renaissance buildings which remain today were in some way designed or supervised by Italians.

Renaissance architecture takes its roots from Classical architecture of the Romans and later from the antique Greeks. In its time it was considered a return to the classical from the excesses of Gothic design.

The Thirty Years War and the slow recovery from its destruction delayed the introduction of Renaissance style into Germany until the end of the 1600s.

Some of the Renaissance style influences seen in buildings are domes and the highly decorated stepped gables found on many public buildings in Eastern Germany.

Baroque and Rococo are both considered variations on the Renaissance theme.

Baroque

A form of Renaissance architecture and design marked by flamboyant designs covering every possible portion of a building. Baroque architecture was at its height in most of Europe from the mid-1600s to the mid-1700s. Its influence in Eastern Germany is mainly during the mid-1700s.

These Baroque decorations took the form of colored marble, bright paints and gold leaf against stark white. Straight lines were eliminated whenever possible.

Rococo

Since Eastern Germany has such a late flowering of Baroque art, Rococo made its appearance in a complimentary fashion more than as a competing style. Many palaces have one or two Rococo rooms, such as the Ballroom, while the remainder of the building displays Baroque touches.

Rococo is a lighter more ornamental, more fanciful form of Baroque architecture with bright colors, mirrors, ivory, gold leaf which disguises the actually building form. Frederick the Great's music room at Sans Souci is an excellent example of Rococo.

Neo-Classical

Neo-Classical styles came into favor as Europe became more democratic. It was the in vogue in Eastern Germany from the late 1700s through the early 1900s. It can still be seen in many governmental buildings across Europe and in the USA as well.

This style is a return to the days of Greek and Roman architecture. It is considered a more "democratic" from of architecture, as opposed to Baroque and Rococo which came to symbolize the excesses of the European royalty.

Columns came back into style and buildings began to look like Green and Roman temples. Many of the buildings in Berlin reflect this neo-Classical style. The rules for buildings were restraint, simplicity and balance.

Journey through the East
From base camp to Weimar

When I was with my friends Goldie and Bomber in Garmisch getting ready to strike out for the East and wondering to make plans with so little information, they told me a story. Bomber, sitting on his couch surrounded by Third World artifacts and sipping on an *Augustinerbrau*, said, "I always think about this when I'm heading into a new place."

"A friend and I were walking the length of Japan and met a monk who took us into a monastery for several weeks. Every night the monks would do intricate sand sculptures. We would wake up and discover something new each morning. One sand box, however, never seemed to change. A monk took my friend to the side of this box. "Sit here with me," he said.

They sat for several minutes. The monk asked, "What do you see in front of us?"

My friend replied, "I see a box of sand, very fine white sand, and three rocks."

"You are blind," the monk quietly said. "Come back tomorrow and sit with me for a day. We will examine this together with time and with changing light."

The next day came, they sat together from dawn to dusk, contemplating this scene. The monk asked as the sun disappeared behind the mountain, "What do you see?"

My friend says, "I see a box of sand with three rocks."

The monk resignedly shook his shaved head, "Still blind. You must look with other eyes. Come back tomorrow. We will sit together again."

As the sun peeked over the landscape to the East, the monk and my friend sat together. They moved to eat rice together when the sun was high and returned to sit and gaze silently. The monk asked again, "What do you see?"

My friend this time was far more specific, "I see glistening white sand and the sun sparkles off the bits of silica mixed with the white sand. The perfect rows of sand lead to three rocks. One is bigger, with crater-like chunks eaten by the weather or the water from its sides; the second is gray and smooth, with a line of white running from one end to the other; the third is flat and smooth, probably worn down from years in a river. It is light, with flecks of black speckled across its side." He looked hopefully at the monk who never shifted his gaze from the rocks in the sand.

The monk slowly spoke. "I see a beautiful ocean with rippling waves and three dolphins leaping through the water. Come tomorrow and we can sit again together."

As the sun rose, they again sat side by side. When the sun was high, they retired to enjoy a bowl of rice, then sat again silently until the sun was low in the Western sky. The monk turned to my friend, "What do you see today before us in our garden?"

My friend, staring directly ahead at the sand and rock garden, says, "Yes, I see what you mean. The ripples in the sand are like the waves on the sea. The three rocks can be three dolphins diving through the waves. You can almost see the sand billowed against their side as if it were water splashing. Yes! I can see what you see." His focus shifted to the monk—still silent by his side. The sun moved lower in the sky, and the shadows grew longer and the flowers had completely turned, tracking the sun.

The monk spoke very slowly, "Today, what I see is a dragon flying through the clouds. You still cannot see. Come with me again tomorrow; we will sit together and learn to see."

The next morning with the dew fresh on the small bushes, the flowers not yet open, the music of birds beginning in the trees, and the glow of the coming sun spilling over the horizon, they sat before what had become almost an altar, this square of rocks and sand. Almost motionless, they gazed directly ahead, not looking to the side, searching for sight. The shadows disappeared and they ate together—simple rice from a wooden bowl—this time not moving from their spots, focused on the sight before them.

As the sun touched the top of the mountains in the west, the monk again asked, "What do you see?"

My friend smiled. "I see much," he said. "I see what I never saw before. I see three turtles crawling onto the beach to lay their eggs. I see your dragon with wings flying through billowing clouds. I see three ants searching the sand for a new home. I see three rocks resting peacefully before two sitting men."

The monk never moved. When the only part of the sun was a tiny red speck shining over the western mountains he said, "Tomorrow you may begin to travel again through the country. You can experience it as only one can who can see." We left the next morning with the rising sun, walking north to Mt. Fuji."

Pre-trip thoughts

I've spoken with scores of people—Americans and Germans. They've all heard stories about "The East," but no one's been there. I've met about five who went overland to Berlin in the old days, but their input is almost useless. They can't answer simple questions like what to see, what to take for barter—money, they say. But there's got to be something like silk stockings, candy bars, ballpoint pens, or Bic lighters that everyone can use and can't find. I'm drawing a blank.

> *I can't remember a trip I've taken where I'm stepping so much into the unknown. I've always had some idea from some fellow traveller about what to expect and how to prepare.*

On this trip, I only get vague comments like, "Watch your car, they steal them." "The drivers are crazy — they have just bought Western cars that can go 140 kpm, but they have never driven faster than 80 kpm in their little plastic cars." "Stop early to find a place to stay. By evening all lodging is taken." "The roads are very narrow—like a paved cowpath." "No one knows how to work. They work an hour or two, then stop for the day. They're used to quotas." This will be like joining a tribe of pygmies in

Africa and slowly discovering their rituals. This evening, I'll deal with the first ones, dinner, then sleep—assuming I'm in the East by then.

Heading toward the east

I've decided to head to the area north of Wurzburg and spend the night, perhaps in the West, and early in the morning head to Weimar, settle in and explore the country from there.

I finally got on the road about 3 p.m. on 1 October and headed North. I had heard such horror stories about getting rooms in the East that I decided to stay just on the Western side of the border. Got a room in the town of Bad Neustadt for DM45, including breakfast. Had lasagna at an Italian place up the road. Got more stories about the bad roads and how poor everything was in the East.

As I sat there by myself, sipping on my last bit of Chianti, it was like spending my last night at base camp before striking out for the summit of Everest. When I was in the Army, this was my intelligence area of responsibility. I remembered battle plans and attack routes over the Fulda Gap and Meiningen, just where I was headed now. My eye looked over the terrain with the care of a commander preparing for battle. It was terrain I had never driven, but knew intimately from maps, aerial photos and helicopter overflights. It's really strange when you know you'll be driving into the land of the Bogeyman in the morning—not to be faced with T72 tanks and artillery, but a people struggling to work themselves into something like your lifestyle.

Early in the morning, I looked out my *Gasthaus* window to the north. A front was moving from West to East—it would be a good day in about an hour. I dressed and went upstairs for breakfast. My toothless host remarked to someone that I looked much younger this morning than when I showed up late last night. Then his face brightened when he realized I could understand most of what he was saying. I had planned on a peaceful breakfast, but instead I heard a litany of stories about how this once border town had changed and now was in the middle of Germany. It proved to be a story I'd hear over and over from folk on both sides of the border.

The border

I was rolling, on my way, jumping off at about 9 a.m. — the time had come. There was a bumper-to-bumper line heading into the East. There wasn't that much traffic, only a series of strategically placed, very slow trucks going up very steep hills. It didn't matter.

I was savoring this moment, perfectly happy to take it as slow as the slowest truck. Even on the Western side, this was no-man's-land, where once upon a time even I couldn't wander. The road steepened and turned, and I saw the first tower.

All its windows were broken. Many of the white shingles on the sides were missing. It looked decrepit, but it wasn't marred by graffiti. It just stood by itself—alone—a solitary sentinel over the countryside. The road swung to the left and down the hill to the right. I could see three guard towers, all dark, stretching to the forest line. Everyone's car was creeping now. The trucks weren't holding anyone up. No one hurried. Life at the crest of this hill was running in slow motion. Two turns later, I passed the old, gray, empty customs station, then 100 yards further was a guard barracks, now turned into a restaurant and truck stop. I should have stopped, but I didn't.

A few turns later, about five kilometers into the East, I passed another series of towers and another checkpoint where they had controlled the local people who lived within this border zone. It had been a phenomenally elaborate and effective system for keeping people in.

From Meiningen to Weimar

The first city of substance after crossing the border is Meiningen, which was up until two weeks ago home of a Russian regiment. I parked on the outskirts and walked into my first East German town . . . one that I had studied militarily but knew only as a spot on a map, a target for long-range missiles. I'm glad I never had to fire our version of a Scud at Meiningen—it is an elegant town. It's not pretty: it's run-down, dirty, unkempt, grey, deteriorated, but you can see a powerful heart in this city—the architecture hasn't been destroyed, just ignored. The people are bustling, and when it's restored over the next five years or so, this will be a gem. The town didn't suffer from Western-style overbuilding and was never "blessed" with becoming an East German industrial center.

This is a pattern that I will see in every East German city. The inner core city is still there—barely alive, looking like a prime candidate for a bulldozer, tiles missing from roofs, flecks of stucco not quite covering the wooden walls inside. The heavy beams in half-timbered houses, which we usually see done in deep brown, are as gray as the plaster which surrounds them. But it's not disheartening.

These towns don't look any worse than small towns surrounding Heidelberg or Frankfurt when I first arrived therein the Sixties. When the West Germans wring their hands and seem concerned about the sorry state of the East, they should remember where they were only a few decades ago.

The East's infrastructure is in worse shape, but it will come around. In Meiningen, I wandered into the church, which was uninspiring, then headed to the Ducal Palace, which turned out to have a good museum.

On the way out, I asked directions to the English Gardens from an old lady. Her face lit up and she asked if I'd like to see some beautiful old houses as well. I said, "Of course," and off we headed. She pointed out the old post stop, showed me where the Communist headquarters had been, explained that the red building had been a clinic and the green one a school.

I was still waiting for my directions to the English Gardens. She looked up at me and said, "I hear an accent in your speech. Are you English or American?" I answered, "American." She said, "It's good to speak with an American again. I haven't spoken with one since the war." My mind reels—that's 50 years! "Ah, here's the house you should see," she says as she leads me through a small door off the town's main street. Beyond the narrow doorway, it became a new world. In a courtyard off the street, it was as if time had stood still for 300 years. The courtyard was surrounded with beautifully preserved half-timbered houses. On the wall were photos of Meiningen after the big fire of 1874—only the church was standing; other photos show the town after the war. Then she took me outside and pointed the way to the theater and the English Gardens.

It was past noon. I decided to head to Weimar and get a room. I had been well warned not to wait till the last minute and show up in town late, as I normally do. I zigzagged through the mountains (big hills, really) and headed north. Each town I passed was relatively untouched by modernity—at least the form we've experienced in the last four decades. Then I came to Sühl, one of the centers of East Germany's firearms industry. This poor town had been saddled with box-like buildings which spread in virtually every direction—up hills and into valleys. I kept going. I began to notice that every factory I passed was closed. No smoke poured from the tall chimneys. No trucks rolled in their yards. No workers scurried between buildings. Only silence.

Arriving in Weimar

The road kept winding and I arrived in Weimar at about two in the afternoon. I was immediately struck with the beauty of this town. It had not suffered the indignities of East German industrialization, and the inner town was very much intact. A beautiful park stretched along the river. After reading that Goethe and Schiller had both decided to live here, I was expecting an aura of quiet studiousness—a place where one could contemplate, then wander back into the real world. That is exactly what Weimar affords.

The room reservation woman set me up only a five-minute walk from the center of old Weimar—cost: only DM18 a day, including breakfast and the reservation fee (that's only $12 a night). The town information desk passed out maps of Weimar. I tried to hook up with a town guide, but because of the next day's unity celebrations, every tour was full. They said, "Come back tomorrow at 10:30 a.m. We'll see what we can manage."

I left the Marktstraße and noticed that the regional tourist office was only a few blocks away from my parking place. I decided to head in that direction. I got there after wandering through gaping streets ripped up for major construction: new water mains, new telephone cables were being laid underground. The regional office was as chaotic as the streets: ladders against walls, boxes piled in the hallways, office furniture spread in foyers—the place was clearly going through an upheaval. My contact had moved to the next town south, but one of the secretaries dug out brochures and typed out a list of new phone numbers for room reservations in all the tiny towns of the region. She circled spots on my map I shouldn't miss. We smiled at each other, shook hands and I was on my way. By this time, I only had about an hour until my room would be available, so I wandered through the town—getting a feel for it, finding the castle, theater, Schiller's house, Goethe's house, restaurants the tourist office recommended, then back into the car and off to my apartment.

My first eastern German private room

When I found the building where my room was located, I was surprised. I had these visions of a palatial old building facing the park. Reality struck as I saw a virtually black-with-soot edifice strategically located on a corner, overlooking the main Weimar cemetery. I rang "Schultz" and climbed to the second floor where Frau Schultz was beaming. I got *ein herzlicher* welcome and saw my room—adequate with a shared bathroom with bath and shower nozzle—what luxury. I lugged my suitcase up and prepared for a three-day stay. Inside, was better than I expected.

Dining with the locals

I headed downtown looking for a place to eat, drink and be merry. Walked downstairs to the Ratskeller, but it was all tourists so headed out again. The town was quiet on the streets, very quiet. Your imagination fired by the old lamplights (not added for effect, just old and kept working by necessity) could run wild. I swear I could hear a carriage around the corner or saw Schiller or Goethe walking by. After wandering up a particularly dark street, I came across a *Gaststätte* which seemed good. Walked in, took a seat at the bar and ordered a beer. They had a good selection of local beers, so I knew I'd be here for awhile. When a table opened, I moved and ordered Thüringer dumplings with a kind of deer stew.

Just after I'd ordered, a group of four came in and asked if anyone else was sitting at my table. "No," I said. "Sit down." It didn't take long for us to start a lively conversation.

Before I get into that, I've been noticing that these East Germans look just like the Westerners. I'd expected a less up-to-date style in clothes—more old stuff, and so on.

It seems clothes came first on their list, then a car, then improvements for their houses, which many of them now own for the first time.

So, on with the conversation...

The group of four was two couples. The two guys and one of the women spoke fairly understandable German. The other woman's German was laced with such dialect, it was almost impossible to understand (not an uncommon problem in any part of the country).

The most outgoing of the group, and also the most understandable, was a forester. His job is provided by the state. Control of forests is a government job. Right now, he's not working since the government hasn't decided what it wants to do—but he gets paid.

He originally came from a town in the Harz, right on the border. The fences went up virtually in his backyard. Kids he grew up with were separated because of the streets they lived on. (In the beginning, before the clear zone was created, they could still carry on conversations across the border fences.) After high school, he moved to Weimar. He has been there since, working in the Thüringerwald. Right now, one of his gripes is that the government is bringing in wood from Bavaria to rebuild half-timbered houses. He understands why—the wood must cure before being used for construction—but he wonders when they will get to work here to build up their stock and bring in money.

I don't think he has long to wait. The East has tract after tract of forest land and farm land—it's much less densely populated than almost anywhere in the West.

I began to ask questions about life in Weimar. I told them that I hadn't heard very much, except that things were tough and no one seemed terribly pleased with unity so far. All the locals at the table were full of optimism. "We know we've made mistakes in making German unity a reality but now we know what to do and can get on with it."

They actually were quite light-hearted about their situation. When we spoke about cars and the problems with *Stauen* (traffic jams) which seem to be everywhere, they joked about driving.

"Before, when we had less than one car for every other home, we all wished that we could have more cars. Now we have cars for every family and we wish only half of them were on the road."

When I asked how life in general was going, they reached into their pockets and pulled out a German mark. Holding it up they said, "Now we have this—we all have the same money." Then with a smile the forester continued, "Before we had lots of money, East German marks, but nothing to buy with it. Stores were empty, you had to wait years for a car. Now we can buy just about anything we want but have no money."

Life with a Trabi

I continued, "You mentioned waiting years for a car. What do you mean? Was there a waiting list? Did you have to do something special to get one?"

The smaller man chimed in,"No we didn't have any special controls on cars—there just weren't enough. We would wait 14 years on the list for a Trabi."

The forester dug into his pocket and pulled out an old East German 10-mark note. "I keep this as a souvenir," he said as he waved the now worthless money at me across the table, "But it is perfect for this conversation." He put the note in front of him on the table and pointed to the beautiful young woman pictured working in a lab. "We used to say that when you first ordered your Trabi you looked like this young woman." He then turned the 10-mark note over and pointed to an old woman pictured on the other side. "When your Trabi finally arrived, this is what you looked like." We all laughed, and the next table roared with laughter as well.

Let me describe the Trabi. I read this to the Easterners and they all laughed again. Sixty percent of the cars on the roads are these Trabies, properly called Trabant, and put together in an auto factory in southern East Germany.

Trabies are tiny putt-putt mobiles with bodies made of plastic and sawdust. They are about the size of the original Honda Civic, with the shape of a Nash Rambler.

The engine sounds relatively smooth when it's running at 1000 rpm or more, but when it's idling it sounds like a misfiring lawn mower and puffs out billowing white exhaust as each piston explodes. You forever see folk by the side of the road fixing these things. Evidently they are as easy to fix with a wire and a screwdriver as the old VW bugs, but need it more often.

Trabi Economics

This description brought more than smiles—the table all declared their love of the Trabi. They began to describe the Trabi's strange economics. Since there was such a long waiting list, many people found they could sell a five or six year old Trabi for more than the price of a new one.

If Trabi owners left their rear window open, potential buyers would drop in offers with their address. Even if the owner hadn't thought about selling, they would sometimes drive to the highest bidder's house with offer in hand, and make the deal. Used Trabies had the added cachet of being ready *now*, and new orders had to age more than a decade.

This process also produced a lively market in waiting list positions. Entire families would sign up for Trabies arranging for one to be delivered every three years or so. The husband ordered one, the wife ordered one, then each of the children ordered one as they reached the right age. A family of five who planned well might have 5 Trabies ordered. They would then sell their waiting list spots to others who didn't plan as well. There was even a barter system where a spot to get a Trabi next year might be traded for two spots five years further on.

Many families spaced their waiting list time by about two years, and as they picked up a new Trabi they sold their old one, making a thousand or so Marks profit on each turnover. They all had loving stories about Trabies and how you had to become a mechanic just to drive one and keep it running.

But everyone at the table agreed they would never buy one today. "In the past we couldn't drive anywhere, so a Trabi was OK—today we can travel anywhere we want and it makes no sense."

The woman sitting across from me leaned over and asked, "What do Americans think about East Germany?"

"We don't really think about it. It's been an empty spot on a map with Berlin in the center," I shrugged, "We know much more about western countries and perhaps Poland than we know about East Germany. Even today there is very little about East Germany on TV and when I went to buy a guidebook in America I was told they don't exist. I eventually found a British guidebook. It's a big unknown."

The woman across the table said, "We had lots of good things, especially our kindergartens, the schools and athletics. There weren't "things" like cars, telephones, washing machines, but some very important things were very good. We have to mix the good from our system with the good from the West. Then we'll be better off. But now everything we had is being swept away. It's a shame."

The barkeep announced that it was closing time. Conversations came to a close. We got up shook hands and said goodbye. I had been through my first night in the East.

The Day of German Unity

When I planned this trip, I had no idea that I'd be in Eastern Germany on such a momentous occasion. It was a year ago today that the two Germanys officially became one. I think everyone went into the union with visions of sugarplums. It's been a tough go—especially for East Germany, which has seen its industrial output drop over 70 percent while unemployment skyrockets. The West has borne the burden with higher taxes—clearly earmarked for East German reconstruction. The situation has created a not-to-be-unexpected backlash on both sides. The East Germans feel they are poor relations or unwanted stepchildren of the West, and the West Germans moan that the Easterners don't appreciate all they're doing.

I got up and had a pleasant breakfast and conversation with Frau Schultz. I found out she's originally Polish and her husband died five or six years ago at the age of 55. Both she and her daughter are delightful hosts and the breakfast include everything from rolls, to bread, to jam, jelly, wurst, liverwurst, sliced meats, cheese or eggs. It's all laid out for you in her kitchen.

After that spread, I wandered downtown to see what was happening and check out what the Weimar Tourist office might have arranged for a tour. When I got to the Marktplatz a horn quintet was playing classical music on the balcony of the Town Hall while a crowd gathered below and wurst, beer, wine, and other eating stands set up shop.

To this day I find it incredulous that there were Germans dancing polkas to ump-pah-pah music played by a Soviet Army Band decked out in perfectly pressed uniforms.

Checked in with the Tourist Office to try and get a tour of Weimar, but no luck until Saturday night. I said thanks, but I had to be in Dresden by then. So I started out on my own city tour with my collection of brochures and books.

I returned several times to the square where festivities continued for the entire evening. Eventually I decided to eat and write at a Gasthaus across the street.

Just as I started to write in the smoky, nicotine-brown dining room, an East German student saw the book I was carrying and haltingly read the English title out loud. That prompted me to say hello, which started a conversation, which prompted the rest of his table to say in uncertain English, "hello," which in turn encouraged half the room to greet me with smiles and an *"Allo"* or *"Guten Abend"* and later with a chorus of *"Guten Appetit"* when my food finally was served.

Out of this group of about two-dozen Germans filling this gaststätte, I was the first American two-thirds of them had ever met! I like being first, but I never dreamed it would be in this situation. During that conversation I was talking with university students who had only known the East system for their entire life. Until that conversation, I don't think I realized there were people here who really liked or accepted amiably the old system. Other than that revelation and the fact that they announced I was their first American, it was uneventful.

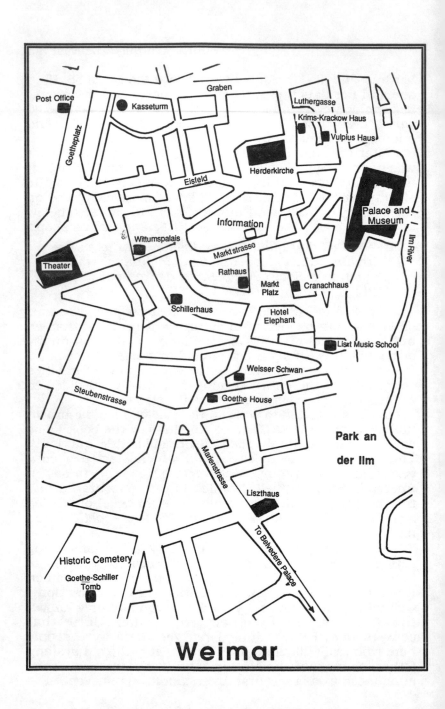

Weimar

Weimar

This is one of the cultural capitals of Germany. The city has preserved a small-town atmosphere amid some of the most beautiful classical buildings, small museums and extensive parks in Germany. Like Heidelberg, Weimar has the air of a not-too-large, not-too-small university town filled with history. It can serve as a perfect center for exploring other nearby towns and the beautiful outdoors of the Thüringerwald to the south.

The Weimar Republic

To most of us here in the States, this name is associated with the short-lived Weimar Republic, created here by the national assembly in 1919.

The Weimar Republic was intended to fill the political vacuum after the loss of World War I. In fact, the Imperial government had already collapsed for the most part before the armistice (which we celebrate on November 11, Armistice Day) was signed. More to the point, it was never really signed by anyone in command—no one was in command. The document only has a nameless signature, "Imperial Chancellor."

Immediately after the war most of the cities in Northern Germany were in the throes of a communist revolution, just like the one that overthrew the Czar in Russia. To make matters worse the armistice was virtually ignored along the contested Polish border. While the Americans, French and British consolidated their peace along the western front, hostilities continued in the east. There was widespread hunger, made worse by the Allied blockade of the North Sea and by the confiscation of 150,000 freight cars, 5,000 locomotives and 5,000 trucks under the terms of the treaty. Widespread starvation was the rule throughout the winter of 1918-1919. The Versailles Treaty wasn't signed until the following spring, and then only under highly vocal protest. To show this displeasure at the treaty, the German navy scuttled their entire fleet before signing.

Under the terms of Versailles, the French managed the virtual occupation of Germany until 1930. The treaty also forced the liquidation of the German Empire—nearly all Germany's overseas possessions and large chunks of her territory on the European continent—and the creation of what became known as the Weimar Republic. This was in essence a government formed by moderate socialists who attempted to maintain as much of the remaining German social and economic order as possible.

The meeting of the National Assembly

The National Assembly met in Weimar only to avoid the chaos, turmoil and open revolution taking place in Berlin at the time. They returned to Berlin after this short meeting. That is about the entirety of Weimar's participation as center of the republic.

This frail government limped through the next ten years, avoiding overthrow and eventually weaving its way back into the world community by means of generous foreign loans negotiated in a series of treaties. The government enjoyed support from a majority of its citizens, and seemed to be on the way to succeeding.

The fall of the Republic

The collapse of the world economy in 1929 destroyed that hope. Eventually one out of every four Germans was unemployed. The government collapsed, and the loyalty of the people to the moderate politics of the Weimar Republic dissolved. The Communist vote steadily grew to almost 15 percent, while at the same time Hitler's National Socialists reached about 40 percent. The question, now that more than 50 percent of the people had no faith in the moderate Weimar Republic, was which way it would fall, to the right or to the left. In 1933, through a series of bumbled political maneuvers, Hitler was appointed Chancellor, even without a majority of the vote. Even then, and while his thugs controlled the streets, Hitler could only claim 44 percent of the vote. Hitler's final rise to power was orchestrated through the burning of the Reichstag building in Berlin and the Enabling Act of 1933 which made him effective dictator.

History and culture of Weimar

The list of luminaries who worked, studied, taught, wrote, painted, played and lived here reads like a Who's Who of German Culture—Lucas Cranach the Elder, Johann Sebastian Bach, Friedrich Schiller, Johann Wolfgang von Goethe, Johann Gottfried von Herder, Franz Liszt, Richard Strauss, Christoph Wieland, Lyonel Feininger, Vassily Kandinsky, Walter Gropius, Gerhard Marcks and Paul Klee, to name a few.

The modern town was first founded about 1250, though there are remains of settlements dating back many thousands of years. Weimar grew to prominence in the 16th century when it became the residence of one of Germany's electors, Johann Friedrich. The city reached its peak in the 18th century under the patronage of the Duchess Amalia and her son Charles Augustus. Christoph Martin Wieland was the first novelist, poet and playwright to dominate the cultural scene. Then Goethe arrived at the court in 1775.

Goethe and Weimar became synonymous. Goethe's presence made Weimar the literary center of Europe in his lifetime and attracted other geniuses such as the philosopher Herder and dramatist Schiller to the city. He established and directed the Weimar theater. In addition Goethe served as architect and designer for gardens, palaces and other buildings in Weimar and surrounding towns while working in the service of Charles Augustus. In his spare time he performed scientific experiments, worked as a botanist and dabbled in geology. He lived his life to show a man's full potentiality. Many believe that he served as a perfect example for the educated, cultured, and fulfilled man. Goethe died in 1832 and the city continued as a literary, artistic, dramatic and musical center based on his reputation.

Franz Liszt was musical director at the Weimar Theater from 1848 to 1859 and Wagner's *Lohengrin* had its debut here under Liszt's direction. The existentialist philosopher Friedrich Nietzsche lived his final tormented years here. The Bauhaus architectural movement was founded by Walter Gropius in this city as well.

Weimar is a town you can easily tour on foot. It is compact, and even sights outside the walking zone in the town center are easily reached. The small museums, the castle, the churches, the narrow streets and the gardens make this a charming and relaxing town to visit.

Start your visit at Weimar-Information, Marktstraße #4, just off the main square.

Goethehaus

This was Goethe's residence for almost 50 years. He was given this house by Charles Augustus in 1794 after his return from travels in Italy. Goethe immediately redecorated the house with a wide Italian Renaissance staircase and filled the house with artifacts, art and sculpture he had brought back from Italy. He also painted each room a different color since he believed that color affected one's mood—the dining room was a bright sunny yellow and the study was a soothing green.

Goethehaus is located at Frauenplan #1 and can't be missed. Unfortunately all the explanations of Goethe's works and the exhibits about his life are captioned only in German, with no English translation, at least on my last visit. There were no English guidebooks available at the bookstore on the second floor, but I was assured that one existed—be sure to ask.

The museum exhibits Goethe's art and scientific collections as well as his extensive library of over 5,000 books. Here Goethe wrote, lived and eventually died.

Just outside the door of the Goethehaus is the Restaurant Zum Weissen Schwan (The White Swan) where many of Goethe's visitors stayed. Today it is an excellent restaurant. A cannonball is imbedded in its wall facing the door to Goethe's house, a remnant of the shelling of Weimar by Napoleon's troops in 1806.

The house and museum are open March through October, 9 a.m.-5 p.m., and November through February, 9 a.m.-4 p.m. (closed Mon.).

Schillerhaus

This small yellow house on the walking street in the center of town was Schiller's residence for only the last three years of his life (1802-1805). Schiller wrote his most famous work, *William Tell*, while living here. The house itself is restored much as it was when Schiller died. At the rear of the house is a modern museum dedicated to Schiller and his work. Unfortunately, again the explanations are strictly in German and here there was no English-language guidebook available (or rumored to be available). If you do not have a good understanding of German, much of the museum will be lost on you, but the house is quaint and provides a good look at how life might have been in those days.

The house and museum are open March through October, 9 a.m.-5 p.m., and November through February, 9 a.m.-4 p.m. (closed Tues.).

Residenzschloß (Ducal Palace)

Though there have been royal residences on this spot dating back to the 15th century, this palace was built from 1789 to 1803. The previous palace burned to the ground in 1774, leaving only a tower. Much of the current architecture was developed by Goethe. The sweeping east wing staircase, the festival room and the *Goethezimmer* (Goethe room) are all spectacular.

The main point of visiting the palace is the **Kunstsammlung zu Weimar** (Weimar Art Collection). This surprising museum contains a fascinating collection of paintings and sculpture ranging from Cranach to modern European masters. There are also many modern German paintings from the Weimar school, such as Buchholz and Hagen; the Bauhaus period, such as Gropius and Klee; and the German Romantic painters.

Upon entering the museum you encounter a room full of Cranach paintings. He depicts Hercules, Samson and Delilah, Salome before Herod with John the Baptist's head, David and Bathsheba, Samson and the Lion, Caritas, and Adam and Eve, as well as a series of portraits. The almost grotesque faces are captivating. (I find Cranach's *Three Pairs of Lovers* to be the basis of a very bad dream.) Other paintings on this level are by Tintoretto and Titian.

The second floor (European "first floor") is a series of wonderfully ornate rooms to the outer side of the palace. Along the inner side opening into the courtyard, they are filled with landscapes, portraits and wonderful impressionist art works by Kessler. The frescoed Ballroom is filled with Dutch paintings and drawings of the 16th and 17th centuries. The landing on this floor features large works—Lambreucht's *Surreal Forest*, and two works, *Boys Diving from Rocks* and the *Grape Pickers* by the idealist painter Hofmann.

The next floor (European second floor) features 19th and 20th century paintings. Many of these artists are unknown in the United States but worthy of discovery. Some of the work is the terrible "state art" created by the communist artists, but much is beautifully created. Of the late material, I found Gunther Brendel's *Nude* done in 1979 sensuous; Gottfried Schüler's *Houses in Winter* painted in 1969 evocative; Heinrich Burkhardt's *In an Air Raid Shelter* painted in 1947 depicts the horrors of waiting to be bombed; and Harold Metzkes' 1974 painting *Girls by the Lake* provides a lovely vision.

After this collection of modern material you'll be surprised by a mixed bag of masterpieces. One of Claude Monet's splendid versions of *RouenCathedral* is hung beside a window where the changing light adds to the effect. Across from this stands a famous Degas sculpture of a dancer and in the next room around the corner is an original Rodin, *Der Eherne Zeitalter*. You'll also find an excellent work by Max Beckmann, *Boys on the Beach*, painted in 1905 during his impressionist period.

The museum also houses a collection of Russian icons, closed during my visits.

The Weimar Art Collection is open Tues.-Sun. 9 a.m.-1 p.m. and 2 p.m.-5 p.m. (on Friday the museum opens at 10 a.m.). There is a small entrance fee of about DM3.

Herderkirche (Herder Church)

This church dominates Herderplatz only a few minutes' walk from either the palace or the Marktplatz. Some residents and maps refer to this church as the *Stadtkirche St. Peter und Paul* (Town Church of Peter and Paul). In the center of the square stands a statue of the philosopher turned preacher and theologian Johann Gottfried Herder, erected in 1850.

Herder was a good friend of Goethe and moved to Weimar to work more closely with him. He was one of the most influential philosophers in the *Sturm and Drang* (Storm and Stress) literature movement. (see *Personalities*) Herder's most famous works written in Weimar ranged from a collection of folk songs to his *Outlines of the Philosophy of Man*, which developed an evolutionary approach to history.

The church itself was originally constructed in 1498 but then rebuilt in 1735-1745 in a Baroque style. The main attraction is the Cranach altar painting started by the artist and then finished by his son. The triptych shows the Crucifixion; below the cross to the left is Cranach standing between Luther (who holds a book of rules) and John the Baptist; to the right is Christ triumphing over death; and in the background you'll see Adam being cast from the Garden of Eden, the flight from Egypt, and angels announcing the birth of Jesus. Side panels depict the ruling families of the day.

Herder is buried in the church under the organ loft. He rests under a simple slab inscribed with his motto— *"Licht, Liebe, Leben"* (Light, Love, Life). Duchess Anna Amalia is also buried here and to the right of the altar you will also find the tombstone of Cranach the Elder moved from the Jakobskirche cemetery to protect it from decay.

The Herderkirche is open on weekdays 10 a.m.-noon and 2 p.m.-4 p.m.; Sat. 10 a.m.-noon and 2 p.m.-5 p.m.; Sun. 10 a.m.-1 p.m. Organ recitals are held in the summer months at 6 p.m.

Goethe's garden house and Goethepark

This simple cottage with its pitched roof is set in a long, beautiful park that runs along the Ilm River. This was the place Goethe lived for his first six years in Weimar; later in life when he was renowned and living in relative grandeur in town, he would still spend his summers here, where he felt he could think more clearly. The rooms are still filled with original period furnishings and many items actually used by the great writer and thinker. Entrance to the cottage is DM3.

Here he worked on some of his most important works including *Wilhelm Meister*, *Iphigenia auf Tauris* and *Torquato Tasso*. He also used the cottage as a rendezvous with his mistress, the noble writer Charlotte von Stein who would walk across the park from her palatial house during a ten-year love affair.

Goethe, getting the most out life, eventually had to take a vacation from his amours. He went to Italy and upon his return two years later became enamored of Christiane Vulpius, a common factory worker—20 years younger than he—who eventually married the great man. (To be fair it should be added that Christine's brother was a well-known German writer.) She walked along these same forest paths from her tiny house, tucked on Luthergasse beside the Herderkirche, to meet Goethe during their courtship.

The park was laid out by Goethe in the free style of an English garden, recalling nature rather than the tight symmetry of formal gardens of the time. The woods must have been the scene of many romantic scenes. One scandal which rocked the court was the discovery of a lady's body beside the bridge leading to Goethe's cottage. Reporters claimed that she committed suicide for unrequited love or jealously, and died clutching a copy of one of Goethe's books dealing with a spurned lover, *Die Leiden des jungen Werthers* (The Sorrows of Young Werther). Goethe, moved by the incident, had a rocky cave created nearby called the *Nadelöhr* (Eye of the Needle).

The park contains other buildings such as the thatched and moss-covered *Einsiedelei* (Hermitage) where Carl Augustus stayed during the summer and another house he had built the classical *Römisches Haus* (Roman House). The park also contains mainland Europe's first monument to William Shakespeare, erected near Goethe's house in 1904 by Theodor Lessing.

At the edge of the park is the *Liszthaus* where Liszt lived from 1869 until 1886 (Marienstraße #17). Hungarian-born Franz Liszt resided in Weimar (though not in this house) from 1848 to 1859 as well, before heading to Rome for several years. During his time in Weimar he taught most of the leading pianists in Europe, served as the musical director for the Duke of Weimar, and wrote the Faust Symphony and several of his Hungarian Rhapsodies. The house contains many instruments reportedly owned and played by the great master of the keyboard as well as the baton with which he conducted the first performance of *Lohengrin.* The Liszthaus is open Tues.-Sun. 9 a.m.-1 p.m.

Goethe-Schiller Tomb and Historic Cemetery

This cemetery, about a ten-minute walk from the center of town, is most visited by those paying homage to Goethe and Schiller. These two great writers, poets and playwrights are entombed in a stark, classical, columned mausoleum at the end of a wide path lined with linden trees. Carl Augustus, who was responsible for bringing Goethe to Weimar, is buried in the same mausoleum.

Immediately behind the Goethe-Schiller Mausoleum is the onion-domed Russian Chapel built in 1862 for the daughter-in-law of Duke Carl Augustus.

The graves surrounding these two buildings are something of a Who's Who of Weimar society in its golden age. One of Goethe's mistresses Charlotte von Stein, his grandchildren, and much of his family are buried here.

The Mausoleum and the Russian Chapel are open 9 a.m.- 1 p.m. and 2 p.m.-5 p.m. (closed Tues.).

Krims-Krackow-Haus

This house at Jakobstraße #10 across from the Herderkirche is refurnished in the style of a rich merchant's house in the first half of the 16th century. It is one of the oldest buildings in Weimar. The restored house with its Baroque façade also houses the Herder museum with memorabilia and papers documenting the life, times and ideas of Johann Gottfried von Herder.

The house is named for two residents—Franz Krims who lived there during Goethe's time and Charlotte

Krackow who lived there from 1825 to 1917 and preserved the house as a monument to Weimar's classical period.

I expect the museum hours to be similar to other official museums in Weimar, but it was closed during my visits. It was the one sight most recommended by just about every Weimar resident I spoke to.

Take a walk behind this house down the short, evocative Luthergasse. Here you'll find a house with a plaque saying Martin Wieland lived here from 1773 to 1777; he was a friend and mentor to Goethe. A few doors down the narrow street is the house where Christiane Vulpius, who became Goethe's wife, lived.

Rathaus (Town Hall) and Marktplatz

The town hall stands along one side of the Marktplatz built in neo-Gothic style in 1841. It replaced the original Renaissance style town hall, built in the mid-1500s, which burned down in 1837. The two Renaissance doorways to the mayor's office are considered its best works of art, and the city's oldest coat of arms hangs over the hall entrance. A Dresden porcelain set of bells plays on the hour.

The Marktplatz is the scene of *Volksfests* and concerts throughout the spring, summer and fall. During my visit, a brass quartet played from the balcony of the town hall and later a Russian Army band played Umm-pah-pah music while the townsfolk danced and wolfed down local *Thüringerwursts* and Mecklenburg chickens.

Opposite the town hall stands the **Lucas Cranach House**. This three-storey Renaissance house decorated with pillars, dolphins, arches and carved vines, built in 1549, is where Cranach the Elder lived from the time he came to Weimar in 1552 until his death in 1553. Cranach lived earlier in Wittenberg where he worked as the court painter under three electors and also served as the mayor for two terms. He was a good friend of Luther and has been called the Painter of the Reformation. This is where he painted one of his masterpieces, the Herderkirche altar triptych.

Along the northern side of the Marktplatz the buildings have been recently restored to add to the Renaissance flavor of the square. The opposite side of the square is dominated by the **Hotel Elephant** with its 1696 façade. Bach, Wagner, Napoleon and Tolstoy . . . yes and Hitler as well . . . are among its famous visitors, but it was made famous in German literature by Thomas Mann in his book, *Lotte in Weimar (The Beloved Returns)*. In Mann's novel this was the location of a tryst between Goethe and one of his lovers, Lotte Kestner. You'll also find on the square two of the original town kellers, today tourist-filled restaurants—The Elephant Keller and the Ratskeller (not under the town hall but across the square under another city office building).

Fürstenplatz

This square, just off the Marktplatz, is built around a massive statue, erected in 1875, of the Duke Carl Augustus riding on horseback and looking much like a Roman Emperor. On the park side of the square stands the Renaissance Grünes Schloß (Green Palace) which was built as a residence for the two brothers of the duke in the mid-1500s. Today it houses the **Central Library of German Classical Literature** which also encompasses a nearby tower of the town wall. This old library has a wonderful two-storey interior with wooden planked floors and built-in bookshelves. Ornate wooden columns add a classical effect to the decor. The library was first founded by Duchess Anna Amalia and was under the control of Goethe for many years. Schiller's skull used to rest inside the pedestal of a bust of him by Dannecker which can still be seen. His skull has since been reunited with his body in the Goethe-Schiller Tomb.

The library is open Mon.-Fri. 11 a.m.-12:30 p.m. and 3 p.m.-5:30 p.m., and Sat. 10 a.m.-12:30 p.m.; the reading room is open Mon.-Fri. 9 a.m.-noon and 2 p.m.-6 p.m., Sat. 10 a.m.-12:30 p.m.

The long side of the square behind the statue is dominated by the Fürstenhaus where the Duke resided. Today it houses the **Franz Liszt School of Music**.

Jakobskirche

Though this church, with its very recognizable onion-shaped tower, is where Goethe married Christiane Vulpius in 1806, it is most notable for its cemetery. This is the burial place of many of the great pre-1800 names of Weimar history. (Many of the names are relatively obscure for casual students of German literature, art and philosophy.) It is also the final resting place of Goethe's wife and was the burial place of Schiller before his body was moved to the Goethe-Schiller Tomb.

Theaterplatz

The German National Theater, where many original presentations such as Goethe's *Faust*, Schiller's *William Tell*, Liszt's Rhapsodies, and Wagner's *Lohengrin* were performed, dominates this square. The current theater is very modern inside and is the fourth to be built in this location. This theater was also the meeting place for the German National Assembly when they created the Weimar Republic.

In the center of the square stands a statue of Goethe and Schiller cast in 1857.

Opposite the theater is the **Wittumspalais** and **Wieland Museum**. This building was the residence of Anna Amalia for over thirty years. It contains many rooms filled with golden crystal chandeliers, ornate period furniture, gilded stucco relief decor, and Weimar classical paintings. The small ballroom or *Festsaal* is beautifully decorated. The Wieland Museum chronicles the life of Christoph Martin Wieland, the first novelist, poet and playwright to dominate the Weimar cultural scene. He also translated Shakespeare's complete works into German. The annex of the palace, actually on Theaterplatz, is a gallery for changing art exhibitions. The Wittumspalais is open Wed.-Sun. 9 a.m.-noon and 1-5 p.m. Admission is DM3.

Schloß Belvedere

This Baroque palace with its extensive formal gardens and spreading forest is about 2 km south of Weimar. The palace was undergoing extensive renovation during my visits, but the gardens, many designed by Goethe, are beautiful, filled with flowers, plants, and singing birds, and provide a wonderful escape from the museums and bustle of downtown Weimar.

The palace was built in 1739 and used as a getaway and summer palace by the dukes of Weimar. This was one of the retreats of Weimar's luminaries. Rooms are reportedly decorated in ornate Rococo style. You'll also find a collection of carriages and coaches here.

The palace houses a practice section of the Franz Liszt School of Music, so often you'll hear piano music wafting from the palace windows. The Orangerie is beautiful, especially in the mornings when it catches the early sun.

The Belvedere Palace and gardens are open May through September, Wed.-Sun., 10 a.m.-1 p.m. and 2 p.m.-5:30 p.m. The palace is an easy drive south of the town, or about a 45-minute walk from the end of the big town park. There are rumors of starting a direct Belvedere Express Bus for the summer, but Bus #11 leaving from Goetheplatz is the only public transportation that gets you close to the palace. Tell the driver you're headed to Belvedere; he'll let you know when to get off and point you in the right direction—then it's another 15-minute walk. The same bus loops you back to town after you've explored the gardens.

Buchenwald

Four kilometers north of Weimar is the site of the infamous Buchenwald concentration camp. This was a death chamber not only for Jews, but Gypsies and thousands of political prisoners including the leader of Germany's Communist Party at the time of Hitler's rise to power. It is estimated that 56,000 prisoners were executed at this camp. Since it was officially a work camp it did not see the massive murder that other camps such as Auschwitz did.

There is a regular showing, in German, of a documentary about the camp, but you have to ask to see an English-language version. I am sure the presentations will be changing with the changing of the political winds—after the war the camp was used by the Soviets as a prison for Germans who didn't prove to be good communists. In the spring of 1990 the mass graves of more than 15,000

Germans killed by the Soviets were found in nearby woods—already a plaque commemorates this massacre.

Both buses and trains connect Weimar with Buchenwald (direction Etterburg). The memorial created by Fritz Cremer to the prisoners from 32 nations is open daily and the camp and museum are open 9 a.m.-4 p.m. (closed Mon.). Signs marked "KZ Lager" lead to the camp, and "Gedenkstätte" point to the memorial. The camp archives are open to anyone researching relatives who may have been at the camp from 1938 through 1945.

Getting around

The Weimar train station is inconvenient to say the least. It is on the far northern side of the town and about a 20-minute walk from Weimar tourist information. There is an extensive bus system, but you don't really need it except to get back and forth to the station (take Bus #4). The inner town is very walkable, much of it is a pedestrian zone, and most of the private rooms available through the tourist office are within walking distance as well.

Accommodations

The most central hotel in town is **Hotel Elephant**, Markt #19 (tel. 61471; fax 5310). It's expensive and historic. The **Russischer Hof** on Goetheplatz is just as expensive and also very centrally located (tel. 62331, fax 62337). A new hotel has just opened far from the center of action, opposite the park at the south side of the city, **Hotel Belvedere**.

Check with the tourist office for youth hostel information since most of the old hostels have gone back to private hands as "Westies" reclaim houses taken by the old socialist government. You can try **Maxim Gorki**, zum Wilden Graben #12 (tel. 3471); **Ernst Thälmann**, Windmühlenstr. #16 (tel. 2076); and **Am Poseckschen Garten**, Humboldtstr. #17 (tel. 4021).

Dining

Most tourists head to the aforementioned **Zum Weissesen Schwan** (tel. 61715) where Goethe and Schiller dined. Here you can enjoy expensive local cuisine excellently prepared. Call for reservations and wear a jacket.

The **Ratskeller** and **Elephantenkeller** (tel. 61471) on Marktplatz both serve up good food at not too expensive prices, but pricey all the same, and filled mostly with tourists. The atmosphere is Functional Kelleresque. The **Gastmahl des Meeres** on Herderplatz serves good fish dishes in a lovely atmosphere. The **Grabenschänke** at Graben #6 (tel. 62107) had good mid-price fare.

Wander through the town and search out some places filled with locals or students. New restaurants and bars are opening nearly every month. I found the **Scharfe Ecke** (tel. 2430) on the corner of Eisfeld and Geleitstraße. They have good wholesome German cooking for down-to-earth prices, and it seems that most of the locals pass through the bar sometime during the night. For more student atmosphere head to the **Goldener Stern** on Jakobstraße.

Nightlife

In Weimar nightlife is quiet, very quiet. Head to good bars such as the **Scharfe Ecke** or the **Goldener Stern**, or for dancing there is late-night disco in the **Kasseturm**, a student club that also serves pizza.

Tourist information

The Weimar-Information office is at Marktstraße #4, only a stone's throw from the Town Hall (ask locals "Vo ist der Rathaus"). Here you can purchase maps of the town, a brochure with a schedule of events, and walking tours of the town; you can also reserve rooms (tel. 2173, fax 61240 for reservations).

Journey through the East
Part II

Erfurt, Gotha and Eisenach

On my third day in Weimar I headed toward the west to Erfurt, Gotha and Eisenach. This from a sightseeing day point of view was going to be a long day. I though I'd have a chance to come home through the Thüringerwald but ended up without the time.

I first arrived in Erfurt. The town has twin cathedrals topping a hill in the center of the town. It's a charming old medieval town with a bridge bearing half-timbered houses and shops—the only such bridge north of the Alps.

Next stop was Gotha—to me this has always been a target: Headquarters for a Soviet 8th Guards Army division. In Gotha they were having a feast which filled the Marktplatz. I parked, asked around for tourist information. This was an interesting exercise—no one seemed to know where the information office was. Seems it had just been moved recently. Finally a Cinderellaesque serving girl came out from the Ratskeller kitchens and pointed me in the right direction—aahh fairy tales—her directions came in slow motion but not slow enough for me—I could have listened to her talk forever. She had to scurry below to the kitchens when the headwaiter howled up the stairway. Just a fleeting moment.

Gotha, it turns out, has a picture-perfect Hauptmarkt-platz and a Neumarkt both in need of some paint. There is also a massive palace topping a hill overlooking the town. The palace houses a small museum with old masters and a surprisingly good Egyptian collection, along with a dozen furnished and restored palace rooms.

The Wartburg

By now it was past 2 p.m. and I had to head to Eisenach. I was on my way to see the Wartburg. This castle is considered one of the the best preserved medieval fortresses and was where Martin Luther hid out and translated The Bible from Greek to German. Perhaps the most important part of the translation was that it created the standard for a modern German language.

As I turned into town signs announced that you must park below, then catch a shuttle up to the castle. Parking cost DM2; shuttle roundtrip, DM4; castle entrance, DM6. The Wartburg was appropriately spectacular—but crowded—45-minute wait even on a weekday in October! It must be hours on weekends and in the summer.

After going through the Wartburg I walked into town and saw the Bach house (he never lived there), a house where Martin Luther stayed as a student, the cathedral and the town center then headed back to Weimar on the Autobahn.

That evening I was a good boy, writing rather than striking up conversations. I spent the evening working on my journal in a café opposite the Weisses Schwan Restaurant and Goethe's house. It was an upscale affair and very quiet, perfect for writing.

Erfurt

Erfurt

Erfurt is the capital of the new state of Thuringia. Unknown and unheard of by most westerners, this is a fascinating medieval city, one of the oldest in Germany with citations in history dating back to the days of St. Boniface. In 742 he requested that Pope Zachary establish a new bishopric in Erfurt. Obviously there was already a thriving town, but 742 is claimed as the foundation year. Erfurt is undergoing massive restoration work in conjunction with its 1250th birthday celebration in the summer of 1992.

Once you work your way in past the built-up suburbs, the old town, spared the indignities of modernization, is quaint and delightful. The churches here are magnificent, the inner city is charming, and commerce thrives.

Hundreds of years ago, Erfurt was a university and religious center as well as a stop on a major medieval trade road, the Königsstraße running from the Rhine to Russia. Erfurt also stood in the midst of some of Germany's most fertile land, with abundant water; the combination was perfect. The city grew to include 36 churches and 15 monasteries. Its main sights are still the two cathedrals that top the central hill and the old town that spreads beneath the church towers.

Erfurt reached its peak late in the 14th century when it had relative freedom as a free city and member of the Hanseatic League, the mercantile association of German towns. The Krämer Bridge was built in 1325 and the university was founded in 1392. In the 16th century the university would become one of the most important in Germany and the second largest in Europe after the University of Prague. It eventually developed into a center of German Humanism. Luther studied here from 1501 to 1505, but the university eventually closed in the early

19th century. The fortunes of the town had crumbled as Leipzig became the more important trading center, and Erfurt eventually became a part of the Electorate of Mainz, under whose control it remained until it was incorporated by Prussia in 1802.

Napoleon came here in 1809 to meet Czar Alexander I. The meeting renewed the Peace of Tilsit, which had dismantled Poland and relegated Prussia to the status of only a buffer state between the Napoleonic Empire and Russia. Napoleon stepped across the boundaries of the peace he had negotiated, and attacked Russia. His defeat in the Muscovite winter was the beginning of his long retreat back to Paris and eventual exile to Elba.

The Cathedral and Church of St. Severus

These two massive churches crown the same hill in the center of Erfurt. I can't think of another site in Europe which claims two such beautiful churches side by side. An expansive stairway sweeps up 70 steps from Domplatz, ringed with restored Renaissance houses, to the spire-topped churches. As you look up at the two churches from Domplatz the *Dom* (Cathedral) stands to the left and *Severikirche* (St. Severus) to the right.

At the top of the stairs to the right is a small yellow house. Inside is a souvenir shop which sells an English language guide to the Cathedral. If you want more detail than I present here, it's well worth a few DM.

Depending on which tour group guide you hear recounting stories, you may hear the one about Luther hurling his Bible across the altar in his first mass. He claimed that he was aiming at the Devil, while others see it a foreshadowing of his split with the church.

The Dom is the older of the two churches. It has a single Gothic spire and is built upon a massive arched substructure which provides most of the interior floor space. The Dom is very unusual, both in its siting and its situation toward the town. Most churches are built with the monumental, most decorated side at the entrance, at the far end from the altar. This church sits with the chancel facing the town and the unusual triangular gate building halfway along the side of the church, barely visible at the top of the wide, sweeping staircase that leads up to both churches. The interior offers stark contrasts between the old and the new. The rear of the church is new reconstruction and the chancel, with altar and choir, is Gothic.

The stained glass windows are exceptional and date from the 15th century. These are among the best preserved in Europe, with 895 of the 1100 original medieval panes still in place. The 15 windows, each 18 meters high by two and a half meters wide, took more than 40 years to complete. The changing light shifts the mood of this room from brightness and joyful color to somber solemnity.

The choir stalls are among the largest built in medieval Germany. The 89 oak seats are in a double row with ornamentation from northern Germany. They have remained here since they were carved in about 1370. The figurative details are amazing and unusual, with more than 36 female figures.

The Cathedral also contains a Romanesque Madonna and Child carved in the mid-1100s. This small statue is enclosed by an arch depicting the heavens with God sitting in judgement above. The sculpture was originally brightly painted and set up in a small chapel of the north tower where it received a halo of sunlight on the Feast of the Assumption. Near the Madonna and Child is an unusual free standing bronze candlestand known as "Wolfram" which was created during the same period for the town's mayor. This is one of Germany's oldest free standing bronzes. In the bell tower the largest free-swinging bell in the world, *Gloriosa*, hangs and rings only on special occasions. It took three years to hoist up, inch by inch with wooden winches.

To your left as you enter is a side altar and an altarpiece showing the Annunciation with a Unicorn. Belief in unicorns was widespread in this part of Germany during the 1400s. On the southern wall of the nave is a very large (27 by 20 feet) painting in oils on the sandstone wall, the familiar scene of St. Christopher carrying Christ on his shoulders across a river; in the background of the painting are Erfurt's twin churches and the stairway to them.

After walking out of the Apostles' Portal, the other door in the triangular-plan gate building, decorated with figures of the apostles, walk around to the exit on the other side of the portal structure. This door with its carvings of maidens is called the Maidens' Portal. Each maiden is different and they seem to dance around the doorway. All the sculptures on these portals were carved about 1330.

St. Severus, built between 1278 and 1400, is in the German 14th-century style. It has five aisles and three spires. The interior is very Spartan, but the massive organ and the baptismal font with its intricately carved open canopy are impressive.

The Cathedral is open Mon.-Sat. 9 a.m.-11:30 a.m. and 12:30-5 p.m. (closed an hour earlier from November to April). Mass is held at 6 p.m.; Sun. 2 p.m.-4 p.m. Mass is held at 11 a.m. and 6 p.m.

St. Severus is open for visits Mon.-Fri. 9 a.m.-12:30 p.m. and 1:30 p.m.-5 p.m. (4 p.m. from November to April). Mass is held 7:30 a.m.; on Sat. Mass is held at 7:30 a.m. then church is closed; Sun. closed.

The Old Town
The inner portion of the city lies within a triangle marked by the Cathedral, the Augustinerkeller, and Anger. Wander across Domplatz from the Cathedral and walk down Marktstraße. Watch out for the mini-trains rolling down the middle of Marktstraße. Note the Renaissance house at #38. You will arrive at Fischmarkt which was the center of trading activity during Erfurt's heyday. The buildings surrounding Fischmarkt include the neo-Gothic Rathaus, which has excellent paintings of early German tales and fables in the entrance; Zum Roten Ochsen (The Red Ox) once a dye dealer's home and today the town art gallery; and Zum Breiten Herd (the Wide Hearth) which was the headquarters for the town's medieval chamber of commerce.

A few steps from Fischmarkt is the Krämerbrücke (Shopkeepers' Bridge), the only bridge north of Florence that is lined with shops. The shops on this medieval bridge over the river Gera date from the 12th century, and artisans still ply their trades here in many of the 32 houses. The tourist office is also located here.

From the Krämerbrücke turn round the corner to the left on the northern side of the river and head to the

Augustinerkloster (*see below*). Then walk down *Johannesstraße* (Leninstr. on old maps) where you'll pass the city museum housed in the Renaissance-style *Haus zum Stockfisch* (The Dried Cod) at #169. It showcases the development of Erfurt from 1500 to 1815 (Open Sun. - Thurs. 10 a.m.-6 p.m.) Another house on this street is *zum Grünen Sittich* (The Green Canary) at #178. Further down Johannesstraße you will *Anger* (originally meaning Village Green) now a pedestrian zone. The Anger Museum in the Baroque building at #18 contains medieval art, and porcelains and glass from the 16th to 18th centuries. (Open Wed.-Sun. 10 a.m.-6 p.m.) A carillon in the *Barthomäusturm*, Anger #53, plays Wed. and Sun. at 5 p.m.

Augustinerkloster (Augustine Monastery)

Martin Luther studied at Erfurt's Augustinian Monastery to take his vows as a friar. The strict regimen included prayers at midnight and again at 6 a.m., then a morning of begging followed by his one meal of the day at noon, an afternoon and evening of prayer and study, then lights out at 8 p.m. Under this order he was not allowed to laugh or talk during his studies.

The Library, destroyed during the war and recently rebuilt, contains many Bibles including those used by Luther, complete with annotations.

The monastery was first built in 1277 and reached its current appearance about 1350. The former monastery is now a Protestant college. It is open to the public April-October Tues.-Sat. 10 a.m.-4 p.m.; during the school year, from November to March, it is open only for guided tours starting at 10 a.m., noon and 2 p.m.

Other churches

This town has so many churches that it would be a shame to leave without visiting several others after seeing the Cathedral and St. Severus. The *Kaufmannskirche* (Merchants Church) just off Anger has a beautiful altar in high-Renaissance style. The *Schottenkirche St. Jakob* (Scottish Church of St. James) was built in the 12th century by Scottish and Irish missionaries; the city's oldest stained glass window is found in the Gothic

Barfüßerkirche (Barefoot Church); the *Peterskirche* is a good example of Romanesque architecture; and the *Predigerkirche* was built in the 13th century by an order of monks who took vows of poverty.

Getting around

Erfurt is an easy town to walk in, and that is probably the best way to get around. There is also an extensive tram and bus system. Buy tickets at automatic ticket machines at most stops. Bus and tram tickets good for 25 minutes cost 80 pfennigs; one-hour tickets cost DM1.30; 24-hour tickets cost DM3; and 24-hour family tickets for up to five members of the family (only three may be over 14 years of age) cost DM5.

Accommodations

The best hotel and most atmospheric and expensive in town is the **Hotel Erfurter Hof**, Bahnhofsvorplatz #1/2 (tel. 51151). The sterile **Hotel Kosmos**, Juri-Gargarin-Ring (tel. 5510) is almost as expensive with none of the Old World atmosphere. The **Hotel am Ring**, Juri-Gargarin-Ring (tel. 22214) was probably a high-rise workers' apartment; rooms are apartment-like and can be a bargain for a group sharing or a family. **Hotel Bürgerhof**, Bahnhofstraße #35/37 (tel. 21307) has shared baths and lower prices. **Hotel Thüringen**, Juri-Gargarin-Ring 154/156 (tel. 65512) once a youth hostel is now a sparse hotel and a bargain if three or four share a room. **Hotel Germania**, Eislebenerstr. #1 (tel. 5732674) is small, with moderate rooms.

Tourist information

The main tourist information offices are at Krämerbrücke #3 (tel. 23436) and Bahnhofstraße #37. The Krämerbrücke office is open Mon. to Fri. 9 a.m.-12:30 p.m. and 1 p.m.-5 p.m.; Sat. and Sun. 10 a.m.-4 p.m. the Bahnhofstraße office, just down the road from the train station, is open Mon. to Fri. 9 a.m.-6 p.m.; Sat. 10 a.m.-3 p.m.; closed Sunday.

Gotha

Gotha, a small town on the road between Eisenach and Erfurt, was once the center of a minor kingdom and makes a perfect spot for a two- or three-hour stop, perhaps including lunch. Gotha is also perfect for anyone who wants to stay in a small town and use it as a base for local exploration of the Thüringerwald. A little train, the Waldbahn, plies the route between here and the heart of the Thüringerwald to the south.

Gotha is dominated by a massive palace, Schloß Friedenstein, built in 1643-1654. Beneath this palace, the town center is well restored with a picturesque **Hauptmarkt** (Main Market Square) featuring Renaissance buildings, brightly painted stucco, and fanciful medieval guild signs. There, a free-standing *Rathaus* (Town Hall), built in the mid-1500s, presides over a beautiful square with fountain framed by decorative colored stonework. Lucas Cranach the Elder also lived for a short time in a house on this square before moving on to Wittenberg. To the left of the Rathaus is a very good and reasonable Ratskeller which serves up heaping lunches.

Marktstraße connects the Hauptmarkt with **Neumarkt** (New Market) which is built around the late-Gothic **Margarethenkirche**. On the other side of the Hauptmarkt follow the Augustinerstraße, running from the top of the square to the **Augustinian Monastery** which features a small, but well-preserved cloister.

Schloß Friedenstein

This massive white Baroque palace sits atop a hill above the town. The palace grounds are also huge, and take up more area than the entire old town center. The palace contains a series of museums and libraries. You'll find several museums, including an art museum with several Cranach paintings and the well-known portrait of of the *Gotha Lovers*, the oldest German double portrait.

Upstairs many of the palace rooms are open to the public. The first room presents a series of scale models showing the development of the palace from its days as a fortress. Next is an ornate **Baroque and Rococo ballroom** with gilded relief statues holding 17 different coats of arms, an ornate ceiling and glistening chandeliers. The other rooms are filled with furniture, porcelains, and crystal, and feature intricate inlaid wood floors. In the next wing there is, surprisingly, an **Egyptian museum**, and a series of rooms with changing displays.

The palace also houses a research library with over half a million volumes, as well as one of Germany's top cartographic collections, the result of Gotha's prominence in map making in the 1700s.

The western section of the palace also contains an exceptional **theater**, one of the oldest in Germany, built in 1683 and still featuring the original stage, and the **Museum of Local History and Folklore**.

Tourist information

Gotha Information is located a block to the west of Hauptmarkt on Blumenbachstraße #1/3 (tel. 54036). This office can make private room reservations and provides an English-language map of the town. Open Mon. 2 p.m.-5 p.m., Tues. - Fri. 9 a.m.-1 p.m. and 2 p.m.-5 p.m., closed Sat. and Sun.

Eisenach
and Wartburg Castle

This was the closest major East German city to West Germany and it was an industrial center for the east and home of one of their automobile factories. Johann Sebastian Bach was born here in 1685. Martin Luther also lived here, both in the town as a schoolboy and later in the wonderful Wartburg Castle above, where he translated the New Testament from its original Greek into German.

A colorful, well-preserved town center

The Eisenach town center today is a surprisingly well preserved and colorful collection of houses with convenient pedestrian zones. If you come by train, a walk through town will take you to the Wartburg. If you drive, I suggest that you park your car at the foot of the Wartburg and take the ten-minute stroll back to visit the town.

The town is easily toured on foot. The **Bachhaus** (he never actually lived in this house) is located at Am Frauenplan #21. It contains a museum with materials of the Bach family, together with an exhibition of Baroque musical instruments—flutes, lutes, cornets, a clavichord and a harpsichord—upon which the guides perform many of Bach's works. (Hours: 9 a.m.-4:30 p.m. closed Wed. Admission: DM4 (students, children and seniors DM3).

Luther's House stands at Lutherplatz #8. Here Luther stayed while he studied Latin as a schoolboy between 1498 and 1501. The house belonged to Ursula von Cotta. The 15th-century exterior is far more interesting than the interior, which contains some of Luther's works, a collection of Bibles, and family-related furnishings. (Hours: daily 9 a.m.-1 p.m. and 2 p.m.-5 p.m.; Admission DM3; students, children and seniors DM1.50).

On Markt not far from Luther's house is the **St. Georgenkirche** (Church of St. George). This church has a spectacular interior, with three levels of continuous galleries and a wonderful 4,835-pipe organ that was played by four generations of the Bach family from 1665 to 1797. This is also the church where Bach was christened in 1685. Luther preached here and earlier sang in the choir. The church is also noted for its good collection of paintings of Luther, the elector Frederick the Wise, and the Holy Roman Emperor Charles V.

Opposite the church at Markt #24 is the **Museum of Thuringia** with local paintings and blue Thuringian pottery housed in a former town palace built in a Baroque style in 1751. (Hours: 9 a.m.-1 p.m. and 2 p.m.-5 p.m. Closed Mon. Admission: DM2)

The Wartburg

For many this is one of the ultimate destinations in Germany. During its time under Communist rule you actually needed a visa to visit this amazing building, but today throngs of tourists climb up to walk in the footsteps of princes, dukes, Goethe and Luther. No other castle is so filled with German history from the medieval days of wandering minstrels, to the Reformation, to early attempts to create democracy, to a standoff between Hitler's National Socialists and the Lutheran Church.

Warning #1: A visit to the Wartburg means a long (long and uphill) walk. I don't mean from the parking lot or from the town. There are now tourist trains and shuttle vans which wend their way up to the base of the castle cliffs. But once you get off the tourist train (Wartburg Express), or your shuttle from the parking lot there will still be several hundred yards of uphill walking before you can cross the drawbridge into the castle yard. If you have trouble walking, don't say to yourself, "Oh, I'll make it." I saw many tottering senior citizens turn back, even determined Germans. Wear comfortable shoes—no high heels.

Warning #2: Because of the aforementioned throngs of tourists, most of the time, unless you arrive in the first wave of visitors, you will have a long wait. My wait on a weekday in October was over an hour for the guided tour of the interior (there's no escape, it's the only way to see it).

Ask about English language for your tour—a few official castle guides speak English, or the staff may try to hook you up with an English-language group for the tour; otherwise, buy a small English guidebook next to the inner ticket office for about DM4 or just follow with this book, which covers the basics.

Warning #3: You will be asked to pay two different entrance fees—the first allows you to enter the courtyard and tower for DM1; the second is for the castle interior and museum for DM5 (for students, children and seniors DM3). If you come by car expect to first pay DM2 for parking and another DM4 for the shuttle van (German: *Pendel*) to the castle.

So much for the basics—we're on our way.

After ascending the paths and stairs from the bus exit, you get your first close view of the castle walls from the drawbridge. After crossing the drawbridge, DM1 gets you into the first courtyard.

The castle is constructed around two connecting courtyards. The first is ringed by half-timbered buildings from the 15th and 16th centuries. The next is older and more impressive, flanked to the left by the Great Hall, centered by the massive well and ringed with crenellated ramparts and towers.

A history of the Wartburg

The first mention of the castle, about 1067, describes two wooden towers and a palisade. The position provided excellent observation of the surrounding countryside. In 1140 Ludwig's son (who had the same name, but we can conveniently call him Ludwig II) began to build a stone castle on this spot. The sandstone arch one passes under when entering the courtyard is considered part of the original fortress.

The first two storeys of the large Romanesque Great Hall were built in the mid-1100s by Ludwig III, and the *Sangersaal* (Minstrels' Hall) served as the center for ceremonies. At the end of the 1100s another storey was constructed on the Great Hall by Hermann I, who became best-known for the minstrels' contest he sponsored and his love of the arts and chivalry.

Hermann was followed by Ludwig IV in 1217, who died ten years later while on his way to fight in the Fourth Crusade. Ludwig IV's wife was Elisabeth, the daughter of the King of Hungary. Elisabeth spent the rest of her life taking care of the poor and sick. She died in 1231 and was later canonized St. Elisabeth of Hungary.

The castle passed through several hands from the mid-13th to the 16th century, all the while remaining more or less part of the Saxon kingdom. During that time the Great Hall was extended to include a chapel, and the half-timbered buildings were erected in the outer courtyard.

In 1521 Luther was brought here by the Elector Fredrick the Wise of Saxony for protective custody, the Catholic Church having outlawed him the Diet of Worms.

Goethe came here and "rediscovered" the castle in 1777 and eventually his influence resulted in the restoration of most of the castle. The architect Hugo von Ritgen directed the reconstruction of the Wartburg which took place roughly from 1846 to 1889 and resulted in the rebuilding, refurnishing and redecorating of most of the castle as well as development of the museum. Since 1922, after the abdication of the German royalty, the castle has been kept up by the Wartburg Foundation. In 1938 the Nazis attempted to replace the cross atop the Wartburg (which had been dedicated to Luther's stay) with a swastika. Massive protest forced them to remove the swastika.

Room by room

Your tour will enter on the ground floor of the Great Hall, also called the *Landgrafenhaus* (house of the Landgraves). The guide will start in the vaulted **Rittersaal** (Knights Hall). The room is square and has cross-vaulting joined at a central column. The capital of the column is decorated by eagles. This room was restored in the 1960s.

Next you'll pass into the **Dining Hall** with its flat wooden ceiling of hewn oak, the fireplace and a large central column. Studies of the oaken beams in the ceiling show that they came from trees felled in 1168. The doorcases and window jambs are painted red in contrast to the whitewashed walls.

The final room on the ground floor is the women's chamber, called the **Elisabeth Kemenate** (Bower or private

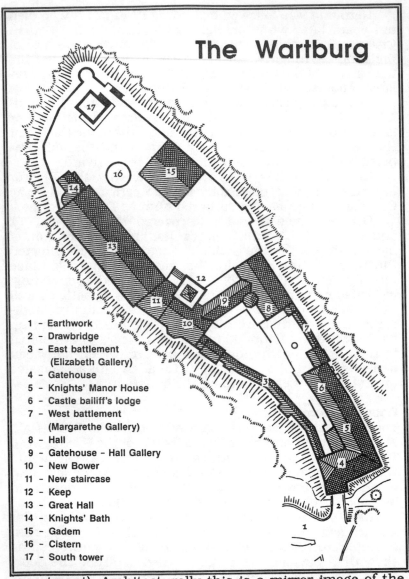

The Wartburg

1 – Earthwork
2 – Drawbridge
3 – East battlement
   (Elizabeth Gallery)
4 – Gatehouse
5 – Knights' Manor House
6 – Castle bailiff's lodge
7 – West battlement
   (Margarethe Gallery)
8 – Hall
9 – Gatehouse – Hall Gallery
10 – New Bower
11 – New staircase
12 – Keep
13 – Great Hall
14 – Knights' Bath
15 – Gadem
16 – Cistern
17 – South tower

apartment). Architecturally this is a mirror image of the Knight's Hall, but the arches radiating from the central column and walls are covered with detailed mosaic deco-

rations and pictures. The mosaic scenes are from the life
of St. Elisabeth. They show her birth in Hungary and depict Hermann I learning of her from a Hungarian mystic
and magician. Another shows her coming to the Wartburg
and being betrothed to the Landgrave's first-born son. He
died when she was only nine and she subsequently married Ludwig IV and had three children. In 1227 Ludwig IV
died on a crusade. She continued helping the poor and the
sick, renounced her worldly offices, entered a Franciscan
lay order, and was canonized in 1235. You can follow these
stories, set in more than a million bits of glistening glass,
mother of pearl, and gold leaf. Many of the vignettes from
Elisabeth's life are also presented in frescoes lining the
second floor arcade, with one notable addition, perhaps
the best known: this is the Miracle of the Roses, which was
said to have been converted her husband, Ludwig III. He had not
always been totally enthusiastic about her good works,
and one day asked her, on her way to town, what was under her cloak, suspecting it was part of her charities. "Only
roses," she answered; and when he demanded to see what it
was, and she opened her cloak, the bread for the poor that
she was carrying was transformed into roses.

Walk out of the room onto the arcade and then ascend
to the chapel on the second floor. The **chapel** was one of
the last additions to the castle. The decor is for the most
part very Gothic. Double Gothic columns stand in the window under round Romanesque arches, and thin columns
support the vaulting. Services and organ recitals are still
held here during summer months.

Tours now move into the **Sängersall** (Minstrels' Hall).
Originally this room stretched through what is now the
chapel. This was the scene of a 12th-century singers' or
minstrels' contest of the sort immortalized by Wagner in
his opera *Tannhäuser*. The contest is shown in the fresco
painted by Moritz von Schwind in 1854. Six minstrels
competed for the favor of Hermann I. They included the
famous poet Wolfram von Eschenbach, Walther von der
Vogelweide, and Heinrich von Ofterdingen, as well as three
other unknown singers. Heinrich was the only singer to
praise his duke from back home in Austria while all the
others sang the praises of Hermann I. Naturally, Heinrich
lost the contest, but as the hangman was being called, he

begged for another chance. Herman said OK and gave him one year to find the famous mystic and magician from Hungary, Klingsor, and submit to his judgement. As the story goes, Heinrich found Klingsor and with the help of a magic carpet returned in time for a replay of the contest. During the time Klingsor spent in Eisenach, he related his visions of the birth of Elisabeth to Hermann.

You'll now enter the **Landgrafenzimmer** (Landgrave's Room). This is a relatively simple room with a series of frescoes high on the walls. Each tells an interesting regional legend. One of the best-known legends is the founding of the Wartburg where Ludwig der Springer is seen resting on a rock and admiring the scenery. Ludwig is said to have shouted "Wait, hill (*Wart, Berg*), I will build you a castle (*Burg*)" ... thus giving Wartburg its name. Another fresco depicts the legend of the Smith of Ruhla. In this story Ludwig disguised as a hunter asks the blacksmith for a room for the night. The blacksmith agrees and eventually recognizes the duke, but doesn't let on. During the evening the smith takes every opportunity to point out how the common people are being mistreated by the duke's men. Ludwig got the message and had his henchmen harnessed to a plough, with a peasant allowed to wield the whip as they plowed the field.

The final room in the Great Hall to which you'll be guided is the **Festsaal** (Banquet Hall). This massive room could accommodate hundreds of guests. Today it is the venue for concerts. The arching carved wooden ceiling is spectacular as is the ornate decoration and lighting. This ceiling was only added, however, during the renovations in the mid-1800s; the original ceiling was flat. In October 1817, the 300th anniversary of the beginning of the Reformation and the fourth year after the Battle of the Nations, which broke Napoleon's occupation, about 500 representatives of German student societies toasted "Honor, Freedom, Fatherland" in the *Festsaal*, and their flag still hangs in the room. This was the first middle-class democratic meeting conducted in Germany, but the group was ruthlessly crushed two years later. Later, Liszt conducted his "Legend of St. Elisabeth" in this grand hall.

The guide will turn you loose in the castle **museum** which is filled with Wartburg memorabilia. Several of the most important paintings are Cranach's portraits of Luther and his wife. There are also portraits of Luther's mother and father, Hans and Margarethe. Another Cranach painting is *The Holy Mother Eating Grapes*.

As you leave the museum a series of stairways and hallways will lead you past **Luther's Room**. Luther stayed here from May 4, 1521 to March 6, 1522 under the disguise of Junker Jörg wearing knight's garb and growing long hair and a beard during his stay. Frederick the Wise, who brought Luther here, hoped that the uproar over Luther's refusal to recant his beliefs before the Diet of Worms would subside. For ten months Luther worked each day on his translation of the New Testament from original Greek into vernacular German. He chose to translate from original Greek to eliminate what he considered scholastic falsifications introduced in the Latin versions, and he translated into a German which was formed from many of the country's dialects. His aim was to create a New Testament understood by both the Low and High German speaker.

Today visitors can peak into Luther's study where he completed his Biblical translations. The small desk where he wrote, the whale vertebra he used for a footrest, a small stove, wooden walls and stone floor present an austere workplace. A mark on the wall is said to have been made when Luther saw the Devil spying on his work late one night and hurled an inkpot at the Prince of Evil. Hanging on the wall are copies of Cranach paintings of Luther and the Greek scholar Philip Melanchthon of Wittenberg who proofread Luther's translations, as well as an engraving of Luther with his beard under the guise of Junker Jörg.

The Wartburg is open daily, May-October 8:30 a.m.-4 p.m.; November-April 9 a.m.-3:30 p.m.

Tourist information

Eisenach Information is near the station at Bahnhofstraße #3/5 (tel. 6161). The room reservation number is 4895. Hours are Mon. 10 a.m.-5 p.m.; Tues. to Fri. 9 a.m.-5 p.m.; Sat. 9 a.m.-1 p.m.; closed Sun. The room reservtions number operate on Mon. to 7 p.m. and on Saturday to 6 p.m., but it is better to call during regular hours or, if your German is weak, go in person and use sign language.

Journey through the East
Part III

My night in Leipzig gets cancelled

Got up on Saturday and at breakfast decided to stay one more day with Frau Schultz. She and her daughter said getting a room in Dresden would be tough—plus the *Zimmervermittlen* (room reservations) would probably close at 1 or 2 p.m., before I was planning to arrive. I was comfortable with Frau Schultz and enjoyed the atmosphere of Weimar. Convincing me to stay another day was not difficult.

I walked down to the Weimar tourist information desk and let them know I was staying another night so they could keep their index cards up to date, then went to the post office and called the Dresden tourist information to try to make reservations for the next night. They told me that their allotment of rooms that could be reserved in advance was gone, but they said they'd be open until 1 p.m. on Sunday and that there were at the moment plenty of rooms. The girl's last statement was "Get here early, the earlier the better."

"Thanks", I said and walked across town and started the two-hour drive to Leipzig to spend a day sightseeing there.

Leipzig is a big dirty industrial city with a surprisingly interesting history which effectively brightens what otherwise would only be a big dirty city. The stories of merchants and traders who were instrumental in developing the town are wonderful. Later took a tour of the outer part of the town—it was very disappointing. One day here is enough—with a good guidebook and enough energy to get around the inner city. You can skip the tour of the outskirts.

Conversations after Leipzig

After visiting Leipzig I returned to Weimar on winding backroads. Got back to Weimar about 8 p.m. and headed back to Sharfer Ecke again after trying the Goldener Ecke—closed again. This time had another Thüringer meal, which was, once again, great: grilled pork smothered with onions and french fries all washed down with Apoldaer Beer from the town next to Weimar.

This night I ended up chatting with a group of four who were at my table. This group was very East German nationalistic—especially the two women. One woman was bitter about the unity and how it was handled—the other was concerned with how to make things better. The conversation started with a trading of name calling—they weren't calling me names but as I described my trip they had slang terms for each of the peoples I met in each region. The people from the Thüringerwald, the wooded, hilly region south of Weimar, were called *Löffelschnitters*—spoon carvers. The people from Mecklenburg, the low-lying level area between Berlin and the coast, are called *Ochsenkopfs*, or meatheads. The folk from the north where I'll be going are known as *Flaklanders* or Flatlanders just as Southern New Hampshire folk are known to Northern New Hampshire folk. I'm always interested in these details, besides they provide lots of laughs—at someone else's expense.

The men and I told stories and jokes for awhile, then I got into a serious discussion with the two women, Uschi and Beatrice. Uschi said, "They forget that we did a lot in East Germany with very little. We didn't have the help that West Germany had from the Americans. They would never have progressed so far on their own? I'm really irritated with their superior attitude. If we had that much money and help, we'd be ahead of them."

Beatrice broke in at this point, "We can fix a car, we know how to make the most from nothing—we know how to survive—they can't repair a thing, life's come to them on a silver platter—sure they work hard . . . all Germans do. The West had the deck stacked in their favor and they were successful at taking advantage of it—they aren't any smarter or better than we are—they lived under different circumstances."

The men were talking with each other about repairing a car then I heard something about a trip to Berlin—but I was focused with the women...they were really getting into the discussions.

Beatrice paused then took a long drink from her beer. She stared at her hands and gripped them together then tapped her fingers together. Thoughtfully, she started,

"My father worked selflessly for years and years and years to make this system work. He believed that he was sacrificing to make a better world for his children and everyone. Yes, he was a "Communist" but he wasn't a greedy monster living off the people that many today point to—My father gave more than he ever took—I know—I saw how hard he worked."

She pauses, takes a deep breath, "I ask myself was his concern wasted? Did we learn nothing in our struggle here in East Germany? Are we a nation of failures?" She shrugs, throwing her hands in the air, settles down and sips her beer.

Uschi, who had been listening intently and nodding in agreement with Beatrice said, "We have done lots of good things—our kindergarten system is unmatched, perhaps in the world—we had a wonderful school system and the best physical education system, which produces Gold Medal winners year after year. Those are achievements that are acknowledged internationally. What we have to do is to mix the good of the East and the good of the West—then we'll have a better country. But they seem intent on sweeping out everything that was "East" and giving us the total "Western" system. It's wrong and if they don't see their mistake now they will later.

Beatrice looked over at me and said, "We've always been told to do this or do that for your country or your fatherland—not only our generation—it seems to be the German tradition."

I nodded and broke in here. "That's the big difference between the German experience with Communism and

America. In America, you never hear anyone say,'do this' because it's good for the country or your fatherland. What we hear is do it for yourself. Do it for you own benefit. I'm not sure why, but when everyone is basically selfish and works to make things better for themselves as individuals it brings the whole society up."

Beatrice looked over resignedly. "We all worked, our fathers worked to build things —that wasn't our problem— but for some reason once something was done everyone stopped. Nothing grew from what we built—it only created more to deteriorate."

Uschi put her hand on Beatrice's. She stared again at her hands. Clenching them tightly, "We are disgusted with the leaders. We believed in the concept of the good of everyone—we still do—you do according to your newspapers, according to West German papers. Today we find we marched in place—going nowhere for over 40 years." She shakes her head. "I know why we worked hard, but why were we like sheep for so long when it was obvious our leaders were steering us nowhere?"

Uschi's husband, across the table heard this last comment and roused from his car talk.

> "We went nowhere for years now we have to start from the ground floor. We have to learn about insurance and credit, redo our pensions, worry about a whole new system of universities, find jobs in new industries. For us it's a whole new world."

"Many people are taking advantage of our newness to the system and they are taking the few DMs we have—again for nothing."

Beatrice quietly groaned, "It's the system—for us a new system—and we have to learn to live with it."

I broke in again. "I know it's the system, we have one in America too, but the big difference is not that you can complain openly without the Stasi following you home or worse, taking you away for bad thoughts. It's all a bigger change and this is something many, many people even in the USA don't understand—you can change the system. If you don't like it you can change it. You can bring back what you felt was important—kindergartens, sports and so on. You can now vote and that is the biggest change. Yes, you traded system for system and you might not like everything about the new system but you now have an announced opportunity to change the system or at least work to change it. You must speak up for change or be sheep again . . . and you more than anyone know the price you paid for being sheep, you know more than anyone else in the West."

The lights were turned up in the restaurant. *"Freier Abend"* the bartender cried. Beatrice and Uschi both hugged me goodbye. "If you come back to Weimar you can find us here several nights a week. It was good to speak with you. All we normally hear is, "You have no problems, lots of money is coming, be patient, wait." You at least let us know you understand how we feel. We want some part of our lives justified—they can't throw it all out...or maybe they can . . . and we can get it back. But, that seems a long way around." Beatrice shrugged as well and tossed her head towards the door *"Gehen wir nach hause. Aufwiedersehen Charlie."*

I could feel my two liters of Alpodaer as my steps echoed through the narrow streets on my way home. I could also smell the coal in the air—it's a smell you almost never get back home. The weather is cooling a bit but not much—I'm still wandering home at midnight with a light cotton jacket.

Leipzig

Leipzig has during the past forty years been known to Westerners as the home of the Leipzig Trade Fairs, where export goods of the Communist Bloc were displayed and sold to an international market. This fair was and is certainly the most important event in Leipzig, but this has always been a city of music, culture, publishing and education.

A city astride two major trading routes

Leipzig was originally a small Slavic settlement which didn't start to develop as a town until the mid-1100s. Trading has been the focus of this city for centuries. Leipzig developed at the intersection of two of the most important medieval trading, pilgrimage and military routes (the King's Highway and the Imperial Highway). In 1497 it was given the right to hold an imperial fair by the Emperor Maximilian and over the next 300 years developed into what many called the Marketplace of Europe.

A city of music

Bach lived here with his brood of 20 children, and his music is played and sung at the Church of St. Thomas where he served as choirmaster for 27 years. Mendelssohn founded an orchestra here. Wagner was born here and conducted here. And one of the world's largest music publishers, Peters Verlag, is headquartered in Leipzig.

A city of literature

From the middle of the 18th century until 1945, Leipzig was the dominant center of German-language book

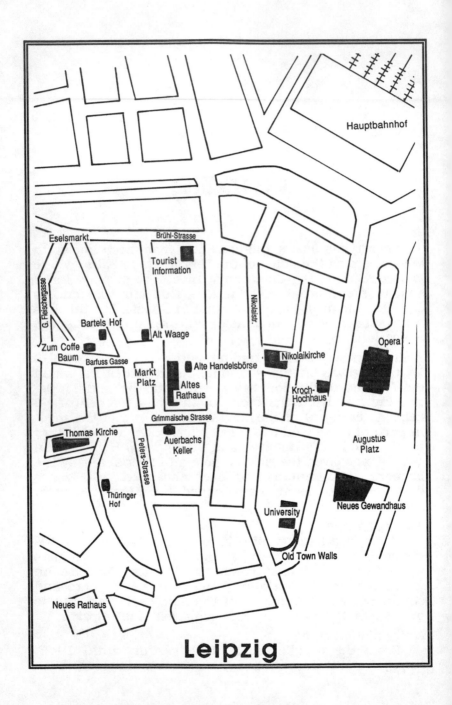

Leipzig

publishing. There were once as many as 900 publishers, and today 35 major houses, including the German Library for the Blind, still publish books.

A city of philosophers

Leipzig has long been a hotbed of political philosophy and at the forefront of many movements of change. Outside the city gates, Napoleon's defeat by the allied armies at the Battle of Nations in 1813 foreshadowed the end of his plans of domination. The city was a center for Socialist thought at the end of the 19th century. Lenin, Wilhelm Liebknecht and August Bebel created many of the tenets of the modern Communist party here in Leipzig and the first issue of *Iskra*, the Russian Marxist newspaper was secretly published by Lenin here. (Ironically, the first open defiance of the communist dictatorship in the autumn of 1989 was the Monday evening marches organized in Leipzig.) Lessing, the dramatist and playwright of the Enlightenment, who first translated Shakespeare into German, and Nietzsche, the German existentialist philosopher, both were associated with the University of Leipzig. This university was the largest in Germany when Hitler came to power and was the largest in the former DDR.

Leipzig has maintained its role as a trading center to this day. It was the venue of the Communist world's largest trade fair and will more than likely be the central focus for trade fairs dealing with goods from the old Eastern bloc in coming years. Besides its major trade fair facilities and the large university it also claims Europe's largest railway station, built between 1901 and 1915, with 31 platforms. It is one of the most densely populated cities in Germany with over 500,000 inhabitants.

To get the most from Leipzig, look behind its façade

Frankly, Leipzig is markedly unappealing at first impression. The city seems big, dirty and unfriendly. But if you know a bit of its fascinating history and walk through the center enjoying it from a historical perspective, you will find yourself slowly being entranced by its smoldering spirit and its vibrant energy. In many of the city's drab buildings, behind the dull façades, lives a bustling world.

An approach to the city
This chapter is organized as a walking tour of the inner city with short historical vignettes which should bring these otherwise grey, dirty, seemingly lifeless buildings to life. The tour follows a path outlined in a small guidebook, the *Little Blue Yellow City Guide* distributed by the Leipzig Tourist Information Office. It provides a much more detailed picture of Leipzig today and in the past. Much of this *Little Blue Yellow City Guide* requires an active imagination to envision medieval activities in the midst of high-rise office buildings, but it does an admirable job of breathing life into Leipzig for the tourist. It recounts stories of fur markets, medieval embezzlements, town politics, and friendships which shaped Leipzig through history.

Eselmarkt, or Richard-Wagner-Platz
This is a square filled with history where you must use your imagination. But imagination will let you to see the colorful world of the past, the site of Leipzig's first street market.
Nearby, the *Haus zu den drei Schwanen* (the House of Three Swans), mentioned as early as 1580, served as an inn for coachmen and merchants from the town of Zwickau. Here the traditions of Merchants' Concerts began which developed into today's renowned Gewandehaus Orchestra. Where the modern department store, Am Brühl, now stands, Richard Wagner was born on May 22, 1813. Here, the city's first market was formed under the protection of the now-destroyed *Libzi* castle in the 11th century. (*Eselmarkt* means Donkey Market, named for the donkeys which transported the wheat traded here to a nearby flour mill.)

Zum Coffe Baum
First opened in 1694, this is the oldest intact coffee house in Saxony and one of the oldest in Europe. Over the door is a carving of a Turk resting under a blossoming coffee tree, being served the steaming beverage by a cherub. Goethe, Lessing, Liszt, Wagner, Schumann, and Napoleon have all savored coffee here. It occupies two floors. The

upper floor, theoretically reserved for writers and artists, is much quieter and filled with changing art exhibitions. The entire coffeehouse at #4 *Kleine Fleischergasse*, is filled with 19th-century nostalgia.

Handwerkerpassage (Craftsmen's Passage)

Coffe Baum opens onto a narrow walkway connecting Kleine Fleischergasse with Markt which was originally created as an interior courtyard of a department store. The walkway is lined with the workshops of active craftsmen ranging from umbrella repairman to printer to cabinetmaker.

Markt

Three times a year, from the early 1500s to 1891, traders from Holland, France, North Germany and the Orient exchanged goods here by sale and barter. In 1891 the trade fair concept changed to the system still followed today, one of sampling and ordering.

Markt is the traditional city gathering place. This was the scene of celebration when Napoleon's troops were defeated in 1813. It had been filled with peasants demonstrating during the Reformation and the Peasant Wars, and served as the site of public execution until 1824.

Just off the Markt is the *Barthels Hof*, the only remaining Baroque trading courtyard, built in 1523. Wagons filled with goods were driven into the courtyard, and cranes then hoisted the merchandise up into the salesrooms. This building has over 200 rooms in four stories. The awe inspired by these buildings in the 1700s and 1800s must have been similar to what modern man feels when gazing up at the Sears Tower or the Empire State Building. Goethe wrote that these buildings "embraced a world in their courtyard rooms which loom as high as the sky; and resemble high castles, indeed half a town." As you walk out of the Hof look above you at a massive Baroque bay window, originally part of the House of the Golden Snake, which is a good example of the popular Leipzig ornamental style.

The *Alte Waage* (Old Weighing Station) stands at the northern end of the Markt. Its reconstructed façade has a

Renaissance gabled roof and a sundail. When it was built in 1555, this was the center for controlling the trade fairs and the main source of income for the town. All goods that merchants brought to Leipzig, as everywhere in those days, had to be weighed, taxed and checked.

The *Altes Rathaus* (Old Town Hall) is the most impressive and most photographed in Leipzig. It is a football field long, lining the eastern side of the Markt. Its preliminary structure was erected in 1556 and has since been rebuilt and restored several times. **The longest inscription in the world** (according to Guinness), with just over 100 words and signs, runs along the length of the building just below the eaves. The building today houses the **Museum for the History of the Town** and concerts are held in the massive 57-yard-long festival hall. The "town pipers" have been a tradition since 1479, when they were first invited to entertain the townsfolk and stayed because of the endless supply of beer. Every weekend they play dressed in traditional garb. The clock tower has a large blue and yellow clock plus a smaller one just beneath it called the *Armesünderglöckchen* (the Poor Sinner's Bell) which tolled during public executions. Under the arched arcade the old merchants' stalls have been turned into small shops and boutiques.

The Old Town Hall including the **History Museum of Leipzig** (undergoing reconstruction) contains the Mendelssohn room, where the composer worked for over a decade until his death in 1947, as well as thousands of exhibits showcasing the city's past.

The Fair Halls near the Markt

This was the heart of the original trade fairs that brought so much wealth to Leipzig. Beneath the Markt is the Underground Fair Hall, chiselled out of red stone and opened in 1925. The fair hall was built here since all above-ground space was taken and this was the best location in town. Across Grimmaischestraße from the Old Town Hall are the *Messehaus am Markt* and the Mädler Passage. These buildings have interconnecting walkways and are almost a world in themselves.

The **Messehaus am Markt** was the center of the book publishing trade. In this area the original booksellers brought their books in casks to the market and sold them from barrels. Until 1989, almost half of the DDR publishers were headquartered in Leipzig. A bit of trivia: it was here that the system of house numbering was first introduced in 1793.

The glass-covered 20-foot-wide **Mädler Passage** stretches almost 200 yards through the trade fair buildings. This is a relatively modern structure built in 1913. It radiates from a three-storey rotunda with a glockenspeil of Meissen porcelain bells echoing the old traditions of the **Auerbachs Keller.** The "new" Auerbachs Keller was preserved when the Passage was constructed. This keller, originally built between 1530 and 1538, became famous when Goethe used it for a scene in Faust: Mephistopheles brings Faust here to show him the pleasures of revelry and sings the *Song of the Flea* The former wine cellar is 13 feet underground and has four rooms, each decorated with murals of scenes from Goethe's *Faust,* painted in the 16th century. Above ground, the entrance is marked by large statues of Faust and Mephistopheles.

There are 17 other trade fair halls scattered around this area. Each building has its own stories. In Leipzig the trade fair was king; as it expanded, anything not directly related to commerce seemed to be pulled down. Around 1900, the **Gewandhaus** was built on the site of the demolished Leipzig Conservatory where the Mendelssohn-Bartholdy Academy of Music was founded. At the same time, the **Städtlisches Kaufhaus** rose on the site of the old Baroque town library. Petershof (St. Peter's Courtyard) is the largest trade hall in the city and was the last to be built in the city center. Further down Petersstraße, the **Drei Könige** (The Three Wise Men) was built in 1917, and the **Stentzlers Hof,** a medium-sized fair hall, was constructed during World War I from 1914 to 1916.

Thomaskirche (Church of St. Thomas)

This is Mecca for Johann Sebastian Bach fans. Here he worked as organist and choirmaster from 1723 to 1750. He wrote much of his religious music here, including the *St. Matthew Passion* and the *Art of the Fugue*. A statue of Bach carved by Seffner in 1908 stands outside the church entrance and Bach's tomb is inside, in front of the altar.

Originally built in 1212 as an Augustinian church, it was modified in the 13th to 15th centuries. The high-pitched roof, rising 50 feet, was built in 1496 and is the largest in Saxony with a surface area of over 24,000 square feet. The roof truss was constructed with only wooden nails.

Mozart, Mendelssohn and Wagner all played here. On Fridays Bach's music is normally performed by the Thomaner Choir at 6 p.m., as well as on Sunday mornings.

Opposite the church at 16 Thomaskirchhof is the Johann Sebastian Bach Museum in the Bosehaus. It is open Tues. - Sun. 9 a.m. - 5 p.m. Bach lived in this building and spent much time here talking and playing music with his friend Georg Bose, a silverware manufacturer. Here you'll find original musical instruments, autographed documents, and other Bach memorabilia and archives.

Neues Rathaus (The New Town Hall)
From 1899 to 1905 the New Town Hall was constructed on the foundations of the old 13th-century castle which protected the city's south side. The base of the main tower from the old castle was incorporated into the central tower of the present building. The Latin inscription on the main clock states *Mors certa hora incerta* (Death is certain, the hour is uncertain). The Rathhaus in the cellar provides good meals in typical surroundings.

Nicolaikirche (St. Nicholas Church)
This church was central in the demonstrations against the East German government during the autumn of 1989. For seven years, Monday evening prayers were openly said inside the church. Then, in October and November of 1989 the crowds began to gather at the church and begin their demonstrations, marching from Karl-Marx-Platz around the *Promenadenring* from Autumn 1989 until April 1990, against the Communist regime.

Architecturally, this is an impressive church. Built in 1165, it is Saxony's largest hall church and the oldest church in Leipzig. The interior is a beautiful mixture of Gothic and Classical styles. The Gothic choir was constructed in the 14th century and the nave dates from the 16th century. The columns are finished with Corinthian flourishes and the colorful ceiling sparkles in rose, green, and gold over the clean white columns. The church also contains the largest organ in eastern Germany. Many of Bach's works were first performed here, including the *St. John Passion.* Fittingly for Leipzig, St. Nicholas is the patron saint of merchants.

The church is open Mon. - Thurs. 10 a.m. - 6 p.m., Fri. noon - 6 p.m., Sat. 10 a.m. - 4 p.m.

Augustus Platz

This massive, modern square, surrounded by modern buildings is about half the size of St. Peter's Square in Rome.

To the south of the square is the high-rise University building, affectionately called the Jagged Tooth by Leipzigers. The view from the 34th floor is spectacular in good weather. Just to the south of the base of this modern tower are a few remains of the 16th-century city walls, Moritzbastei, and to the north of the building is the **Neues Gewandhaus** (New Drapers' Hall), the home of the Gewandhaus Orchestra, founded in 1781 and once conducted by Felix Mendelssohn. The modern building has two concert halls.

On the northern side of Karl-Marx-Platz is the 1600-seat Opera House which has regular theater, ballet and opera performances. Just to the west of the Opera House stands Leipzig's first "skyscraper," the Kroch-Hochhaus. This building was constructed in 1928 by a banker. The town elders only gave him permission to build a seven-storey building, but allowed him to finish off a façade of the remaining top four floors. When the townspeople saw the final building form, they approved it and allowed the construction to be finished. The top of the 60-foot tower is crowned with Europe's highest free-standing carillon, the *Glockenmänner* (the bellmen), modeled on the Bronze

Moors of the St. Mark's bell tower in Venice. The bellmen strike every quarter hour.

Alte Handelsbörse (The Old Stock Exchange)

Behind the Old Town Hall is another unique Baroque building, the Alte Handelsbörse built in 1687. Its ornate façade carvings depict Mercury, Apollo, Venus and Minerva.

The Burgkeller

This is the oldest restaurant in Leipzig. It is located in the basement of the Handelshof, behind the Old Town Hall on Grimmaischestraße. During my visits it was closed for renovation. When opened, it should be a spectacular eatery if it is restored to resemble the sketches seen on old postcards. The restaurant was officially opened in 1419.

Outside of the center

The **Leipzig Zoo** is a 10 minute ride from the center of town on Tram #20. It has an excellent collection of tigers, panthers and lions, and is known for breeding these large cats in captivity. One of the largest aquariums in eastern Germany is also a part of the Zoological Gardens. The zoo is open daily 7 a.m. - 7 p.m. in summer and 7 a.m. - 5 p.m. in winter.

The **Schillerhaus** is a small farmhouse at Menckestraße 42 in a northern suburb of Leipzig, Gohlis. Here, in 1785, Schiller wrote *Don Carlos*, a play, and his poem, *Ode to Joy*, which was set to music by Beethoven in his 9th Symphony. It is open on Tues., Wed., Fri. and Sat. 11 a.m. - 5 p.m.

The **Gohliser Schlößchen** is a Rococo palace built in 1756. Once a gathering place for Leipzig's literati, it is a short walk from the Schillerhaus at Menckestraße 23. The wrought iron tower and the painted ceiling are its main drawing cards. This small palace is open Mon. - Sat. 9 a.m. - 5 p.m.

The **Völkerschlachtdenkmal** (Battle of the Nations Monument) is as ugly as any monument can possibly be. It was built between 1898 and 1913 to commemorate the battle fought by the allies against Napoleon for four days in October 1813. The 150,000-man French army was defeated by an allied force twice its size. More than 100,000 soldiers died during the fighting. Ironically, although the monument was dedicated to remind the people of the horrors of war, World War I broke out the following year. The observation platform, with good views of the southern part of Leipzig, is a 500-stair climb.

The **Russische Gedächtniskirche**, just down the road was built about the same time as a memorial to the Russian troops fought in the campaign against Napoleon.

Getting around

The bus, city rail, and tram system in Leipzig is excellent and reaches every corner of the city and most of the surrounding suburbs. Pick up a map of the system at the main tourist office or at the Hauptbahnhof (main train station).

Special tourist tickets are available for 36 hours, 72 hours, seven days and for seniors.

Accommodations

For the well-heeled crowd and those on generous expense accounts, head to the **Hotel Merkur**, Gerberstraße 15, tel. 41/7990, fax 41/7991229. You can also choose the expensive **Astoria** at Platz der Republik, tel. 41/72220, fax 41/7224747. Both hotels have restaurants and all amenities. For the next level down in price try **Stadt Leipzig**, Richard-Wagner-Straße #1-5, opposite the station, tel. 41/288814, fax 41/284037; the Baroque and classy **Hotel International**, Tröndlinring #8, tel. 411/71800; or the **Zum Löwen**, Rudolf-Breitscheid-Straße #1, behind the Astoria, tel. 41/72230.

The best bet for more affordable accommodations here is the *Zimmervermittlung* at the Leipzig-Information office. They can make reservations at several pensions and gasthauses as well as private homes.

Tourist information

Leipzig-Information is located at Sachsenplatz #1, tel. 41/79590, fax: 41/281854. Open Mon. to Fri. 9 a.m.-7 p.m.; Sat. 9:30 a.m.-2 p.m.

Journey through the East
Part IV

Weimar to Dresden
Had my last breakfast with Frau Schultz and her daughter. We all ate with another woman (about 35) who spent the previous night with them. She had studied in Leipzig and now lived in East Berlin. At any rate, this woman was about as hostile and distant as anyone I've ever met (or in her case, didn't meet). I spoke with Frau Schultz about my plans and then struck out for Dresden. I was on the road about 9:15 a.m. and arrived without too much strain around noon.

As with my approaches to most East German cities I drove until I found something that seemed to be the center. In Dresden I finally found the train station from a map in a guidebook I bought. Luckily, I had called Dresden and knew the tourist office was across from the Bahnhof.

They gave me a room about 5km outside of the center—at first I was a bit disappointed—but when I saw there really wasn't a center to Dresden, with homes and apartments to speak of, I was more understanding. The tour board was very helpful with maps, even those that cost, and they gave me virtuallly everything they had printed in English. I couldn't check into my room until after 5 p.m. so I stayed downtown. The car was in a good spot, I had all the info I needed, so Dresden, here I come.

Exploring Dresden
The only knowledge of Dresden I had up to this time was that this was our example of saturation bombing to break the will of the people to resist. Churchill ordered the

bombing of the city strictly to encourage Hitler to surrender, and quickly. Dresden was not a major military center—it was one of Germany's prized cities. I also had vague ideas of Dresden china and Meissen china which comes from this area.

According to what I had read, Dresden was pretty well destroyed during the night of saturation bombing. Now, standing in front of the tourist office, I could see how much of the city virtually disappeared overnight. It's impressive—perhaps not the power of an A-bomb but the cleared area between the train station and the palace takes a good 10 or 15 minutes just to walk across in any direction. Photos of "before" show a densely populated city with beautiful medieval core, the "after" photos show rubble.

The architectural treasures of Dresden

What remains of Dresden is breathtaking—the Zwinger Palace, the Royal Palace, the Semper Opera, the Cathedral. The museums are all beautiful and many have been beautifully restored. What the Communist regime didn't get around to restoring, the new unifed German government is hard at work on—it's obvious from the scaffolding and cranes. The local guidebook from the tourist office to Dresden is not nearly as good as that to Leipzig—it goes back to the routine of merely describing things rather than what gave them life.

The Dresden art collection really gave me an idea of the power of the Saxon kings during their day—just as powerful as French, English or Russian kings—only their greatest collections and castles were over here in the East—away from our wondering eyes. The collection included a dozen Rubens, a half-dozen Rembrandts, Vermeers, Bols, Van Dyke, Dürers, Cranachs, Holbeins, Courbet, Gaugin, Rodin, Degas, Renoir, Monet, Manet—the list goes on.

I particularly taken with a wonderfully beautiful and sensous picture of St. Agnes painted by the Spaniard Ribera. Legend has it that she was taken by the infidels and had her clothes ripped off, but she covered herself with her long hair, and an angel came to give her another cloak to cover her nakedness.

The treasury of the Saxon kings rivals if not surpasses the Queen's jewels in the Tower of London. It's like an orgy of gold and jewels plastered on anything and everything from models to spoons, cabinets, clocks and swords.

There were two special exhibitions—one of sculpture made from crumpled parts of automobiles which might have been better displayed in a junkyard; the other was a wonderful collection of Canaletto paintings depicting Dresden in the 1770s. (Even then the Cathedral was covered in scaffolding.)

After the final museum visit I was exhausted and stopped at a small wine fest for a glass of wine, then hiked back to the train station and drove up to my room.

Staying in "new" Dresden

The house I was staying in looked like it had been transported from a new development in West Germany. The owner was very officious and directed me to the room which was in a section of his house with my own entrance and which could be shut off from his living area. There were two rooms-one with a single the other a two-bed room—we shared shower and toilet.

Tried to find a local Gasthaus the house owner had recommended but after driving around for a half hour, I decided I didn't need to eat any more and headed back to my room. I was astounded at the lack of restaurants anywhere in town, especially up here in the suburbs. When I returned to my room, I noticed restaurants were marked on the map that the tourist office had given to me. I was amazed when I counted them—less than a dozen in the center of Dresden, a city of half-a-million people. Though I was staying in the midst of a group of high-rise apartment buildings with more residents than my hometown, there were no restaurants or snackbars within walking distance. I did some writing, then reread some *Crime and Punishment*, then it was off to sleep—early.

Dresden

Once known by virtue of its art and architecture as the Florence on the Elbe, this city was founded, as far as modern civilization is concerned, in the early 1200s. By 1287 the first stone bridge was erected across the Elbe, insuring the permanence of Dresden. Martin Luther preached here in the early 1500s and by mid-century Dresden was a firmly in the Reformation camp.

In the 16th century Dresden began to develop as a center for government, art, architecture, culture and crafts—the first museum, which eventually developed into today's Dresden art collection, was founded; an orchestra was established which drew musicians; and Dresden became a residence of the dukes and kings of Saxony. The 17th century saw city laws to preserve the architecture of the town, new parks and gardens, the first newspaper, and the rise of the goldsmiths to become the leading crafts guild. Some of Europe's best organs were constructed here and the art of porcelain was introduced to Europe, though nearby Meissen became the production center.

In the 18th century Baroque and Rococo architecture flowered under Augustus the Strong. The fabulous Zwinger was constructed and the Church of Our Lady was built. The city was repeatedly occupied by the Prussians during the 1700s—first during the Silesian War in 1745, and then after the Seven Years War in 1756. Eventually, at the dawn of the 19th century, Dresden was declared capital of the Kingdom of Saxony, ironically by Napoleon, who won his last major victory just outside of the city gates. In 1813 when Napoleon was defeated near Leipzig, the Prussian and Russian troops again occupied the city and made Dresden the capital of Saxony. They released the king after he gave up two-thirds of his lands to Prussia.

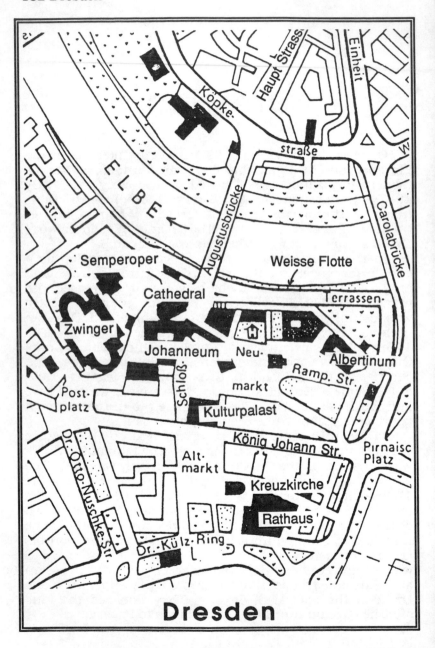

Dresden

After the Congress of Vienna Dresden again turned to commerce, art and architectural treasures. The first German long-distance train began running between Leipzig and Dresden. Richard Wagner conducted the Dresden Orchestra. Karl Marx began one of his publications here.

In the late 1800s and early 1900s Dresden grew into a large city. More bridges were built, railroads connected the country to the port on the Elbe, and industries manufacturing pharmaceuticals, sewing machines, typewriters, cigarettes, cameras and electrical materials all expanded. Universities were founded, art institutes were established. The population passed 500,000.

In 1933 at the beginning of Hitler's rapid rise Dresden was earmarked as the Nazi center for defamation of the arts, and in 1938 the systematic persecution and holocaust of the Jewish population began here on *Kristallnacht*.

In 1945 just before the end of World War II Dresden was subjected to the most concentrated saturation bombing attack of the war. Overnight between February 13th and 14th bombs rained down on this city reducing more than 15 square miles to rubble. The Allied Forces carried out this bombing attack to break the will of the German people to resist and to forcefully encourage them to renounce Hitler. There has been much political second guessing about the effects of the the bombing raids on the the people, but the destruction wrought is very evident. Three months later Soviet troops entered the city.

During the past four decades many of the city's buildings have been reconstructed and reopened to the public. You can still get a sense of the architectural splendor of Dresden, but the center of the city, surrounding the old central market, is unfortunately cold, sterile, gray socialist government architecture.

This is not a typical European city bustling with people. It seems strangely quiet, busy during the day and empty at night. But Dresden does offer plenty to keep you occupied for several days. The Zwinger, the cathedral, the remaining buildings and the museums are spectacular. And should you decide to make Dresden your hub for exploration of this region, the surrounding cities and countryside are beautiful.

The tourist information office has several booklets with English translations which will help visitors. The *Dresden Information* pamphlet published monthly and sold for DM1,20 provides important times for current concerts and exhibitions, as well as hours for most surrounding castles and museums, but you will need to understand some German to use it.

The Altmarkt

Though the *Altmarkt* (Old Market) is the historic center of the city, little remains that requires more than a glance. The main street running along the northern edge of the square is the Wilhofstraße, once Ernst Thälmann Straße.

The *Kreuzkirche* (Church of the Cross) stands at the eastern edge of Altmarkt. It was named for a supposed relic of the cross upon which Christ died. A church has stood on this site since 1200, but these churches have been burned down, remodeled, leveled by war, ruined by poor construction, bombed by the Allies, and always reconstructed. The interior of this church is void of any decoration but the church is home of the wonderful *Kreuzchor* (Choir) which performs regularly.

The *Kulturpalast* at the north side of the Altmarkt is a modern concert hall which features a full program of music. Tickets may be purchased at the tourist information office or reserved by calling 48668.

Your exploration of Dresden should start at the Tourist Information office located on the walking street, 10 Pragerstraße, across from the main train station, the Hauptbahnhof.

From the tourist office it is a long walk to the historic center; you may prefer to catch Tram #7, which will take you to the *Zwinger*, one of the most impressive Baroque buildings in the world.

Zwinger

Zwinger in German means Keep, as in a castle. This was the center of Dresden's kingdom. This Baroque, ornate quadrangle of buildings was built between 1709 and 1732 for Augustus the Strong, King of Poland and Elector of Saxony.

The architect was Mathäus Daniel Pöppelmann and the chief sculptor was Balthasar Permoser. This symmetrical structure consists of seven pavilions, all connected by a gallery, surrounding a football-field size central courtyard, complete with splashing fountains and pools, called the *Zwingerhof*. In the olden days this was the site of carnivals and tournaments. Reportedly Augustus kept a bevy of concubines here. He is generally described as a lusty king with a great love of art—this group of buildings stands in testament to his love of beauty and life.

The *Kronnentor* (Crown Gate) is topped by a large cupola and four Polish eagles. The *Nymphenbad* presents a scene of nymphs frolicking with dolphins in cascading water in a shell-lined stalactite grotto. The *Wallpavillion* appears to be almost a piece of sculpture in itself. The curving building blends into the overall quadrangle, and Hercules carries the globe above. Opposite the Wallpavillion is the *Glockenspielpavillion* (Carillon Pavilion) with its bells.

The northeast side of the Zwinger was built in 1846 by Semper, the same architect who designed the Opera House. Its quality of blending in with the other portions, built more than a hundred years earlier, is remarkable. Today it houses two major museums—The Gallery of the Old Masters and the Historiches Museum; they have been closed for a few years for restoration, but may open by late summer 1992.

The Gallery of Old Masters contains one of the continent's best collections of art. Some of the pieces are on display at the Albertinum until restoration is completed. The Historiches Museum is filled with costumes, clothing, and ornamental weaponry (About five percent of the collection, including the massive Winged Helmet of the King of Denmark and a horse literally covered with bells, can be seen housed temporarily across the street in a restored section of the castle. Open Thurs. 9.m.-6 p.m., Fri.-Tues. 9 a.m.-5 p.m.).

The Albertinum

This is another museum complex. This glass-domed building was built in the 1880s as a museum on the foundations of the old (16th century) arsenal along the Brühl Terrace overlooking the Elbe.

It contains the *Galerie Neue Meister* (Modern Masters Gallery), the Green Vault, the Sculpture collection and the Numismatic collection. During the reconstruction of the Semper building at the Zwinger, the Albertinum is also housing some of the paintings from the Old Masters Picture Gallery. I honestly have no idea which paintings will remain here and which will move to the restored Gallery of Old Masters when it is reopened.

In any case this museum, together with the Gallery of Old Masters, is mind-boggling and magnificent. When you walk up to the main gallery level you are met with no less than seven Canaletto paintings at the top of the stairs; the first gallery is packed with many of the famous and priceless Old Masters Collection—a dozen Rubens paintings, a half-dozen Rembrandts, as well as other paintings by Van Dyck, Vermeer, Bol, Dürer, Cranach the Elder and Holbein.

The next rooms are filled with German landscape artists—Richter, Friedrich, Blechen, Dahl and Oehme. Then move to the Modern Masters rooms displaying

works by Courbet, Gauguin, Lautrec, Monet, Renoir and Manet. There are also two Rodin sculptures and three sculptures by Degas in addition to his paintings.

Make sure to find the Portrait of St. Agnes by Giuseppe de Ribera in the Spanish section. This incredible painting showing St. Agnes covering herself with her long flowing hair is delightfully sensuous.

Other rooms contain masters from Italy. There are four giant paintings by Correggio, and another group of massive canvases by Veronese, and works by Lotto, Raphael (the famous Sistine Madonna), Tintoretto, Titian, and the mannerist Parmigiano.

Turn-of-the-century art is marked by a half-dozen Max Liebermann works and by three wonderful paintings by Menzel. And the modern age is marked by what I find its collection of relatively soulless art.

Downstairs at the Albertinum is the *Grünes Gewölbe*, or Green Vault. This is the richest collection in the world of precious jewels, silver and gold. It was also the first such display ever presented to the public when it opened its doors in 1730. The collection was founded by Augustus the Strong from items selected from the Electoral Art Chamber, the Silver Chamber and the Royal Secret Depository. The Museum is filled with spectacular, dazzling, bejeweled wall mountings, swords, clocks, and models.

Here many of the works come from Dresden's own goldsmith guilds. The earliest is Saint George and the Dragon, created in 1694. It is made of cast gold enamelled and studded with emeralds and diamonds. Other works to search out are *The Bath of Diana*, Augustus the Strong's golden coffee set, and the spectacular and detailed creation, *Keeping State at the Delhi Court on the Birthday of the Grand Mogul Aureng Zeb* , with 137 colorfully enamelled golden cast figures. This work kept 14 artisans busy for seven years and contains 3,000 diamonds, rubies, emeralds and pearls. It cost more than the nearby Moritzburg Palace.

The Numismatic collection is one of the largest in the world. It includes 200,000 different coins, medals and bank notes. There is also a complete collection of Saxon coins, a reference library of 15,000 volumes, and a stamp archive with thousands of coins and stamps for educational work.

The Sculpture Collection was started by Augustus the Strong in the early 1700s. It includes over a thousand pieces, of which half are on display. The sculpture includes Greek masterpieces, Etruscan art, statues from Pompeii and Herculaneum, and more modern works.

The special exhibition halls often house contemporary shows or special collections. During my visit, modern sculpture created from junked automobiles was displayed in one series of galleries, and in the other a grouping of Canaletto paintings of Dresden.

The Old and New Masters Galleries in the Albertinum are open Tues.-Sun. 9 a.am.-5 p.m. (6 p.m. Wed.). The

Grünes Gewölbe, Sculpture Collection, and Numismatic Collection are open Fri.-Wed. 9 a.m.-5 p.m. (6 p.m. Wed.).

Hofkirche or Cathedral of the Holy Trinity

This is the largest church in Saxony, built by Augustus III to provide an effective Catholic counter to the Protestant Frauenkirche. The Italian architect Gaetano Chiaveri was commissioned to design it, and the cornerstone was laid in 1739. Owing to a series of disagreements between Chiaveri and almost everyone else involved, construction was halted in 1748 when Chiaveri left Dresden. The church, one of the last examples of the Italian Baroque style, was eventually finished in 1751 with some changes to Chiaveri's plans.

The exterior is ornamented with 78 statues of saints standing on the parapets and over the entrances of the church. The bell tower is elliptical in its floor plan, and above roof level rises in two tiers of open columns, surmounted by an onion dome to the height of 279 feet. (Setting the columns in an elliptical ring provides a unique view of the tower from any viewpoint an observer takes.) The church is also connected to the palace by a small bridge which leads to the gallery seating area used by the ruling family.

The interior contains the largest organ created by Silbermann, considered Germany's best organ builder. Built in 1755, it has 2,896 pipes, 47 voices and three manuals. The altar was destroyed during World War II and rebuilt with colorful marble donated by Pope Pius XII in 1962. The altar picture, the *Ascension of Jesus Christ*, evacuated before the bombing, is by Anton Mengs.

This is also the burial place of the Saxon royalty. Four vaults contain the bodies of 49 electors, kings and princes. The heart of Augustus the Strong is here in an urn—the rest of his body is buried in a cathedral in Cracow, Poland.

The cathedral features organ concerts almost every Wednesday at 11:45 a.m. and Saturday at 4 p.m. Special guided tours of the church are given Mon.-Thurs. at 11 a.m. and 2 p.m., Fri. and Sat. at 1 and 2 p.m., and Sun. at 2 p.m.

Frauenkirche

This church stands destroyed as it was after the great bombing raid of 1945. It was designed by Georg Bähr and built between 1726 and 1743; it was almost round and with a massive cupola, constructed so that the Protestant congregation could cluster around the preacher. It was considered the most magnificent Protestant church of its time, a combination of late Baroque and classical architecture. It had survived bombardment from Prussian cannon during the Seven Years War and was still standing after the raid in February 1945, but collapsed the next day from the heat stress of the raging fires.

The interior was filled with hand-carved pews, the cupola was painted by the Venetian Giambattista Grone and the organ was also built by Silbermann.

In front of the ruined church is a statue of Martin Luther copied from an original in Worms.

Brühl Terrace

As you gaze at the palace and cathedral from the Augustus Bridge, (formerly the Georgi Dimitroff Bridge) to your left is a terrace overlooking the Elbe. This garden terrace was created upon the former walls of the city by Count Heinrich von Brühl. It has undergone many renovations over the years, and the only original section is the Dolphin fountain created by Pierre Coudray and the wrought iron railings. The gardens still contain bronzes by Schilling—*Night, Evening, Noon* and *Morning*. Most of the original palaces along the terrace have been replaced over time with other buildings.

Procession of the Princes

This 110-foot-long wall decoration runs along Augustusstraße, a narrow street next to the castle. Originally the picture of a procession of princes was created in 1589 as a mural using the sgrafitto technique (employed by Greeks and Egyptians, and by the Italians during the Renaissance; layers of paint are scraped away to reveal other colors underneath). In 1908 the painting was recreated on 25,000 porcelain tiles made in Meissen and set into the wall.

The picture includes 93 figures including 35 rulers of the Wettin Dynasty, plus influential artists, scientists, and professors. The procession ends with the painter Ludwig Richter, the sculptors Schilling and Hähnel and lastly the creator of this work, Wilhelm Walther with his assistants.

The Royal Palace

This palace was first built about 1530 on its present site. It was modified by Augustus the Strong after a fire and later redesigned in the Renaissance style from 1890 to 1901. The palace is still in ruins but restoration has been moving at a feverish pace since 1990. The Georgian Gate has already been restored and provides a beautiful example of Renaissance decoration. The central courtyard can be seen if you look past the barricades at the entrance near the Hofkirche. The Long Passageway with its 22 open Tuscan arches has also been reconstructed behind Augustusstraße, and the stables—where 128 horses were kept—are also open to the public.

The Semper Opera House

This opera house was only reopened forty years after its destruction in the war. This is one of the masterpieces of Gottfried Semper and considered one of the best examples of 19th-century German architecture. The sculpture adorning the exterior of the building is some of Germany's best from this period. Schilling's bronze panther chariot at the top of the monumental entrance way and the statues of the Three Graces with Apollo and Pan by Paul Kiessling also add to the ornamentation.

The interior has excellent acoustics and the main curtain depicting Imagination sitting on a high throne is considered a masterful reproduction of the original. Tours of the Opera House are given regularly.

Opera, theater, and concerts are also held here on a regular basis. Call 48420 or fax 4842692 for ticket information and reservations. Tickets may be reserved by calling 4842323. Unreserved tickets are sold at the Opera box office an hour before the performance, often for less than DM10. Advance tickets cost about DM40 or more.

Transport Museum

This building was constructed as part of the palace, and its portal on the west side is considered the most perfect of German Renaissance. It was the first building reconstructed after the war and was turned into the Transport Museum, which opened in 1956. More than 100 historic locomotives are included in the collection as well as hundreds of cars, airplanes and ships.

The museum is open Tues.-Sun. 10 a.m.-5 p.m.

Porcelain Museum

This is considered the second largest porcelain collection in the world. (The largest is in Istanbul.) It was started by Augustus the Strong in 1717. The collection includes much Meissen China but also pieces from Chinese Ming, Tang, and Sung Dynasties. There is also pottery from Japan and Korea.

The museum is housed in the Zwinger and is open Sat.-Thurs. 9 a.m.-5 p.m.

Dresden Neustadt

This new section of Dresden on the opposite side of the Elbe. The *Goldenen Reiter* statue was created in 1736 and the gilding was added in 1965. It is a likeness of Augustus the Strong.

The walking street which stretches northward from the statue is the Hauptstraße, once called Straße der Befreiung (Street of Liberation). This plane-tree shaded street makes for an interesting walk from the river to the Albertplatz, once called Platz der Einheit. Cafés, cabarets and restaurants line the promenade. Baroque burgher houses and new building styles are more or less blended into a unique atmosphere. Number 11 used to be a Bierkeller and though the exterior is modern the vaulting dates from 1695. At #13 you'll find the Museum of Romanticism in the Kügelgen House, where leading members of the Romantic movement used to meet. It is open Wed.-Sat. 10 a.m.-5 p.m., Sun. 10 a.m. -4 p.m.

The nearby **Museum of Folk Art** at 1 Köpckestraße is open Tues.-Sunday 10 a.m.-5 p.m.

And just past the Hotel Bellevue is the **Japanese Palace** built by Pöppelmann from 1727 to 1735. This building was named for the oriental porcelain collection of Augustus the Strong rather than for any exterior oriental motif. It contains the **Museum of Prehistory** and the **Museum of Ethnology**. The palace is built in the Baroque to early Classical style with four wings surrounding a courtyard. A gallery supported by Chinese busts runs three quarters of the way around the courtyard.

The Museum of Ethnology is open Sat.-Thurs. 10 a.m.-5 p.m.; the Museum of Prehistory is open Mon.-Thurs. 9 a.m.-5 p.m., Sun. 10 a.m.-4 p.m.

Getting around

If you arrive by train you will step into the Hauptbahnhof on the southern side of the center of the city or the Dresden-Neustadt station on the north side of the Elbe. The Hauptbahnhof is more convenient to a majority of the trams and buses and is only a short walk from the main tourist information office. Trains connect the two stations about every twenty minutes and Trams #3 and #11 connect the two train stations. Tram #11 rolls right past the Zwinger.

The bus, city rail and tram system in Dresden is excellent and reaches every corner of the city and most of the surrounding suburbs. Pick up a map of the system at the main tourist office or at the Hauptbahnhof (main train station).

The Weisse Flotte operates boats which cruise up and down the Elbe. These are excellent for trips to Meissen and southwest through the Sächsische Schweiz. They stop just below the Bruhl Terrace on the Elbe, tel. 051/4956436.

Accommodations

If you have big bucks or DMs, head to the **Hotel Dresdner Hof** (tel. 051/48410), considered one of the best in Eastern Germany. It is smack in the middle of the city and has more restaurants than the entire surrounding area. Expect to pay in the range of $250-$300 a night. **Hotel Bellevue** (tel. 051/56620) is across the Elbe from the historic center of Dresden with great views back to the city. It is built into the former Royal Chancellery which survived the bombing of 1945. Rates will be similar to the Dresdner Hof.

A bit out of the center, but with excellent views up on the hill across the Elbe is the **Hotel Schloß Eckberg** (Bautznerstraße 134) which was built in former youth hostel. Rates are more reasonable than upscale downtown hotels. Be sure to ask for a room in the old palace section rather than in the modern part.

The next level of comfort seems to be grouped near the tourist office on Pragerstraße, a walking street. Try **Newa** (tel. 051/48560), **Hotel Königstein** (tel. 051/48460), and **Hotel Lilienstein** (tel. 051/48560).

There are two youth hostels in Dresden:

Jugendherberge Rudi Arndt, Hübnerstraße 11, Dresden. Tel. 470667. This 73-bed hostel is located in a mansion that used to be owned by the the Singer sewing machine family, 5-6 blocks south of the train station.

Jugendherberge Oberloschwitz, Sierksstraße 33, Dresden-Loschwitz. Tel. 36672. This hostel is a long tram ride, then a train ride, then a five-minute hike. If you like beautiful locations, it's worth it.

Tourist information

Dresden-Information is on Pragerstraße #10-11, across the main street from, and within sight of, the Hauptbahnhof. The office has an agent who handles room reservations in private homes, distributes maps and tourist literature, and sells tickets to most cultural events in the town.

City bus tours and walking tours also leave from just outside the tourist office. The long (3 hours) city tour leaves daily at 10 a.m. and will cost DM34 per adult and DM17 for children 6 to 12; children under six are free. The short city tour (2 hours) leaves four times a day and costs DM22 per adult and DM11 for children 6 to 12; children under six are free. There are also city tours which include some of the surrounding area.

NOTE: The city has been busily renaming streets, but maps printed before the summer of 1991 still refer to streets by their old names. Many of the residents do not know the new names, so be ready for some confusion. Where we know of changes, both the old and new street names have been mentioned.

The tourist office hours are Mon.-Fri. 9 a.m.-8 p.m.; Sat. 9 a.m.-2 p.m.; and Sun. 9 a.m.-1 p.m. Tel. 495-5025, fax 495-1276.

There is also a small branch of Dresden-Information under the Goldener Reiter in the Neustadt section. It only hands out tourist literature and sells books, maps, postcards and souvenirs.

Journey through the East
Part V

Down the Elbe from Dresden

The next morning I went downtown to change money then headed for the Sächische Schweiz . . . off to find what I could find. This was a day of traveling blind. I know this "Schweiz" was supposed to be beautiful rock formations, but where exactly and what's on the way, were questions I hadn't been able to answer when I began my drive.

I had read of a Baroque Garden in a local tourist brochure and saw it marked on the map, so I decided to head there first. I carefully checked every possible sign along the road and ended up in the next town. Turned around and asked a street worker who pointed to the top of the hill and gave me complex directions in dialect. The only part of the directions I understood was the pointing. I headed up. Finally, I found the gardens—no signs—but spectacular nonetheless. It is hard to imagine why any king would want such an expenditure of time and money on top of this hill...

Wound my way back down the mountain and drove into the next town on the route to Pirna. Noticed an interesting steeple and a palace on the hill so decided to stop in there. The town was delightful but everything is closed or under construction. The young woman at Tourist Information explained that the palace I saw at the top of the hill was a sanitarium and wouldn't be open but the church and museum would be opened by next summer. They gave me several excellent maps of the "Schweiz" area and recommended a route. Finally, I had a plan to my day, and hopped back into the car.

First stop was Festung Königstein, I has no idea of what this was. From the few photos I had, I assumed it was some model Medieval Village or such. Was I mistaken! This is the most fascinating fortification I have ever visited. The giant fortress sitting on this massive rock is impressive in its own right, but when you couple the magnitude of the construction effort with the magnificence of the views over the Elbe, which the fortress dominates, it's a unique combination.

I went back down to my car and drove along the Elbe, crossed at Bad Schandau then headed to Hohnstein Castle which had been recommended by the Pirna tourist office. The road up to the castle was through a deep gorge and tall trees hung over the road, making it seem like dusk at midday. The village of Hohnstein is a half-timbered picture postcard-perfect town. This would be a good place to relax at the cafe in the castle on Hotel AmHohnstein.

But there was to be no relaxing today. I was running late and had to be to Pillnitz on the outskirts of Dresden by 4:30, I figured, expecting that it would close at 5 p.m. I made it, and the gardens turned out to be open until about 8 p.m. but the museums would close soon. I wandered into the museum which housed old furniture from the period of Pillnitz—the actual space is a bit limited but you get a good idea of the furnishings of the time. Now don't believe that everyone had bejeweled beer steins—but the king did.

Dinner in Dresden

Headed back to my room on the hill behind Dresden and hooked up with my landlord and paid for these two nights (DM60). I decided to head out to eat—I hadn't grabbed anything since my breakfast of a cup of coffee and two rolls at the train station after changing money. This time I was determined to find the Phantom Gasthaus—after much circling I found the place, but it was closed. Alas. I headed back ready to do without dinner again, but then decided to drive to the next town. Smaller towns always seem to have at least one *Gaststätte*. The road drove into total darkness turning down off the hill into a valley then up the next hill where a darkened villlage sat.

It looked lifeless, as many East German towns appear as soon as the sun goes down. I wasn't very hopeful but took the first left into what seemed to be the only part of the village with any light. Alas, the lights only lit advertising. Made another left back toward Dresden and found a hotel with a restaurant—finally—food.

I sat down with a large dark man who looked more like an overgrown Sicilian than a German—but with accents in this area, I really had no idea of where he was originally from. He sold bread products all over East Germany and lived near Weimar—he was on a business trip. We chatted about the food he wolfed down with amazing speed, and about the local brew, but not much else. As he scraped his plate, he grunted, "Ich muß gehen" and took off to visit restaurant customers.

A few minutes later a young guy (35-40) and his girlfriend (40-45) sat down at the table. He was an accountant. She worked at the Semper Oper downtown. It seems that when he has clients who come to Dresden, he puts them up at this small hotel. Our conversation remained only small talk about where I've traveled and a series of jokes. Another friend of his arrived whose impossible-to-understand accent said he was from Munich. He was leaving the next morning very early (3 a.m.) to avoid traffic jams and had a series of sales calls to make. The final result was that they maintained small conversation and I could throw in some small jokes here and there . . . and then we parted.

Dresden's Environs

Surrounding Dresden are a collection of towns, castles, gardens and natural sights which can take several days to discover. The following short descriptions detail the spots which I enjoyed most during my stay. I start with a hunting chateau to the north of Dresden followed by a palace a bit to the southeast, then a drive looping generally southeast along the Elbe valley.

Moritzburg

This beautiful hunting palace sits glistening yellow, surrounded by a shimmering blue lake. It rises from the water just as anyone familiar with fairy tales would imagine. It is the most visited palace around Dresden.

This gem is only 14 km. northwest of the city, and the goal of many day tours. Moritzburg is also only a short drive from Meissen, and many visitors tour Meissen in the morning and early afternoon, then finish off the day here.

The hunting chateau was built for the duke of Moritz in 1546, then rebuilt in the present Baroque style in 1730 by Augustus the Strong according to plans created by Pöppelmann, designer of the Zwinger, and a group of other architects. The Baroque interior has remained unchanged for centuries.

Set in a protected forest

Behind the palace and surrounding the lake is a massive forest with hundreds of kilometers of well-marked walking trails. The *Fasanenschlosschen* (Little

Pheasant Palace) was built in 1782 and today houses a natural history museum focused on the wildlife of the Moritzburg region. This protected area is home to more than 200 species of marsh and water birds, birds of prey and songbirds.

This forest is a good example of the "animal gardens" where royalty of the past kept the game for their royal hunts, and you can still find deer, boar, marten, foxes, pheasants and falcons.

One of Germany's top stud farms and equestrian centers, founded in 1828, is open here during the summer months. It presents competition throughout the season and features a parade of stallions which draws over 50,000 visitors. Along the banks of the lake, fishing exhibitions and competitions also are held.

The interior

Entrance to Moritzburg Palace costs about DM3.50. Arrows direct visitors through the palace. After walking up the first flight of stairs you'll enter what I call the

Antler Room, really a reception room with four fireplaces and about 50 gigantic sets of elk horns adorning the walls. The next room is fully covered with frescoes, and has more antlers, crystal chandeliers, and two grand pianos. You can also see paintings by Lucas Cranach the Elder and Alexander Thiele.

After strolling through several more rooms you'll enter the chapel, which is finished in white with gold trim. Over the altar is a painting of the Assumption of Mary into Heaven. The marble statue of the Man of Sorrows by Balthasar Permoser is considered a masterpiece. The next rooms include a billiard room with an inlaid table from the 1700s; there are beautiful views out over the manicured gardens. The dining room features more antlers, this time 56 numbered sets. Here you will also find the world record rack (#8), with 24 points and weighing 19.86 kilograms. The ground floor features a museum with carriages, sedan chairs, porcelains and models which show how the palace grew from fort to hunting palace.

Opening hours
Moritzburg Palace is *normally* open Tues. - Sun. 10 a.m. - 5 p.m. Check with the tourist office in Dresden or call the tourist office in Moritzburg (tel. 356 or 439—check with the telephone operator for the correct prefix) to make sure the palace is open when you visit. During December and January it may be closed; and in November and February the palace is often closed Monday and Tuesday. It is a shame to get all the way out to Moritzburg and then not have a chance to see the interior of the palace. The Rococo Fasenenschlösschen is open April - October 9 a.m. - 4 p.m. daily.

For a change of pace, you may choose to rent rooms nearby and paths through the woods. The tourist office at the entrance of the palace serves as agent for about 20 local houses that rent out rooms and for the Hotel Waldschänke, Hotel Seefrieden, and Pension Rosengarten. The tourist office has maps of the region and trails, and can arrange for guided tours of the palace and park, bicycle rentals.

Pillnitz

This palace complex is in a suburb of Dresden on the north side of the Elbe River. The cluster of palaces is set in a carefully tended garden, surrounded by vineyards to the north and bordered by the river along the south. These palaces, also the work of Pöppelmann, were erected in 1765. The *Wasserpalais* (Water Palace) and the *Bergpalais* (Mountain Palace) mirror each other and frame the *Lustgarten* (Pleasure Garden) filled with beautiful fountains. On the southeast these two twin palaces are joined by the *Neues Palais* (New Palace) which was added in 1822.

Both main buildings house museums. You'll find ironwork, porcelains, beer steins, silverware, and Baroque furniture. There is also also the Museum of Arts and Crafts in the *Bergpalais* with work from the Middle Ages to the present. (There are also temporary exhibits housed in the *Wasserpalais*, but its main attractions are the gardens and architecture.

The central Pleasure Garden, framed by the palace buildings, leads to a series of other smaller gardens, each surrounded by high hedges. Within each hedge enclosure is a different type of garden—one features evergreens, another small fountains, yet aother is filled with flowers and so on. Behind the Bergpalais is the **Orangerie** with its camellia house and the **English Garden**. Then behind the Orangerie visit the **Flora Garden** and the **Chinese Garden** with its Chinese pavilion.

If you do not have a car, you can get to Pillnitz on the Weisse Flotte boat, or take Tram #14 or #9 to the end of the line and take the small ferry across the Elbe. To get back into town you can retrace your steps or, once on the other side, take Bus #85 back to the Loschwitzer Bridge and then change to Tram #18 back to Altmarkt or #6 to Dresden Neustadt Bahnhof.

The gardens are open daily. The museums are only open May - October 10 a.m. - 5:30 p.m. (*Wasserpalais* closed Mon.). Entrance fee is charged only for the museums.

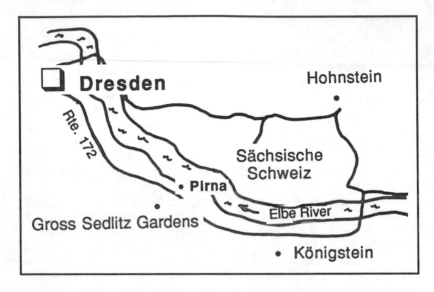

The following towns, gardens, palaces and castles may be visited on a long day trip from Dresden.They are listed in the order that they are reached by automobile looping to the southeast from Dresden—Gross Sedlitz, Pirna, Königstein, Hohnstein and the Sächsische Schweiz.

Gross Sedlitz Baroque Gardens

About 16 kilometers southeast of Dresden in the suburb of Heidenau, these are considered the most perfect remaining Saxon Baroque Gardens. They were planted and shaped at the top of a hill above the Elbe. Again, these gardens were part of Augustus the Strong's royal holdings and again he turned to his favorite architect, Pöppelmann to help design them.

The gardens were started in 1719 and didn't come into Augustus's possession until 1723. They were contested during the Seven Years War and by Prussian troops in 1813, and in both wars were for the most part destroyed. The orangerie was rebuilt from 1872 to 1874, but the new palace was never as grand as the original. The gardens, the pools, the terraces and the massive staircases all serve as a reminder of how grand this palace must have been.

Today the gardens are still beautifully kept. The Orangerie is still beautiful and 52 of 360 sculptures still surround the gardens. They provide a quiet and elegant step back into time once you find them.

Finding the gardens

You will really need a car to reach the gardens. Though well maintained, they are not well marked. Take Highway 172 from Dresden toward Pirna. You will see the signs for Heidenau. Stay on the main road. When you reach a stoplight where Reiffenwerk Heidenau is on your left, turn right; this is Geschwister Scholl Straße. Go up the hill and look carefully for signs. If you see a garden sign follow it, otherwise follow the signs to Hotel Heidenau, which will direct you to the left. Pass the hotel and when you reach a "T" where you must turn left or right, turn right. Then take the next left on Parkstraße and drive past the Heinrich Heine School to another "T" and there turn left. The garden parking place will be easy to see at that point. If there are any signs they will read "Barockgarten." Entrance to the gardens is free for those who find them.

Pirna

This is a small, picturesque town just to the south of Dresden, on your way to the Sächsischen Schweiz, Königstein, Hohnstein and the Großsedlitz Baroque Gardens. This loop will require a car, or you might plan on a two-day bicycle tour.

The town doesn't offer much other than a quaint atmosphere, but it might make a good alternative to Dresden for a place to stay. There are excellent train connections to Dresden and even Meissen, or upriver to Königstein, and the Weisse Flotte boats on the Elbe stop here three or four times a day in both directions. There is also a good collection of small restaurants, and the tourist office is one of the best places to get maps for a drive through the Sächsische Schweiz.

Standing over the town is an old palace, Schloß Sonnenstein, built in its present form during the mid-1700s on the site of one of the most important fortresses along the Elbe. It all looks imposing, but today it is not open to tourists. However, a visit to the grounds does provide beautiful views. The view from the end of Schuhgaße opening onto the central town square with the town hall, the church behind and the palace above, was immortalized by the Italian artist Canaletto in 1753.

A picturesque town square

The old town square itself is interesting with a free-standing town hall showing influences of Gothic, Renaissance, and Baroque architecture. It is ringed by a group of nicely restored medieval buildings. Markt #7 is the house where Canaletto lived from 1753 to 1754. Markt #9 was a trader's house with a late-Baroque doorway from 1673. Markt #17/18 has a carved door from 1578. Markt #19 has been a Gasthaus since 1699 and Napoleon is supposed to have stayed in Markt #20 in 1813.

Our Lady's Church has been used as a storage barn for years. It was built in 1502 to 1546 in Gothic style. The Baroque tower soars almost 100 feet above the town square. It should be reopened sometime in 1992.

The town museum in the Klosterhof, originally a Dominican Monastery, was under restoration in1991 and is scheduled to reopen in the summer of 1992. The monastery was originally built in the 15th century.

Pirna can be easily reached by train or by boat (Weisse Flotte) from Dresden. Tourist Information is located in the center of town at Dohnaische Straße #31 (tel. 2897. It offers private room rentals and reservations, maps and a small souvenir shop. Tourist information is open Mon.-Fri. 9 a.m. - 5 p.m., Sat. 9 a.m. - noon. It may be closed for lunch at times.

Festung Königstein

Festung, in German, means fortress. This is the quintessential fortress in Europe as far as I am concerned. Everything from the strategic site, to the massive walls, to the panoramic river valley views, to the monumental entrance, is spectacular. Words fail me when trying to capture the grandeur and power this edifice evokes as it crowns its giant jutting sandstone rock.

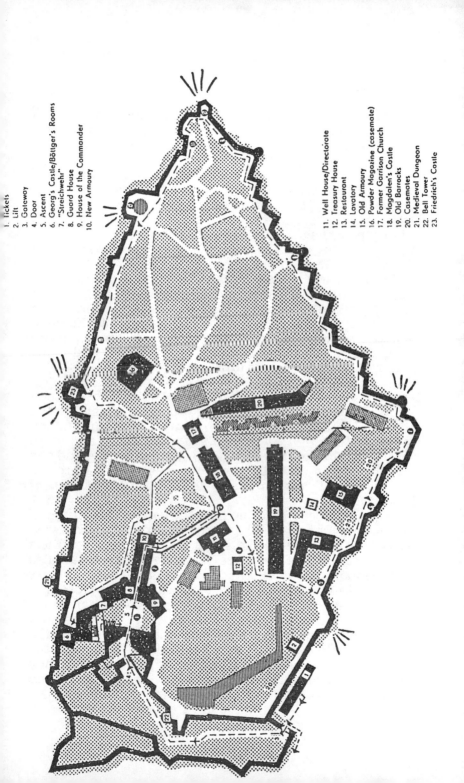

1. Tickets
2. Lift
3. Gateway
4. Door
5. Ascent
6. Georg's Castle/Böttger's Rooms
7. "Streichwehr"
8. Guard House
9. House of the Commander
10. New Armoury

11. Well House/Directorate
12. Treasury House
13. Restaurant
14. Lavatory
15. Old Armoury
16. Powder Magazine (casemate)
17. Former Garrison Church
18. Magdalen's Castle
19. Old Barracks
20. Casemates
21. Medieval Dungeon
22. Bell Tower
23. Friedrich's Castle

Through history the rock has been a strategic location and its ownership negotiated by many monarchs as they moved the boundaries of their kingdoms. In 1359 emperor Charles IV resided in the building then known as Kaiserburg. Königstein fortress eventually became one of the mightiest fortifications built by feudal man, but thanks to the fortunes of history it never became a strategic point, nor was it ever conquered. It has served as military post, haven for royalty during wars, state prison, archives for Dresden's treasures during World War II, and POW camp.

The fortress is situated at a major bend in the Elbe and sits almost 1000 feet above the surface of the river. To get up to it, take the Festung Express, a carnival-like train which shuttles you from the parking lot just off the main highway. Make sure to ask for an English translation to the fortress guide. If they can locate one, it will add many interesting stories to your tour.

Inspiring views from the top of the walls

You have a choice of walking around the walls to the left and entering by way of many stairs and steep walkways through the drawbridges, or of taking an elevator to the top of the walls. I suggest you spend the half-Mark or so and take the elevator, then walk around the walls and wander down the stairs and series of drawbridges.

When you get out of the elevator you will be on top of the massive fortress walls. Turn left along the walkway: the view is beautiful to the south and west over the Biela River, a tributary of the Elbe. On a clear day you can also see the mountains of Czechoslovakia to the south. You are standing on top of a 150-foot high wall—three storeys of fortifications which have protected soldiers for centuries. (There are even bakeries, storerooms, and dungeons built inside them.) The stones used to shape the exterior of the walls were almost ten feet thick. Take a look over the walls: from here, the reality of this fortress will only then begin to strike you. The size of this fortress is amazing and as you walk counterclockwise around the wall you will continue to be amazed by the integration of the walls with the sheer cliffs and the views.

The buildings in the interior served as barracks, armories, military headquarters and royal apartments.

Enjoy a walk around the fortress wall
The walkway around the walls narrows, enclosing a part of the stronghold, a wooded hill more like a forest than a fort. Keep walking around to the east and you will get your first views of the Elbe valley and the town of Königstein. OK, take a picture here, but remember the views keep getting better as you continue. On the opposite side of the river the rock rising almost as a twin to the Königstein fortress is called the *Lilienstein.*

The walkway curves around the walls, and pathways then take visitors to the New Armory where a museum shows the development of the castle and its cannon from medieval to modern. Upon leaving the museum you can work your way down to the entrance. In one of these buildings above the entrance Johann Friedrich Böttger, the inventor of European porcelain, was held in captivity from 1706 to 1707 when he was moved to Meissen to start the factory in the Albrechtsburg.

The entrance is protected by three drawbridges. They have been in operation since 1589. The entrance was modified many times, but still bears the mark of Augustus the Strong, with Polish eagles, a crown, Augustus' initials and the crossed Electoral swords.

After walking down through the gates you eventually reach the parking lot where the "Festung Express" will take you back to the parking lot.

Festung Königstein is open daily, 8 a.m. - 8 p.m. The museum is open 9 a.m. - 5 p.m. The fortress is located approximately 30 kilometers southeast of Dresden. The entrance fee is DM3.50 and the elevator will cost an additional 50 pfennigs. Parking is about DM2 and the "Festung Express" costs about DM2 for the round-trip ride.

Hohnstein
This half-timbered village clustered around the Hohnstein castle is among the prettiest in the region. The castle stands on a commanding 300-foot-high precipice over the Polenz River and the views from the tower over

the surrounding wooded valleys and mountains are wonderful. This river was one of the regional borders for centuries.

A castle has been here since 1241 and served as one of the border outposts of the Meissen bishopric. The present castle was constructed in 1353 on the then border with Bohemia, and for almost a hundred years belonged to the Bohemian kingdom to the south, becoming part of the Saxon kingdom in the 15th century.

The castle served as a hunting lodge and a royal residence, and then as a prison until 1924. In that year the castle was made available as a youth hostel and hundreds of children worked for months to create the hostel which still stands today. Between 1924 and 1933 this was a hotbed of Socialist and Communist ideas. In the first year of the Nazi regime, the castle was a concentration camp; in 1934 this was dismantled and a Hitler Youth camp set up. The castle served to house resettled ethnic Germans from former eastern territories after the war, and again became a youth hostel in 1948.

Today this castle is still a youth hostel with 200 beds, and according to hostel experts is about as good as hostel living gets. There is also an excellent restaurant with beautiful views, and concerts are held during the summer in the gardens below the restaurant and tower. The castle tower can be climbed for a 360-degree view.

The drive up to Hohnstein from Bad Schandau where the bridge crosses the Elbe is beautiful. You twist and turn about 12 km. through a primeval forest set in a deep gorge before coming upon the town. Drive right to the castle. There is metered parking in the Marktplatz.

This town makes a perfect spot to have a meal or coffee, either in the castle gasthaus or in the nearby Hotel Am Hohnstein or Café am Markt.

Burg Stolpen

This castle is located about 25 km. east of Dresden. It is one of the most popular day-trip spots for tourists. The castle is dramatically built on an imposing rock formation of pentagonal and octagonal basalt columns.

(Similar basalt formations, forming the Giants' Causeway, are found in Northern Ireland.)

The small town surrounding the castle is relatively unspoiled. The castle itself was first built about 1100 and expanded in 1300 as an administrative and frontier post. In the 15th and 16th centuries the castle reached its present size as a fortress and troop garrison. It is the scene of several historic tales, including that of Countess Cosel, the celebrated mistress of Augustus the Strong who was held prisoner here for 40 years.

To reach the castle take Highway #6 toward Fischbacher Kreuz. Burg Stolpen is open daily 9 a.m. - 4 p.m., with the last visitors allowed to enter at 3:30 p.m.

Weesenstein Palace

This palace is located just to the south of Dresden. Take Highway 172 to Heidenau; from Heidenau turn right on the road to Altenburg; the castle is about 5 km. south of Heidenau.

Weesenstein Palace was built in the 16th century around the core of an old castle first erected in the early 1300s. The Renaissance doorway dates back to 1575. The rest of the modern palace is built is in Baroque and Rococo styles surrounding the chapel, the first major part of the modern structure. The gardens surrounding the palace were added in the 1700s. Weesenstein Palace contains one of Europe's best collections of wall hangings and tapestries.

Weesenstein Palace grounds are open Tues. - Sun. 9 a.m. - 5 p.m. The tapestry museum may only be visited with a guided tour. Hours are Tues. - Fri. 11 a.m. - 2 p.m., Sat. and Sun. 10 a.m. - 4 p.m. Tours leave every hour.

Sächsische Schweiz

This region of Germany is sometimes called "Saxon Switzerland." this is a land of wonderfully shaped sandstone rock formations. If you have seen Bryce Canyon in Utah, these few spires are not very spectacular, but for most Europeans and for visitors from all over the world they represent some of nature's most fascinating work. The region is perfect for hiking and climbing and provides a very different natural view of Germany. If you are looking for a chance to enjoy natural beauty this region would be a good place to spend some time. Stay in Hohnstein or on the river in Bad Schandau and use it as a base. There are hotels and private rooms available in both towns.

The sandstone formations have been formed over the eons by erosion. The shapes are most dramatic in the region of the Bastei, where they have been developed into a natural park of sorts. Bridges connect many of the sandstone spires and paths wind between these towers. The Bastei area has a large hotel and a restaurant with an excellent viewing platform overlooking the Elbe River. A bit below is a natural open-air theater, the *Felsenbühne* (Rock Stage) where plays are staged during the summer months.

If you want to get away from the tourist crowds, the best bet is to take a hike into the countryside, rather than crowding onto the viewing platforms surrounding the Bastei. The *Lilienstein* (Lily Stone) and the *Pfaffenstein* (Priests Stone) are popular rock formations for a hike or climb. The *Lilienstein* offers views across the Elbe to the Königstein Fortress—a restaurant and the ruins of a medieval castle as a reward after your climb.

Bautzen

This southeast city in the land of the Sorbs is the center of the very special culture of those people. The town, which has been established for more than 1000 years, is called Budysin in the local Sorbian language. The language is Slavic with similarities to Polish and Czech. In reality little Sorbian is spoken in Bautzen, but there are nearby towns which still speak it as their everyday language. Street signs are bilingual in both languages.

Bautzen also provides one of the best examples of town fortifications to be found in Germany. Much of the original walls still remain and are virtually complete on the northern edge of the town. A walk along the walls is beautiful and interesting.

The **Sorbian Museum** is open daily 10 a.m.-noon and 1 p.m.- 5 p.m. more or less. **St. Peter's Cathedral** is an interesting joint Catholic and Protestant church with the congregations separated by a twelve-foot-high fence. The **Nikolaiturm** is one of the old town gates with a gruesome legend of a traitor being sealed inside the tower after he had opened the gate to enemies.

The **Tourist Office** is located on Fleischmarkt and is open Mon. 9:30 a.m.-1 p.m.; Tues.-Fri. 9:30 a.m.-4:30 p.m.; in the summer months, May to September the office is open on Saturday morning.

The Tourist Office has a room reservation section, but be ready for prety rough board and don't head in this direction if you only stay in first class hotels . . . you'll be looking for a long time.

Meißen

Meißen, one of the oldest German towns, is as picturesque, architecturally fascinating and historically interesting as they come in Europe. It is filled with 1000 years of history and did not suffer massive damage in World War II as Dresden did. The magnificent Albrechtsburg and the Cathedral lord it over the small town of spires, half-timbered houses, narrow cobblestoned streets, Gothic buildings, and fountains.

Meißen, only 26 km. northwest of Dresden, was originally founded in the early 900s as a a fortified castle. Otto I in 968 created a Meißen bishopric, but it is about thirty years later, at the turn of the century, that the first references to the town at the base of the castle appear. The town reached its power peak during the mid-1200s when the cathedral was constructed. In 1543 the Elector Moritz set up the "School of Princes" in St. Afra's. This important provincial parochial school prepared boys, regardless of their social standing, to attend a university. Gotthold Lessing the 18th-century philosopher, Christian Fuerchtegott, the inspiring poet and teacher of Goethe, and Samuel Hahnemann, the medical pioneer, are its most famous graduates.

Meißen was attacked by the Swedes and destroyed during the Thirty Years War in the early 1600s. The town also suffered much damage in the Napoleonic Wars when the French troops repeated the favor. The founder of the German women's movement, Luise Otto Peters, was born in Meißen in 1819.

Since 1710 Meißen has been the center of Dresden and Meißen porcelain manufacture. To protect the process of making fine porcelain, Augustus the Strong kept the inventor prisoner here in the Albrechtsburg.

Unfortunately this precaution couldn't keep the secret, although the town still has its reputation for the finest porcelain created in Europe.

Meißen is also known as one of Germany's premier wine towns. The surrounding vineyards produce some of the country's best, and vintners welcome you to test and purchase their wines throughout the year and see them in production during the harvest seasons. The tourist office can point you in the direction of the vineyards in the Spaargebirge area, where you'll find a dozen taverns serving local wines. Or slip into a cozy *Weingaststätten* in town to enjoy a meal with the local wine.

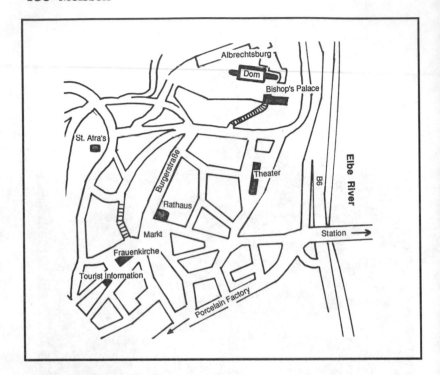

Frauenkirche

This is probably the first sight you'll visit, since it is across the street from the tourist office. The *Frauenkirche* (Church of Our Lady) was built in 1460 over an old chapel from the 12th century. On either side of the altar the thin columns are from the original 12th-century chapel.

The **altarpiece** is carved from limewood by an unknown artist. Several **Cranach paintings** hang in the church and the organ is a good example of a Jehmlich-Dresden organ. It was built in 1937 and has 4000 pipes.

The **bells hanging in the belfry** are made of china and were formed in 1929. They ring at 6:30 a.m., 8:30 a.m., 11:30 a.m., 2:30 p.m., 5:30 p.m. and 8:30 p.m. Each time the carillon plays during the day, it clangs out a different tune. Every quarter-hour a smaller clock in the bell tower strikes. Hardy sorts may climb the **bell tower** to see the porcelain bells and enjoy the view over the old town.

The church itself is open daily (except Mon.) with free entrance 10 a.m.-12:30 p.m., and 1 p.m.-5 p.m. The bell tower is open Tues.-Sun. 1 p.m.-4 p.m. There is a DM1 entrance charge to climb the tower, half as much for children. Tel. 3016.

Beside the Franuenkirche is the vine-covered **Weinstube Restaurant Vincenz Richter** (tel. 3285). This establishment has been serving Meißen wine in one form or another since 1523 and has been offering food since 1873. The wine list goes on for pages; the rest of the menu only takes up a few lines. It is open 4 p.m.-11 p.m. Tues.-Sat., and 10 a.m.-3 p.m. Sun. Alongside this eatery is a stairway which leads up to the Albrechtsburg and the Cathedral.

Dom (Cathedral)

This cathedral stands on the same hill as the Albrechtsburg. Construction was begun in 1270, the main part of the building was completed in 1380, and the original towers finished in 1410. The west towers were struck by lightning in the mid 1500s and finally re-erected 1903-1908.

The only way to see the cathedral is to take a 20-minute guided tour (in German) which is given every hour, 10 a.m.-5 p.m. (4 p.m. October through March) The tour includes the interior of the cathedral, the nearby bishop's house and the small cloister which shelters weathered statues across the cobbled street. Behind the altar in the interior of the cathedral are four spectacular **statues carved by the unknown Master of Naumberg** including a likeness of John the Baptist and of Otto I, the founder of Meißen. The altarpiece features a painting by Cranach the Elder.

If you arrive with a group you can arrange for an organist to play during your visit for a donation of DM30. Call ahead for reservations for the guide and organist.

The town also organizes organ and choir concerts from May through October. These concerts normally last about an hour and take place each Saturday at 6 p.m.

Albrechtsburg

This is one of Europe's great unheralded palaces. It has remained almost new, having been rarely used, and has never been subject to destruction since it was first built and decorated. The castle is one of the best examples anywhere of the conversion of a military structure to civil use. It was built from 1470 to 1525 on the foundations of the old castle that protected the town.

To create this masterpiece, the architect Arnold von Westfalen used creative vaulting, an integral part of the beauty of the palace. This building is his only world-famous work, but his **vaulting techniques** were copied throughout much of Eastern Europe, especially Bohemia. The vaulting begins to arch outward from about shoulder level, curving gracefully to the ceiling, rather than starting high overhead as we are used to seeing it. Just examining the pattern of the vaulting, the play of light, and the decorative effects of the vaulting in each room is fascinating.

After purchasing a ticket on the ground floor ask for a guidebook printed in English. They have only a few, and you will be asked for a DM50 (steep!) deposit which will be returned when you return the guide. The book adds much to the tour of the castle. As you go through this castle there are occasional boxes of large felt slippers which you slide right over your shoes. The management asks that you wear these slippers in several rooms to protect the finish on the floors.

After winding up the first level of stairs you enter the **Large Hall**, which has windows overlooking the Elbe. This was the reception hall for the castle.

To your left is the **Large Courtyard Room** which is adorned with murals showing the story of the castle. There are three on your right as you enter: he first shows the abduction of the princes from the castle, the second shows the knights setting them free, and the third illustrates the princes' triumphant return to the castle. To your left two murals depict the first victory of the 17-year-old prince Albrecht in a jousting tournament and the Emperor Friedrich III giving land to the princes in 1464.

The next room, the corner of the castle, is the **Small Banquet Hall** with a large mural of the betrothal of 16-year-old Albrecht to 10-year-old Zedena, daughter of the King of Bohemia in 1459.

You then pass back through the reception hall and walk up the architecturally fascinating **spiral staircase**. This massive staircase projects into the courtyard and curls up three storeys. The stairs shift from concave to convex to add strength, and the strength added by the vaulting also makes this continuous stairway possible.

The rooms on the upper floors of the castle are smaller and were used primarily for the administration of the kingdom. Arrows direct you through the chambers used by different parts of the government and then to the private apartments of the Duchess, who remained here for ten years before moving to the Palace of Tharandt. The play of light on the unadorned vaulting in the Duchess' rooms changes as the sun moves across the sky and again shows the genius of the architect Arnold von Westfalen.

The Albrechtsburg is open Tues.-Sun. 10 a.m.-6 p.m., but the last visitors have to enter by 5 p.m. Admission is DM3 for adults, DM2 for children 6-16 years, students, seniors and handicapped. Closed January.

Porcelain Factory

China from this area of Germany has been called "white gold." Meißen was the site of the first commercial porcelain production in Europe. The first factory was built in the Albrechtsburg in 1710, and only in the mid-1800s moved down into the city to larger factories.

Though the porcelain-making process was for years a state secret, today we have tours through the factories. The tour takes about 35 minutes. Here you will see how the material is made and fired, and how the decorations are painted and shaped on these delicate works of art.

The factory is about a ten-minute walk from the tourist information office at Talstraße #9 (tel. 541). The way is well-marked. Entrance is DM 3 for adults and DM 2 for children, students, seniors and handicapped. The factory tours are given from 8:30 a.m. to 12:30 p.m. and from 1 p.m. to 4:30 p.m. (the last tours are allowed to enter at noon and 3:45 p.m.) Get there early, because the lines are very, very long for this factory tour. Closed Mondays.

Entrance to the showroom is DM3 for adults, and DM2 for children, seniors etc. I suggest that you skip the display hall and go to the porcelain factory outlet (*Fachgeschäft für Meißner Porzellan*) at Markt #8. The outlet is open Mon.-Fri. 10 a.m.-6 p.m., Sat. 9 a.m.-noon.

Getting there

Meißen straddles the Elbe. The old town is centered on the western bank of the river. It is easy to visit, but has only limited hotel facilities for the overnight visitor. Most often it is visited as a side trip from Dresden. Boats of the **Weisse Flotte** ply the river twice a day between here and Dresden, May through October—the cruise takes two to three hours. The double-decker Dresden **S-Bahn** connects the two towns, and Meißen lies on the main Dresden-Leipzig rail line—the **train** ride takes just under an hour. The Meißen Hauptbahnhof is on the eastern side of the river, about a five-minute walk from the old town. The views of the old town from the bridge are spectacular.

Where to stay

The youth hostel, **Jugendherberge**, is located at Wilsdrufferstraße #28, up the hill about a 20-minute walk south of the city center. Tel. 3065. Rooms here are priced from DM10 to DM15 depending on the visitor's age.

The nearest campsite is Campingplatz Scharfenberg, Siebeneichen #6b, tel. 2680. The campsite is just south of the city in the hills near the Elbe.

Tourist information

Meißen-Information is located directly across from the steeple of the Frauenkirche, at #3 An der Frauenkirche in a restored brewery.

Tourist office hours are Mon.-Fri. 9 a.m.-6 p.m., Sat. 10:30 a.m.-2:30 p.m. They offer maps, guided tours of the town, vineyard tours, room reservations and a small souvenir shop. Tel. 4470.

Journey through the East
Part VI

Arriving in Potsdam

On my drive from Moritzburg to Berlin, I decided not to fight with the madness and traffic of Berlin itself and headed for Potsdam, just next door. I thought rooms would be easier to get there. I arrived at the tourist office *Zimmervermittler* at 3:30 p.m.—later than normal, but I figured in a big city it wouldn't be that big a problem. I was surprised when the tourist office said, "No room at the inn—any inn in Potsdam." The lady did ask if a small pension 20 km north of Potsdam would be OK. I said sure— my car didn't seem that comfortable, and the price she quoted was only DM30 a night including breakfast. So off I went winding my way north through back roads, and one of the largest concentrations of Soviet troops in East Germany.

I drove through kilometer after kilometer of Soviet barracks. I had Soviet Army trucks driving by, Soviet helicopters hovering overhead, Soviet troops strolling along. The troops looked so young, fresh and sharp. Unlike the Kasernes near Gotha and Weimar, the attitude here was much more lax. No one kept you moving past the barracks and motor pools, the troops wandered along sidewalks and even went shopping with a small market of vendors—probably trading hats and belt buckles for the goodies of life.

Settling into my Seeburg barracks

The lady's directions to this pension were simple. "Drive to Seeburg. You'll see the town on your left, at the first road turn right. You'll arrive at a place where the road forks into three streets. Take the far right road and drive until you reach the last house and there are only fields across from you. That's where the pension is."

I followed these directions, along with a small scrawled map she drew for me. I looked and looked for a pension sign—I didn't see anything and ended up in the fields. Turned back, stopped at the last house and rang the bell. A young man came out and said I was in the right spot—but the pension was the barrack-like building next door. I followed him to survey my fate . . . We passed the men's showers, men's toilets, women's showers and women's toilet. I had Room #1. He must have tried six keys before one turned in the lock. After each failure he'd look up at me and grin. When the door finally swung open, I was expecting bunk beds or worse, but it was a very pleasant surprise—two beds, two large lounge chairs, and plenty of good light. Across the hall the breakfast room had plenty of tables with good light for writing.

I asked him the best way to get to Berlin from here. He said waved his arm in the direction of the road, "Keep driving down this road 2 km, you'll pass The Wall—it's still just lying there—then turn left and you're right in Spandau."

I asked, "You mean, we're right against the wall?"

He nodded his head, "Yeah, you'll see it just lying there when you drive by."

Wow, I never expected to end up right on the border and in such a great spot. I took out my map and got a fairly good reckoning on where I was...this is not too bad. I might just stay right here the entire time instead of moving into Berlin—this is just as good, and at DM30 a night including breakfast, much more affordable than dealing with Berlin prices!

My first foray into Berlin

By now it had gotten dark—the traffic up from Potsdam had been very heavy, and I drove through constant construction. To get my bearings, I decided to head into Berlin. My map book had maps of downtown Berlin—but how useful they'd be was another question . . . no better way to discover this than by driving.

Immediately, I hit construction only a kilometer inside the city limits of Spandau. I drove with the other traffic looking for signs. Ended up on a wide main street which seemed to go in the direction of the center and decided to follow it. Berlin's traffic was heavy but not moving at the crawl everyone had told me to expect, except where construction had eliminated most of the streets. Miraculously, I ended up heading directly for the Kurfürstendamm (Ku'damm)—the Europa Center end of the street—the main center of old West Berlin. I could see no parking spaces, and I knew that with the massiveness of Berlin just parking and walking made little sense, so I turned around and backtracked to Seeburg.

An evening in Seeburg

I ducked into the local Gasthaus filled with a very working class crowd, most still wearing their overalls and with folding rulers and hammers poking from various pockets. They were all curious about me—we smiled at each other a lot. I ordered a local *Potsdamer Pils* beer and and an *Erbsen Eintopf* (a hearty pea soup) with a *wurst*.

An American couple was sitting only a table away with German friends from Hamburg. It was a real surprise to hear them—I hadn't spoken English for the entire past week. They were also staying here in Seeburg. It seems that they couldn't find a hotel in Berlin or Potsdam . . . and had ended up in my barracks. I told them about the border only 2 km away and the best way into town. They had planned only one overnight, so as to walk through the Brandenburg Gate and down Unter den Linden as their parents had done before the war.

Early morning at the Berlin Wall

The next morning, I woke up about 7 a.m. and washed up in our communal washroom. I then headed for the nearby section of the Wall. I wanted it to myself for awhile—I had heard the Wall was all but gone, but at least I could walk the former border.

In this section the Wall is still very much evident—I picked up a few concrete fragments of the fabled wall. There's lots of it (The Wall lying beside the ditch). You can

still see towers, the lines of double fences which first faced
escapees, then the open area with the patrol road, then a
ditch, then the actual location of the concrete wall, then
the final fence. Old concrete light posts and rusting light
fixtures lay scattered by the roadside. The poles are used as
barricades now, to keep cars off the old patrol road. I
walked along the patrol road reconstructing The Wall in
my mind. It's hard to imagine the millions who were held
prisoner by so few. I always wonder—why, why, why?

As I drove up to the border. I could see the entire layout
of the defenses. About a 1000 yards from the border the
houses stopped. The road narrowed to basically one lane
and there was a berm of brush and logs. From this berm to
the border was 1,000 meters of flatness—still. As
mentioned the border was relatively complete—The Wall
was knocked down, the fencing removed, the light posts
knocked down . . . but otherwise still ominous and empty.

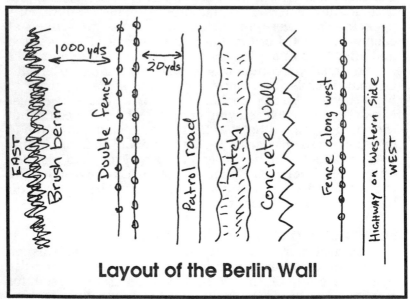

Layout of the Berlin Wall

You could clearly see the double row of fencing, the
clear zone, the patrol road, the ditch, the wall, then the
open area to the West. I walked down the patrol road
wondering how so many can be held by so few. But today
after being in Eastern Germany for more than a week—I've

spoken with many East Germans. From most of their points of view, the Wall was there to shut out the West, it seems.

I returned to the pension and to a surprisingly good breakfast. My expectation was a stale roll with some butter and runny jam. But this place puts out a great spread—everything from cold cuts, to cheese, to 6-minute eggs, to liverwurst, to poundcake served with coffee. Can't complain. It was wonderful. In fact, I've decided to set up camp here for at least three nights, maybe four. It makes a perfect base for exploring Berlin as well as Potsdam.

A day in Potsdam

The next morning at breakfast there was another table of English speakers—a man and two women from the Dallas area. He had been a POW and was traveling with his wife and twin sister to find the camps where he had been held. He had found one former camp near Baarth on the north coast. Now they were in Berlin where he had been assigned to the Airlift, and they were headed west to Braunschweig then Frankfurt and Heidelberg. He agreed to send me a map of POW camps which I may be able to use.

They said they were headed to Potsdam before driving back to the West. They asked directions and wondered what they should see. "I'm headed to Potsdam myself," I said, "First I'm heading to Cecilienhof where they signed the Potsdam agreement, to partition Germany after World War II."

"Mind if we follow you?" they asked.

"Not at all," I replied, "But I'll be headed out in a few minutes."

We crossed the old Wall and headed down Rte. 2 toward Potsdam. Construction was everywhere. After long stoplights controlling alternating in and outbound traffic and a lengthy detour we turned into the New Gardens, lining the edge of the Heiliger See, where Cecilienhof is located.

We found the parking lot but signs to the palace weren't easy to find and we ended up following a tour group. Great, wrong group. This bunch of people headed toward the lake where they saw the remains of the old Berlin Wall which skirted the edge of the gardens. We spotted the palace across the lawn and headed there before the group.

The Cecilienhof

Cecilienhof is a beautiful English-looking mansion rather than a palace. Part of it has been converted into a hotel, the remainder is maintained as a museum. You walk through the Russian and American work rooms, see Stalin's and Truman's desks, and see the round table where the Soviets, Americans and British negotiated the final settlements.

An interesting aside is the story of Churchill at these negotiations. There was an election in Britain during the conference and the negotiations were postponed for a few days to let Churchill and Attlee return to London for the results. Attlee had originally come with Churchill so that, if there was a change in prime ministers, no continuity would be lost. Hard to believe for us Americans (who hear Churchill mentioned together with FDR and God), but Churchill lost the election and Attlee returned to finish the conference.

This conference changed the face of Europe and set the lines for the Iron Curtain which eventually divided Europe. The physical walls and barbed wire have been removed but far-reaching decision such as the movement of Poland's border westwards into formerly German territory still affect European relations.

After contemplating the momentous decisions made in this manor we headed in the direction of one of Europe's most spectacular palaces—Sans Souci.

Sans Souci

We parked our cars and headed for the gardens and palaces. The main palace was painted a brilliant yellow and the terraced hillside dropped down to a gushing fountain. The folk who had been following me decided that they were not up for the walk down and the climb back up. So we said goodbye and I padded down the stairs. The look up at the palace was spectacular and I noticed that each terrace has small glass house enclosures built in to protect the plants during the cold winter months, I was amazed at the ingenuity the gardeners had even back in those days.

The walk through the series of gardens was beautiful. I had been so busy rushing around that I hadn't stopped to enjoy the beautiful weather. Another day of sunshine. Come to think of it I had been blessed with sunshine virtually everyday since my stormy entrance into Eastern Germany. I wandered with the sun on my back and saw another building on a hill to my right. I climbed up to it and discovered the Orangerie, which is a massive affair with a large balcony that affords wonderful views over Potsdam and the San Souci gardens. Inside the main rooms is filled with reproductions of paintings by Raphael, one of the favorite painters of German royalty. I also had a chance to visit the guest apartments which were used by the Czar and Czarina during their visits to San Souci.

I worked my way back to the car and slowly drove down to the Neues Palais, which looks from a distance like Capitol in size . . . and this wasn't even the main palace. I walked up to the ticket office and asked to speak with the director. Now my usual routine is to explain that I am a journalist and I would appreciate free entrance into the palace and if possible could one of the curators come along with me to point out special rooms and outline the history of the building. When you plan ahead and have everything arranged, this is normally how it works, but when you travel as I did, you have to deal with whatever the person in charge will allow at the time. Sometimes they give you the world, and sometimes you get no cooperation. But, I had never received this response.

"Oh mein Gott, ein *journalist*" was the reaction of the ticket seller. She called her supervisor, who asked me to come into her office and wanted to know just what I was planning to write. You'd think I was planning an exposé about waste in German museums. She made a series of calls, wrung her hands, muttered something to herself and looked up at me.

"I'm sorry," she said. "When journalists come they have to write in advance," she paused, "that is the only way that I can allow you free entrance."

I shrugged my shoulders. "O.K. it's no big deal. If you could helped me, that would be nice, but I can wander through by myself."

"Fine, but you can't work, or take photographs . . . we need official permission for that," she said sternly.

I nodded, "OK, I understand, no photographs." That was normal in many museums throughout the world. So I paid my few DM and headed for the entrance. The palace was wonderful. I took out my notebook and began to take notes. I had been through about three rooms when the supervisor came charging towards me.

"I thought I told you that you could not work unless you had the proper permissions," she told me in a loud whisper.

"I'm not taking photos. That's what you said I couldn't do, and I'm not doing it."

"No, you can't do any work here, or write anything about us, or about the palace without permission from the authorities."

I was amazed. "Fraulein, I'm sorry but I came with a letter of introduction from the National Tourist Board. That wasn't official enough for you. I asked you for help to get some background about the history and art in the palace. You are too busy to help. Now you tell me I can't write. You must be crazy (here I shifted into the familiar). I paid my entrance fee and as long as I don't break any of your rules, I can stand here and write all day." I was sputtering.

She was sputtering as well. "You think you can come here and do what you want. You can't. Leave right now. I don't want you doing any work."

I condescendingly told her, I was going to stay right here and continue writing, even if she insisted on following me around and howling for the entire time. "I'm very sorry that you are so unhappy, but this is now a free country, if you haven't heard the news. I can write what I want when I want. If you are so upset, call the police. *Ruff der Polizei an.* You know where to find me. I'll be here writing."

By this time our whispers had escalated to subdued shouts. The other German tourists were amazed at the confrontation. I'm not sure whether they were aghast at my lack of respect for the woman's authority or at her ridiculous demands. In any case, she stomped off. I continued my walk through the palace, expecting to see the police rounding the corner at any time. I stayed another hour and a half, then left.

Babelsberg and Berlin by the Wannsee

The rest of the day in Potsdam was spent wandering through Babelsberg. This palace and the gardens surrounding the palace are fairytale jewels. But they are a pain in the neck to visit if you insist on easy parking and clear instructions. If you are up for a long walk through a park and don't mind asking people for directions, Babelsberg is a grand adventure. The palace itself is turreted with slit-like windows and crenellated walls.

After visiting the palace, I drove across the Glienicker Bridge which connects Potsdam with Berlin, and which was the scene of the most famous exchanges of spies during the cold war. This was the bridge where Francis Gary Powers, the U2 pilot, was exchanged for Col. Rudolf Abel. The view from the bridge up the Havel is spectacular.

Across the bridge is another small palace, Schloss Klein Glienicke with a garden and forest which lines the Wannsee. There is a good café that makes a nice spot to relax during explorations. Parking during the week near the bridge and palace is abundant. These forests on the shores of the Wannsee were the city's country in the years of encirclement. I have been told that the forests and beaches are still crowded on weekends, but are very peaceful in mid-week .

Waking through the woods here has been a pleasure pastime for centuries. In fact, this was probably the Prussian's version of lovers' lane. Even royalty got into the act with Friedrich Wilhelm III building a love nest for his daughter in the early 1800s. The cabin is now a small restaurant on the way to Pfaueninsel or Peacock Island.

Peacock Island is a wonderful spot complete with fanciful gardens, a white castle and hundreds of plants and animals. It is a place with very strict rules and no cars or restaurants. And if you are dreaming of heading there for a picnic on the grass, think again. It's strictly *verboten.*

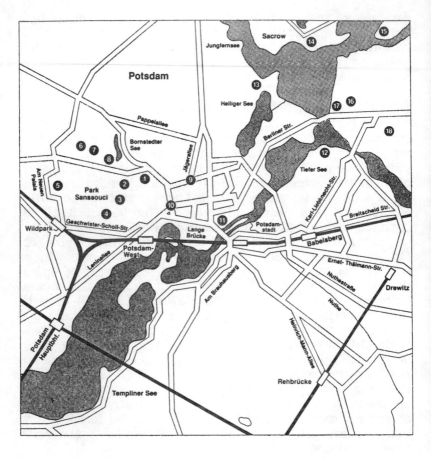

1 Schloß Sanssouci
2 Chinese Teahouse
3 Roman Baths
4 Schloß Charlottenhof
5 Neues Palais (New Palace)
6 Belvedere
7 Drachenhaus (Dragon House)
8 Orangerie
9 Jägertor (Hunter Gate)

10 Brandenburg Gate
11 Nikolaikirche
12 Schloß Babelsberg
13 Schloß Cecilienhof
14 Sacrower Heilandskirche
15 Schloß Pfaueninsel (Peacock Island Palace)
16 Schloß Kleinglienicke
17 Glienicker Brücke
18 Böttcherberg

Potsdam

Potsdam is a fascinating suburb of Berlin. It is home to Sans Souci, Germany's most fascinating palace and most extensive royal gardens and other palaces described below. It is also home to Cecilienhof, site of the Potsdam conference, and Babelsburg Palace. Postdam was the royal residence during the reign of Frederick the Great and is Germany's version of Versailles.

Potsdam is actually older than Berlin. It was first mentioned in history when a group of villages were given by the then Holy Roman Emperor Otto III to his aunt in the late 900s. It remained a backwater town until Friedrich Wilhelm, the Great Elector, picked it for his capital of the Brandenburg-Prussian state in the mid-1600s. From here he issued the Edict of Potsdam allowing the Huguenots, fleeing religious persecution in France, to settle in Germany. The Huguenots, well-educated and many with special skills as artisans, proved to be a major boon to expanding local industries. Friedrich Wilhelm I continued the welcome of foreigners for the same economic reasons, and went so far as to build a Dutch Quarter in Potsdam to attract workers from Holland. Though not many Dutchmen made the trek to Potsdam, people from other countries did and the town developed into an industrial center of its day.

In the case of Prussia's rulers, what drew many of them to Potsdam was the beauty of the country and the chance to escape Berlin. It's been that kind of place ever since. The Hohenzollern royal family continued to use the area as a hunting ground, and when Frederick the Great took power he could have maintained residence in Berlin at the Charlottenburg Palace, but Frederick, who also considered himself a man of the arts, found that by setting up his residence in Potsdam with the army headquarters nearby he could keep in touch with his General Staff and relax, read, play music and write poetry in his palace and gardens.

From 1806 to 1813 Potsdam was under the control of Napoleon. When Russian troops drove him back to France, Potsdam settled into a quiet working mode. The last emperor fled Potsdam in 1918 and the palaces were opened to the public in 1927. Potsdam eventually turned into one of the hotbeds of communism toward the end of the Weimar Republic.

In World War II Potsdam was severely bombed and was chosen as the location of the meeting, in the spring of 1945, between the leaders of The Allies to divide Germany and set the terms of peace. Potsdam, outside of the Berlin zone occupied by the western Allies, was made a part of East Germany and still has one of the largest garrisons of Soviet troops in Germany—if you drive north from the town you'll pass miles of Commonwealth of Independent States army barracks where most of these troops still stay until room can be found for them back in Russia.

Cecilienhof and The New Gardens

This palace was one of the last built by German royalty, constructed by Kaiser Wilhelm II from 1913 to 1917 in an English Tudor style. Cecilienhof is set in the 200-acre **New Garden** which was originally laid out by Friedrich Wilhelm II, successor to Frederick the Great. This area had been covered with vineyards which were the source of Heiligsee Riesling and Pfingstberger Auslese, wines sold throughout Germany.

The New Gardens are laid out in an irregular manner with none of the carefully constructed geometric patterns of the Baroque, but rather a much more natural, woodsy design. When the gardens were conceived, four garden houses—White, Brown, Red and Green—already stood on the grounds and were carefully integrated into the landscape. The **Marble Palace** was the first built in these gardens. It was under construction from 1787 to 1789 and reflects subdued Neoclassical architecture. It remained the primary residence of the Hohenzollern royalty until the last German Kaiser escaped to Holland in 1918. The palace

served a variety of purposes, and then after World War II
became an army museum. In 1988 large-scale restoration
began, and still continues. You can wander past the
detatched kitchen connected with the palace by a tunnel,
servants' quarters and a beautiful **Orangery.** The Marble
Palace is scheduled to reopen at the end of the century, so
don't make any immediate plans for more than a walk
around it.

At the northern end of the New Gardens, the last palace
built by the Hohenzollerns was the **Cecilienhof**. It is a
cluster of several buildings around a driveway with the
half-timbered look of a Tudor home—ornate brick
chimneys, each in a different design. The ex-crown prince
returned from Holland to this palace in 1923 and
remained here until 1945, when he escaped to the western
part of Germany.

Here, in 1945, the Allies met to determine the division
of Germany and the terms of the surrender document at
the **Potsdam Conference**.

This was the last of the Big Three conferences. The was
held in Teheran when the Russians had fended off the Nazi
invasion in Moscow, Stalingrad and Kursk. Roosevelt,
Churchill and Stalin met to coordinate attacks on both
fronts and exchange ideas about the future of Germany.
The second conference was in Yalta with the same three
leaders in February 1945. After the linkup of American
and Soviet troops on the Elbe River on 25 April 1945, the
capture of Berlin on 30 April 1945 and the signing of
unconditional surrender by the Wehrmacht on 8 May
1945, the Big Three decided to meet again. They chose the
Cecilienhof in Potsdam because of the damage sustained
by Berlin in the final offensive.

An amazing amount of work took place before the
actual meetings. Montgomery, Eisenhower and
Antipenko, the Soviet rear services commander, took over
six to eight villas for each national delegation, then
combed the city for furniture to fill the Cecilienhof for the
conference. When the houses were ready to be occupied,
mini-security zones were set up for each party, and access
roads had to be made usable. Almost of 15 miles of roads
were built or repaired, and a pontoon bridge was erected
across the Havel River. They even planted shrubs and

flower beds—the agreement for setting up this meeting was so specific that it states a flowerbed was to be laid out in the inner courtyard of the Cecilienhof, made of geraniums and roses forming a five-pointed star and surrounded by a ring of blue hydrangeas—it still centers the entrance to the palace.

Truman, the new American President after the death of Roosevelt, Stalin, the Chairman of the People's Commissars, and Churchill, British Prime Minister, began the meeting on 17 July 1945. Churchill was accompanied by Clement Attlee, who had run against him earlier that month in the British elections, the results of which would not be announced until 26 July. Since they didn't know who the winner would be, the British sent Attlee as well, to ensure continuity. Every day, subcommittees would meet at 11 a.m., and then the three leaders would meet at 5 p.m.

The decisions made here have affected the map of Europe ever since. They not only divided Germany into four occupation zones—American, British, Soviet and French—but they also changed the German-Polish borders, taking much of the Prussian part of Germany and transferring it to Poland.

The conference was interrupted on the 25th as Churchill and Attlee flew back to Britain to hear the election results; only Attlee returned on the 28th. The meetings continued for another six days and ended on August 2nd. Truman also received the cryptic message, "A baby is born," the code that the atom bomb has been successfully tested.

At Cecilienhof you can visit each delegation's offices and conference rooms as well as the main circular conference table where the heads of state met, flanked by their advisors.

Open April to October, daily 9 a.m.-5:15 p.m.; November to March, 9 a.m.-4:15 p.m. Closed second and fourth Monday of the month. Admission DM3 adults; DM2 seniors and students; free for children under 6. Normally only guided tours are allowed, but if there is no immediately scheduled English-language tour, you can wander through the palace on your own, if you ask.

A portion of Cecilienhof has been turned into a hotel, a wonderful place to stay if you have deep pockets and make reservations very early (tel. 033/231141).

Sans Souci (without a care)

This is a massive palace complex which includes a 730-acre garden stretching more than a mile and a half in length and a mile wide. There are two main palaces, Sans Souci Palace itself and the monumental Neues Palais; two smaller (but not much smaller) palaces, Schloß Charlottenhof and the Orangerie Schloß; and a collection of fascinating smaller royal houses built to satisfy different kingly whims and fantasies.

NOTE: If you are not a great walker, then covering this entire garden may be a strain. Your best bet in that case is to visit the Sans Souci Palace and the nearby *Bildergalerie* (Picture Gallery), and then drive or take a cab down to the *Neues Palais* and skip the gardens themselves (it's 132 steps from the palace down to the gardens and the circular fountains you see splashing below).

The gardens mix formal flower beds and fountains with a surrounding of natural wooded areas. Most of the gardens were enlarged after Frederick's death by Friedrich Wilhelm III and Friedrich Wilhelm IV.

Brief descriptions of the major buildings and gardens included in this palace complex follow.

NOTE: The Sans Souci Palace and Schloß Charlottenhof restrict entry to those in guided groups. When I visited, tours were only in German, but I expect this to change in the not too distant future. Charlottenhof is no problem to visit whenever you have the time, but the Sans Souci tours fill up rapidly, especially on weekends; they leave every 20 minutes and each lasts about 45 minutes. **Get there early and go directly to the Sans Souci Palace to make sure you get a chance to visit this Rococo masterpiece.** If you have a bit of a wait spend it in the nearby *Bildergalerie* (Picture Gallery), the *Orangerie*, or the gardens.

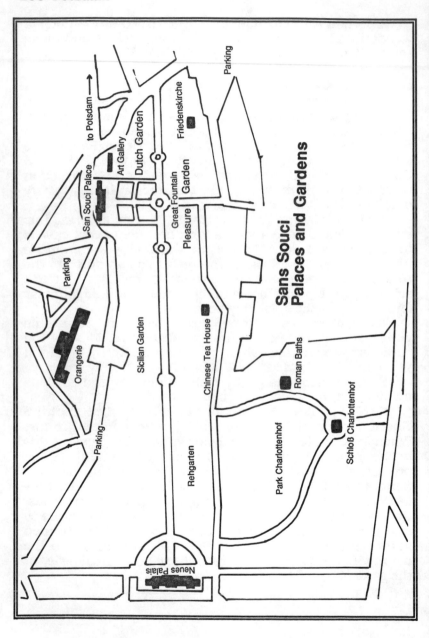

Sans Souci
Palaces and Gardens

Sans Souci Palace

Sans Souci is the most famous of the palaces. It was built by Frederick the Great in the midst of the second Silesian War. Some say it demonstrated the ultimate combination of his loves—combat and beauty. I don't know what psychologists would say today. In any case this was his favorite place to ponder the complexities of life, examine philosophy and enjoy the arts. Obviously he found enjoyment here and visitors still can luxuriate amidst the architectural and natural beauty.

This was the original building in the complex. It was designed by Knobelsdorff, with a great deal of influence from Frederick himself. It was Frederick's insistence which resulted in the single-storey plan, looking southward down a terraced hill to the great fountain. The extended façade is only interrupted by a central dome. Along the eaves 36 Bacchanalian cherubs top supporting pilasters and the edge of the roof is studded with vases and draped with arabesques. In the rear near the modern entrance stands a semicircular colonnade with 88 Corinthian columns, and fake ruins in the far background designed to hide one of the fountain pumphouses.

The interior of the palace is laid out in a French double apartment manner, with smaller rooms behind the larger ones that look out across the gardens. There are plenty of trumpeting cherubs and and dancing nymphs, mixed with women fondling grapes—expressed in a Rococo version of multimedia. At the far eastern end of the palace is Frederick's room, which is filled with portraits of himself inspecting the troops, surveying his kingdom, or pondering philosophy. A smaller, much more modest, wood-paneled back room was where Voltaire resided from 1750 to 1753.

Stories abound about the feisty friendship between the monarch and the poet philosopher. Frederick was pleased to have such a great mind with which to share his thoughts and Voltaire, who espoused individual freedoms, seemed to feel that the opportunity to influence one of Europe's most powerful kings might lead to more acceptance of freedom of expression. In the end, it seems, the great men parted on less than favorable terms. In fact, when Voltaire left Sans Souci for France, Federick had him arrested in Frankfurt for not returning some personal notebooks he claimed Voltaire had stolen. Time didn't seem to heal any of the wounds; their retorts reverberated for years. But Frederick got in the most lasting insult: after calling Voltaire an ape, the monarch immortalized the concept by having a close likeness of Voltaire's face carved on one of the monkeys adorning the Chinese Teahouse.

Frederick's room still has the chair where he died and a clock he always wound himself, and which legend says stopped ticking when he passed away: 2:20 a.m. on 17 August 1786 at the age of 74.

The **Little Gallery** is filled with statues and art including a remarkable bust of Frederick created from his death mask. The **Music Room** is the supreme example of Rococo with mirrors, painted walls, and murals of scenes from Ovid's *Metamorphoses* by Antoine Pesne. The central **Rotunda** is fashioned as a miniature Pantheon of Rome. The elliptical **Marble Hall** is the largest in the palace.

You must take a guided tour. Open Apr. - Sept. 9 a.m.-noon and 1:30-5 p.m., Oct. 9 a.m.-noon and 1:30-4 p.m., Nov. - Jan. 9 a.m.-noon and 1:30-3 p.m., Feb. - March 9 a.m.-noon and 1:30-4 p.m. Closed the first and third Monday of each month. Admission DM6 adults; DM3 children, students and seniors.

Neues Palais (New Palace)

At the far end of the Sans Souci grounds stands the Neues Palais, a majestic building, its façade stretching almost 700 feet. There are more than 322 windows, 230 pilasters and 428 statues adorning the palace. The large copper dome is topped by a statue of the Three Graces holding Frederick's royal crown. Built after the Seven Years' War in the late 1760s, it was described by Frederick the Great as a fanfaronade, a boast, to show Prussia's status after the long battles. It was designed as living quarters for the royal family and is a Rococo delight.

When you enter the palace you step into the fanciful **Shell Room**. Descriptions fail me. The room is covered with shells of all types cemented to the walls and ceilings in fantastic patterns of sea foliage and monsters. Mixed with the shells are corals and semiprecious stones. The floors echo the shell motif with inlaid marble in shell designs.

To the right of the Shell Room is the **Mirrored Room** with an expansive frescoed ceiling and a light airy feel. The tall mirrors set opposite 14-foot high french doors which open to the gardens amplify the daylight.

To the left of the Shell Room you enter a smaller room with a white ceiling of gilted relief work. The room is dominated by a large painting, *The Captured Sultan before Tamerlane*. You the enter the **Men's Bedroom** which is covered with paintings, the most impressive of which is the *Coronation of Wilhelm I*. The **Women's Bedroom** follows with two other matching bedrooms for royal princes and princesses.

The upstairs mirrors to a degree the lower floor plan with bedrooms strung along the western side of the palace. The **Hunting Room** has relief decor reflecting a hunting motif and centered by a beautiful Meißen china chandelier.

Next you enter the breathtaking **Grand Ballroom**. Almost 2500 square feet spread under a 100-foot long ceiling which soars more than 50 feet.

The **Marble Room** has eight massive chandeliers and a ceiling filled with frescoes depicting Olympic Gods eating together. Four other massive oil paintings show the Triumph of Bacchus, The Rape of Helena, The Sacrifice of Iphigenia, and the Judgement of Paris.

The final major room is the **Dance Room** which is very ornate Rococo with a ceiling painting of Venus and the Three Graces.

If you have a chance, a glance at the **Palace Theater** is memorable, but you have to be there at the right time of the day and year. It is open irregularly during the summer and normally has several performances scheduled as well. Check with Potsdam Information for the performance schedules.

Open Apr. to Sept. 9 a.m.-noon and 1:30-5 p.m.; Oct. 9 a.m.-noon and 1:30-4 p.m.; Nov. to Jan. 9 a.m.-noon and 1:30-3 p.m.; feb. to March 9 a.m.-noon and 1:30-4 p.m.

Closed on the second and fourth Monday of each month. Admission DM6 adults; DM3 children, students and seniors.

Orangerie

The Orangerie is an impressive building in Italian Renaissance style dating from the 1850s sitting on the same hillside as Sans Souci Palace. It has a terraced garden leading down to the main gardens and was used to entertain guests, especially the Russian Czars.

It is topped by two towers connected by an observation platform. The views from the upper level over the Sans Souci Gardens, the city of Potsdam and Berlin are wonderful on a clear day. Unfortunately you will have to climb about 120 stairs to reach the viewing level.

The large Raphael Hall is filled with 47 copies of Raphael's works. Smaller well-furnished rooms off to the side were the guest apartments of the Czarina Alexandra Feodorovna and Czar Nicholas I of Russia.

Open mid-May to mid-October 9 a.m.-5 p.m. Closed the fourth Thursday of each month. Admission DM3 adults; DM1.50 children.

The other buildings of Sans Souci

The **Bildergalerie**, next door to the Sans Souci Palace, is filled with Frederick's great collection of 17th-century Dutch and Italian art. (Open Apr. to Sept. 9 a.m.-noon and 12:45-5 p.m.; Oct. 9 a.m.-noon and 12:45-4 p.m.; Nov. to Jan. 9 a.m.-noon and 12:45-3 p.m.; Feb. to March 9 a.m.-noon and 12:45-4 p.m. Closed on the second and fourth Monday of each month. Admission DM3 adults; DM1.50 children, students and seniors.)

The neo-Classical **Schloß Charlottenhof** was built between 1826 and 1829 (Open mid-May to mid-October 9 a.m.-5 p.m. Closed the fourth Monday of each month. Admission DM3 adults; DM2 children. Guided tours only.)

The **Roman Baths,** based on bath houses found in Pompei and decorated with similar frescoes. (Open mid-May to mid-October 9 a.m.-5 p.m. Closed the third Monday of each month. Admission DM2 adults; DM1 children.)

The **Chinese Tea House** was built when Chinese decor was the European royalty rage. (Open mid-May to mid-October 9 a.m.-5 p.m. Closed the second Monday of each month. Admission DM1.)

A walk through downtown Potsdam

The reasons to wander through downtown Potsdam are limited. But if you find yourself heading there to shop or spend the night, make sure to see the following:

Since most of Potsdam was destroyed in World War II this stroll shouldn't take too much time. The **Nicolai Church** behind the Tourist Information office was built by Schinkel in 1837 to 1849 following plans for St. Paul's Cathedral in London. The massive dome is impressive, but not as good as the one it attempted to copy. The inside is virtually bare. Nearby the 1752 **Rathaus** has a gable with Atlas bearing the world on his shoulders.

Take a walk through the **Dutch Quarter**, built in the mid-1700s to attract workers to Potsdam. It consists of more than 130 narrow gabled houses. Next visit to the **Alexandrovka Settlement** originally built in 1826 for 12 Russian singers who formed a choir when the Russian Army liberated Potsdam from the French. The houses are built in Russian style and near a Russian church. The **Nauener Tor** (Nauen Gate) is an example of a town gate from 1755 constructed in an English Gothic style.

Babelsburg Palace

This palace, resembling a Crusaders castle, is located in a garden on the other side of Potsdam set in a large park overlooking the famous spot for spy exchanges, the Glienicker Bridge and the Wannsee spreading beyond the bridge.

If you have plenty of time to spare and want a beautiful walk, this palace might have something to offer. Otherwise it can easily be forgotten. The Tea Room is particularly pretty and the Ballroom features soaring Gothic vaulting set on eight sets of five-column groupings.

Open June to September 9 a.m.-5 p.m. Admission DM3; DM1.50 students, seniors and children.)

Getting around

Potsdam has an extensive train, tram, bus and boat system and is tied into the Berlin transportation network.

You can arrive by **S-Bahn** via the Wannsee Station. For downtown get off at Potsdam Stadt; for Sans Souci Palace and Schloß Charlottenhof stop at Potsdam West and for Neues Palais at the far end of the Sans Souci Gardens get off at Bahnhof Wildpark. Avoid the Hauptbahnhof; it's well out of the way.

The **Weisse Flotte** plies the Havel River with a series of stops. You can catch it from Wannsee for a different approach to Potsdam or leave Potsdam for Wannsee from any of three boat stops near Sans Souci and the town.

There is direct **bus service** from downtown Berlin, but it is not as convenient as the S-Bahn. If you insist, Bus #113 links Wannsee S-Bahn station with the downtown Potsdam bus station at Bassinplatz, or catch Bus #116 over the Glienicker Bridge and connect with Tram #93 heading into town. Once in Potsdam, Bus #695 is extremely useful linking Cecilienhof with Sans Souci every half-hour.

Your bus tickets for the Berlin system are good in Potsdam as well.

Normal transport fares are: DM3 for an hour worth of riding, DM12 for a 24-hour ticket, or DM18.50 for a 24-hour ticket including some boat lines. These tickets include bus, tram and S-Bahn transport.

Accommodations

By far the most romantic spot to stay is at **Schloß Cecilienhof**, the site of the Potsdam Agreement, tel. 33/231141. **Hotel Potsdam**, Lange Brücke, tel. 33/4631 is a high rise towering over the Havel with all tourist amenities. For budget accommodations try the **Hotel am Jägertor**, tel. 33/21834; or the much more reasonably-priced, **Schwielochsee Tourist Hotel**, tel. 33/2850.

My suggestions it to check in early in the day with Potsdam Information and stay with a local family.

Tourist information

Potsdam Information is located on Friedrich-Ebert-Straße #5; tel. 21100; fax 23012. Open Mon to Fri. 9 a.m.-8 p.m.; Sat. Sun. Holidays 9 a.m.-6 p.m. Accommodation service by phone: tel. 23385. This tourist office is busy year round, but especially in the summer—be prepared to be patient: their help is worth the wait, especially with the room reservations.

Daytrips from Berlin
Spreewald, Wittenberg, Brandenburg, Magdeburg

Many travelers use Berlin or Potsdam as a base and drive to these towns or take trains to visit. In fact the Spreewald, Wittenberg, Brandenburg and Magdeberg are all served by daily tours from Berlin.

Spreewald

About an hour's drive from Berlin you can visit a system of picturesque and evocative shallow and often marshy canals crisscrossing through green fields. This area is a nature preserve with hundreds of animals who have adapted to the canals.

This region still has its traditional architecture along the rivers and canals since it was spared any destruction during World War II. Unfortunately, tourism is growing rapidly and the backwoods area will soon be a tourist trap of sorts. Already busloads of tourists arrive every day from Berlin and take rides along the canals on colorful boats paddled by traditionally clad men and women. Fortunately there are now plans to control tourism based on the mating seasons of the wildlife.

Plan ahead if you want to stay in this region. Rooms are relatively scarce and first class doesn't exist. There is a tourist office in Berlin which offers assistance—**Spreewaldbüro**, Zwinglistraße 5a, Berlin, tel. 391-5678 or 392-3022. Expect to pay between DM30 and DM50 per person each night in private rooms.

Lübben is the starting point for many tours through the region. The local tourist office is open 9 a.m.-5 p.m. on weekdays.

Lübbenau is the other hub town. The Spreewaldbüro has its local office here which will help with lodging if you didn't contact them in Berlin prior to showing up. The tourist information office, near the train station, has information on the Gondola tours, which leave whenever the boats fill up in summer, or you can rent your own paddleboat just down the canal.

While in the Spreewald try to visit Lehde where townsfolk still have to paddle home every day, as in Venice. Get directions from the tourist office or the paddleboat rental office and float down the canals to the town.

Wittenberg

Wittenberg is on the western route linking Berlin with Dresden. This is the town where Luther nailed his 95 Theses to the cathedral door. This is also where he spent most of his life, married, led the Reformation and today is buried beneath the pulpit of the Schloßkirche. (*Much of Luther's life and the Reformation are covered in the History section.*)

This town is an easy daytrip from either Leipzig or Berlin. It lies right on the main railway lines. When you arrive you can easily see the main sights of the town in a morning or afternoon.

Luther's Oak Tree marks the spot where Luther burned the pope's order of excommunication—the spot is original, but the tree was replanted after the Napoleonic wars. Within the **Augusteum** is the Lutherhaus, which is the world's most important museum dealing with the Reformation, **Lutherhalle** (open Tues. to Sun. 9 a.m.-5 p.m.). Here you can see where Luther lived, and copies of his original translation of the Bible into German. Make sure to pick up an English-language brochure before starting the tour.

Just down Collegien Strasse is **Melanchthon's house** with more Reformation memorabilia. Melanchthon was Luther's closest assistant and was responsible for much of the political maneuvering which allowed relatively easy conversions from Catholic to Protestant for many. (*See Personalities*) The house itself has survived remarkably well.

The two towers which most people associate with Wittenberg and where Luther preached and was married belong to Stadtkirche St. Marien. It is filled with wonderful religious art. In front of the church is the Renaissance Rathaus with its statues to Luther and Melanchthon.

At the opposite end of town from the Lutherhalle stands the Castle Church or Schlosskirche where Luther supposedly nailed his 95 Theses. Today the once wooden doors are bronze, the originals burned in the Thirty Years War.

Wittenberg Information is (at press time) at Collegien Strasse 29, tel. 51144. It is open on weekends April to October 10 a.m.-2 p.m. and throughout the year on weekdays 9 a.m.-5 p.m. It will move at the end of 1992.

Brandenburg

This town only a short train ride from Berlin, has a quaint old center. Brandenburg's situation is exceptional with plenty of water and unspoiled nature. The original town was created on three islands.

The town also has an interesting cathedral, the **Brandenburger Dom** which is more than 800 years old. It was begun as a Romanesque church and finished in the Gothic style. The 15th-century, brick **Rathaus** has a beautiful **statue of Roland,** the commander rear guard of Charlemagne's who died at Roncevalles in the Pyrenees while retreating from Pamplona. His legend, The Song of Roland, was the first song written in the French vernacular. There are also several sections of the old wall which are worth exploring.

Brandenburg is also a good center for boating excursions on the Havel. Boat tours link the town with the Lehnin Monastery built in the late 1100s and early 1200s, 20 km. to the southwest. It is considered an excellent example of local brick architecture.

The **tourist office** is located at Plauerstrasse 4, tel. 23743; open Mon. to Fri. 9 a.m.-noon and 1 p.m.-7 p.m. They may begin to open on weekends, for room reservations, but don't plan on it unless you call ahead.

Magdeburg

Magdeburg is a rather sterile city. It was rebuilt in Socialist splendor after being about 90 percent destroyed by American and British bombers during World War II. Very little remains, but for some reason tourists are hell-bent to come. I think it's because they think they recognize the name and seem know that *something* famous happened here.

They are right. Magdeburg's main claim to fame is that it is here, Otto von Guericke proved the strength of vacuum with what have become known as the **"Magdeburg Hemispheres."** In his experiment he placed two empty half-spheres, or iron cups with smooth common surfaces, together and then pumped the air out between them. He attached each hemisphere to a team of horses, which pulled in opposite directions. The vacuum held up much to the surprise of everyone except Otto. These famous cups have been preserved in the **Kulturhistorisches Museum** together with other scientific gadgets and much art. Open Tues.-Sun. 10 a.m.-6 p.m.

The city's most impressive building and, in fact, reason enough to come to Magdeburg is the **Magdeburger Dom**, the second largest cathedral in Germany. Construction was begun in 1209, making it Germany's first Gothic church. Its outside may be austere, but the interior is filled with treasures. Under the choir, another Otto, the Holy Roman Emperor Otto I is buried. Open Mon. - Sat. 10 a.m.-noon and 2-4 p.m.

The other building worth visiting is the old cloister of **Unser Lieben Frauen** built from 1064 to 1230. It has been recast as a concert hall today and serves as a modern art gallery as well.

The **tourist office** is at the Alter Markt 9, (tel. 31667). It is normally open Mon. -Sat. 10 a.m.-5 p.m.

Journey through the East
Part VII

Downtown Berlin

I left my car in Spandau and took the S-Bahn. The drive into the center of Spandau was quick and the familiar green S-Bahn sign was easy to find. However, after parking, I learned that the S-Bahn didn't stop in Spandau any more, but the U-Bahn station was only a three-minute walk away. I figured out the fare structure and decided on a day pass for DM12, which allowed unlimited travel for 24 hours, and I was off.

For the rest of the day I walked through the Ku'damm area and took the two-and-a-half-hour city tour. By the time I was through with the tour it was 4 p.m. and I headed back to Seeburg.

On the way home I decided to break with the tradition of German food and have pizza at an Italian restaurant at the edge of Berlin. While living in Heidelberg, I learned to loved the Italian/German version of pizza. The pizzas themselves aren't that great, but I pour (or rather, slather) olive oil over them, shake on more pepper and salt, then sprinkle hot peppers on the basic ham, cheese and mushroom pizza. The one I had this night also had those long, green butter peppers, tangy but not jalapeno-hot. I loved the taste sensations and it was nice to shift into speaking Italian with the waiters for an hour.

After my pizza experience I headed back to the Seeburg Gasthaus in East Germany, but it was closed for a private party. Ended up heading home, then sleeping early. Guess I needed it.

The amazing history of my pension

Next morning while having breakfast in my barracks building, I stopped the owners and asked what this place had been like in the past. They looked out the window wistfully. "Ah, it used to be a wonderful place, filled with joy, and children." Frau Gerlitz sat down at the table with me and continued,

"This used to be a youth camp and a fruit orchard where teenagers came from all over Eastern Europe to work together harvesting fruit throughout the summer. We had children here from Poland, Romania, Czechoslovakia, Hungary, Bulgaria, China, Yugoslavia. Today it's all gone."

She looks out the window to the barren fields and her husband gestures with a shrug. "I can't understand it," he said, "It was a good camp and a good thing to do with children. It taught them to get along with others, it taught them that working together makes the work easier for everyone, it gave them a chance to learn about what life was like in other countries, and we had great fruit as well— much better than the hothouse fruit they make us buy now." He swept his arms out, "We were all together here. We would work during the day, then in the evenings we would cook dinner on the grill and sing songs and play games. It's too bad that it's over. We ran this place for 15 years. Every year was wonderful. Now, it is like hell."

"Look out there. Look at the empty fields. It is hard to believe, but only a year ago we had 10,000 apple trees and 4,000 cherry trees. We had strawberries and plums and fruit which could be harvested at all times throughout the summer and fall. The new government came in and ripped everything out," he paused and looked at his wife. She gave a look of resignation, "We have to try to run this place as a pension now. We don't have any choice. But we are lucky that we still have our place—we built it.

Friends in town are fighting now to keep their houses where they have lived since they came back after the war. Children of Germans from the west are trying to take the houses back. I don't know what is going to happen. It is all very difficult.

We'll just keep on working and keep on hoping that something will slowly change."

I nodded in sympathetic agreement. I hoped that things would work out for them as well. They worked hard and seemed sincere, and heaven knows that the changeover was difficult enough without having your fruit orchards uprooted.

This conversation with the pension owners stuck with me on my way to Berlin. As I thought about what used to be I conjured up scenes of kids from all over Eastern Europe sitting around a campfire. I could hear their counselors telling them stories and at some time during the night with the stars above gesturing towards the glow of lights of West Berlin in the not-too-far distance. "Over there, it's like living in a hell hole. There is so much light no one can see the stars. Everyone is fighting one and other an the rule is each man for himself and forget your brother. If one of those capitalists falls, no one reaches down to help him. No, forget helping, they step on him to get ahead themselves." I can almost see the wide-eyed teens with their eyes glistening in the firelight. The counselor goes on. "Here we all work together to get a job done. We help each other. It makes our lives easier to help our fallen comrades. When there are more hands for work everyone can live better."

A day along Unter den Linden and visiting Museum Island

I parked my car in Spandau again and walked to the U-Bahn. I transferred to the S-Bahn and got off at Friedrichstrasse. Looking up the street, it was difficult to accept that this was currently the highest-priced real estate in Europe. This was going to be the new prime shopping and diplomatic area for Berlin.

I wandered down Unter der Linden. East Berlin has a certain ponderous monumental sense to it. The kind of sense only old massive grey buildings can exude. But along the way I passed Humboldt University and followed a group of students into the building and wandered around a bit. Inside the doors of the University Karl Marx's dictum has been carved in two-foot high letters. "Philosophers have only interpreted the world in different ways; the point, however, is to change it."

I stepped back onto the street and walked down to the Neue Wache. I remembered back to when I came to Berlin as an Explorer scout. We travelled overnight on the Berlin troop train which was an experience in terror and curiosity as we peeked out the windows trying to get forbidden nighttime glances of East Germany. We took a tour of East Berlin. I only remember the massive monument to the Soviets and the goose-stepping changing of the guards at the Neue Wache.

I still remember the hair standing up on the back of my neck and the goosebumps raised by the thud of slapping East German troops' jackboots on the pavement.

I stepped inside and stood beside the flickering eternal flame inside the the somber gray neo-Classical building. I pondered the changed world and how reality had been transformed within my lifetime. It all seemed a bit ridiculous looking back on the attitudes each country had about the other.

I spent the rest of the day in downtown Berlin wandering through the museums I had never visited in the Eastern sector.

In search of Spandau prison

On my back to the pension I took time to wander through Spandau. Though it is a part of Berlin, it has its own pedestrian center. I stopped in a bar and while drinking a beer I asked how I could find the Spandau prison where Rudolf Hess had been held prisoner. I wanted at least to see the place.

"Forget it, mein freund," said the bar tender. "It's gone. They took it apart brick by brick and built a supermarket there."

"What do you mean? And who are *they*?" I asked.

"I mean it is gone. Poof." He made a kind of blowing up gesture with his hands and his eyes got big and round over his bushy mustache. "It's absolutely gone. And *they* are the American, British, and Soviet soldiers. They don't want any remains of the prison. They don't want it to become a tourist sight. But if you must, you can go there and buy potatoes."

I finished my beer and headed back to the car and drove to the pension. I fell fast asleep after watching some of the soccer game on TV with the workers.

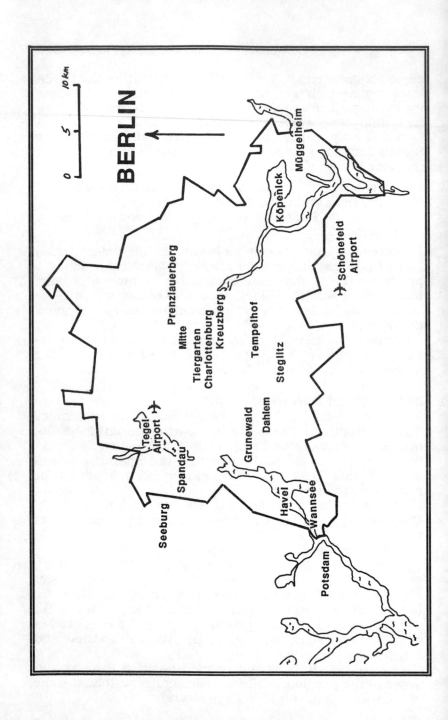

Berlin

Berlin is the new capital of reunited Germany. It is a massive city covering 340 square miles, which makes it larger than New York City and in fact larger than Atlanta, Boston, Cleveland and San Francisco combined. Over 40 percent of this area is covered with lakes, rivers, forests, parks and farmland. The population exceeds three and a half million, more than the combined populations of Hamburg, Munich and Frankfurt, and about the same as Los Angeles.

Berlin is big by any measure: It has more bridges than any other city in the world, with more than a thousand; it has more major museums than any city in the world (and also more rock music groups); the aquarium has the world's largest collection of fish; the zoo has the world's largest collection of animal species; the Olympic stadium is the largest such in Europe; and Berlin is Germany's largest industrial city.

A city of dramatic change

Berlin is a city in the throes of great change . . . and this will continue. Though construction cranes and scaffolding herald feverish restoration work on buildings and the two transport systems have been reconnected, the changes in Berlin are far more profound than the collapse of the Wall.

Berlin is a city which is not only changing physically with the unification of the Eastern and Western sectors, but fiscally as well, with the elimination of the controlled economy in the East and the subsidized isolated society of the West. The change is also psychological—for the first time in 40-plus years, Berlin is not faced with the spectre of imminent invasion by the Russians. And for the first time in modern history Berliners and Germans understand true totalitarianism—the Soviets taught them the brutality and uncertainty that Hitler had practiced with Gypsies, Jews and political foes, but carefully concealed from the masses.

The rebirth of Berlin

The German Federal Government has decided to make Berlin its capital city. The city government has already moved its offices from Schöneberg, where John Kennedy delivered his famous "Ich bin ein Berliner" speech, to the Rotes Rathaus, the traditional seat of city government in former East Berlin.

The physical changes are the most obvious. Reconstruction and restoration are the order of the day in former East Berlin. Cranes rising hundreds of feet punctuate the city skyline. Scaffolding adorns many of the monumental buildings in the Eastern sector. City streets are being torn up for installation of new sewer, water, electrical and telecommunications systems. Traffic seems to be continuously bumper-to-bumper throughout the city, and detours are the rule.

Economic changes

Changes that are more subtle but perhaps much more important are fiscal and political in nature. The West German government formerly rewarded West Berlin residents with what amounted to a 10 percent bonus on their income for residing in Berlin. This tax bonus encouraged residents to stay within the limited confines of the city rather than migrate west and start life over. The elimination of these subsidies and federal assistance programs will place an unprecedented economic strain on the western Berlin population at the same time that unemployment skyrockets in eastern Berlin.

This combined economic effect of having to learn how to deal with a market economy, in both East and West Berlin, has resulted in hundreds of businesses being hurt, the development of a "big city" social agressiveness, and increasing rates of crime.

An ideological island

Ironically, while Berlin was a bastion of freedom in the midst of a Communist sea, the laws of the occupation meant that Berlin residents were also exempt from service in the West German armed forces. This form of effective draft dodging combined with Berlin's excellent universities, which attracted students from all West Germany, created an island of leftist liberalism second to none in Western Europe. This unusual ideological island, now without the menace of invasion, will no longer serve as a "workshop of the society of the future," but will be forced into the mainstream of German society.

A new psychology

Psychologically, Berliners for the first time in over two decades must cope with simply living together with one another. While the population in East Berlin had to cope with Communist brutality and greater repression than elsewhere in the German Democratic Republic (DDR), they still enjoyed the best that system had to offer. As capital of the German Democratic Republic (DDR), East Berlin was relatively a showpiece. The city services were better, cultural offerings were superior and there was a bit more glamour than anywhere else in the DDR.

On the opposite side of the Wall, West Berliners had to deal with a simple, everday fact of life—Soviet troops could sweep in at will and subjugate their city. This threat of invasion contributed to a devil-may-care attitude in West Berlin that became legendary throughout Europe. For decades this was the scene of some of Europe's wildest nightlife, experimental lifestyles, and avant-garde art.

Berlin not only allowed Germans to draw comparisons between the democratic system of the West and the Communist system in the East; Berlin also served as a workshop for opposing totalitarian systems. Its citizens learned what a totalitarian system really can be. In *A Train of Powder*, Rebecca West quotes a Jew who returned to resettle in Germany after the last World War:

"Berliners . . . at last learn from the Russian Sector what totalitarianism is . . . You see under the Nazis, strangers did not come by night and takes you away unless you were a Jew or an important Social Democrat or an important liberal or party member who had got in wrong with the high-ups. If you were not a Jew or a conspicuous politician or a party member, and were an unimaginative person as well, you did not realize what this meant, and perhaps persuaded yourself that it did not really happen. And if you were a sufficiently unimportant German, who only knew the people next door and had no Jewish friends, and never joined the party, then you might very well never get any intimation that it did really happen. But now any German in the Russian sector, whatever his race or politics or degree of distinction, may hear a knock on his door at night and know that he is to be taken away and may never come back. And in the other sectors anybody may be kidnapped. So now the Berliners have learned, all of them, what totalitarianism is."

Berlin's History

Berlin, as European metropolises go, was somewhat unusual even before its post-World War II partition or the headlined crises and dramas since. One thing that set it apart was its marvelously short time as the capital of a major power: where a city like London or Paris may have been the political and cultural center of a generally united country for nearly a thousand years, attracting the best of learning, commerce, art and science, and gradually accumulating the monuments to these efforts, Berlin enjoyed this status for only seven decades, beginning in the 1870s. It became the capital of Germany bcause it was the capital of Prussia, which led the 19th-century unification of dozens of German states into one nation; at the same time, Berlin was one of the prime movers of German economic expansion, becoming the greatest industrial center in Europe. It was later flattened, then isolated, then interfered with in numerous ways by various parties for the next 40 years—but let us look back a little further.

Berlin: A relatively young European city

This European capital is different from its fellows in another way: where others tended to be a geographic nucleus for the growth of their countries, Berlin spent many centuries on the outskirts of German territory, and many more outside it entirely. If we pick up our story at about 1100, when the Slavic area that is now Brandenburg is about to be added to the Holy Roman Empire, we can look toward the west and see that quite a lot of German history has already happened; most of the larger cities in today's western Germany are established: Frankfurt is a royal residence, Mainz has been an archbishopric for several hundred years, Cologne is a city of over 10,000 and eleven centuries have passed since it was founded by the Emperor Claudius. Berlin does not yet exist.

Enter Prince Albrecht the Bear, who conquered the Slav inhabitants and began the systematic settlement of these lands east of the Elbe—the March of Brandenburg—so that in the early 1200s the towns of Berlin and Cölln were founded, like so many capitals, at a natural ford on a river. The settlements of Köpenik and Spandau, at the eastern and western edges of the city, already existed. Berlin was a natural center of commerce, at the intersection of several trade routes for wood, grain, spices and furs from the east, and fish from the Baltic; its economic growth was swift, helped along then as now by customs exemptions and other inducements.

The arrival of the Hollenzollerns

For the next 200 years prosperity continued, with such interruptions as fires and the coming and going of the Black Death, as well as the customary tug of war between the authority of the Holy Roman Empire and the interests of the local magnates. Berlin, without a standing army, was still subject to regular invasions. It made an appeal to the Holy Roman Emperor, who sent Friedrich von Hohenzollern to defend the area and its valuable ford across the Spree River. His descendants would ultimately rule a greatly enlarged Germany and an overseas empire.

Successful in this protection of Berlin, Friedrich was named Margrave of Brandenburg. (German: *Markgraf*. A march or *Mark* is a border territory, a *Graf* is a count). He was also made an Elector of the Holy Roman Empire, another step up in Brandenburg's status as a German state, and in 1448 finally built a royal residence. Under the Hohenzollerns trade routes were redirected and Berlin fell under strict administrative rule. This combination of a confluence of trade routes and stability made Berlin a focal point for bankers and tradesmen.

The Reformation, the Thirty Years War and the rise of Prussia

The Reformation came to Berlin with a relative lack of strife, when Joachim II, the Elector in 1539, converted to Lutheranism; the Thirty Years War, terrible for all of Germany, was worse for the countryside than for the city.

With the conclusion of the Thirty Years War in 1648 it was time to rebuild, and with Friedrich Wilhelm, who would be known as the Great Elector, we begin to see the Prussian pattern of centralized government, large-scale public works, patronage of the arts, importance of the military, and measures to increase trade and manufacture that would come to full flower in the next century. Friedrich Wilhelm even cut personal taxes and introduced the city's first Value Added Tax.

In 1688 when Friedrich Wilhelm died the population of Berlin had almost tripled from about 6000 after the Thirty Years War.

Of particular interest for Berlin, and for the understanding of the character of Berlin as a city, is Friedrich Wilhelm's strong encouragement of immigration by certain groups, notably Jews from Vienna and Huguenots who could no longer live in France. These groups prospered and created a strong middle class.

Immigration had been vital for Berlin from the beginning, and these two additions of wealth, intellect, and energy would be far from the last. Many people came to Berlin, and still do, for the same reasons that settlers went to the American West in the last century, and they brought the same freewheeling rough-and-ready openness, audacity, and familiarity. While Berlin was never exactly Dodge City (it was always bigger and often wilder), the visitor may get a feeling for Berlin more quickly if he expects a touch of the frontier spirit, expressed in a German context.

Bohemians would come, Poles, Russians fleeing the 1917 revolution, the Turkish guest workers of today. These workers were the ones who had their eye on the main chance, those who had nothing to lose, those who had lost nearly everything, and always those who had a little extra hustle and scramble.

The Prussian Kingdom

The first king, the king of Prussia, was Friedrich III, who continued the policies of the Great Elector, but the vain, ugly, hunchbacked Friedrich III was focused on culture, not conquest, and surrounded himself with beauty. His wife Sophie Charlotte, intelligent and curious, played an important part in attracting philosophers and thinkers to Berlin and personally oversaw the construction of her Charlottenburg Palace. Much of Berlin's Baroque architecture was begun, with numerous palaces being erected and art collected in massive quantities. Berlin also became a center of learning—Leibniz, who shares credit with Newton for inventing the calculus, was brought here to found the Prussian Academy in 1701. It was a time of very un-Prussian personal indulgence.

Berlin was reintroduced to Prussian discipline under Friedrich Wilhelm I, the Soldier King. There was a massive shift away from court-sponsored art and learning toward the Prussian army, which grew to the fourth largest in Europe. The Soldier King maintained such a strict regimen that many of his subjects and soldiers tried to desert. Eventually he erected a wall around the entire city which served more to keep his subjects in rather than protect them from without (amazing how history repeats itself). But this Soldier King fought very few battles.

Frederick the Great

His son Frederick the Great, however, made plenty of use of the army. He launched the Silesian Wars and then proceeded to fight all comers—Russians, Poles and Austrians. It is impossible to read about the early campaigns of this brilliant, complex commander without feeling some of the excitement of all concerned—the sense that they and Prussia were being launched on a great adventure and that they were equal to it.

The five decades that Frederick the Great ruled were not only a time of military conquest, coupled with an aggressive diplomacy that made Prussia a European power to be reckoned with; they also transformed Berlin from an ordinary town into a capital.

While building Sans Souci at Potsdam, Frederick with his architects carried out a grand scheme, including an opera house, the first Catholic church in Berlin, a royal palace, and another palace that was to be the home of the University of Berlin—all grouped around a great square, the Forum Fredericanum. Likewise, the Tiergarten began to take some of its present shape, as well as the opulent residences of the important merchants and nobility.

Although it was nothing to the industrial expansion that would give Berlin such wealth and such growing pains a century later, there was very healthy manufacturing growth in this time too—textiles, especially for army uniforms, continued to boom, and, important for the future, metalworking began. Frederick built his own porcelain factory, with Royal Berlin as its trademark. Skilled workers from other parts of Europe, an absolute necessity, continued to arrive; this varied population made a good match with Frederick's philosophy of statecraft, which was very much in the spirit of the Enlightenment. Berlin's and Prussia's success were possible because of the religious toleration practiced here. Frederick's reign may have been authoritarian, but totalitarian it was not.

The arrival of Napoleon

For a couple of uninspired reigns, little happens in the twenty years after Frederick's death except for the building of the very symbol of Berlin—the Brandenburg Gate. It connected the center of the city to the new suburbs, such as Charlottenburg, to the west.

With the defeat of the Prussian forces at Jena and Auerstädt in 1806, Napoleon was able to ride in triumph through the Brandenburg Gate, and the spirit of Berlin turned in a new direction. Napoleon during his two-year occupation of Berlin planted the seeds of change, if only as reaction against his rule.

Beginnings of unification and the Industrial Revolution

After the Congress of Vienna in 1815, Berlin was the capital of a Prussia not only restored but also consolidated and increased. And in the years that followed, practical steps toward eventual unification began in the form of the German customs union, the *Zollverein*—this would do away with the trade barriers within Prussia's territories and would later be used to extend Prussian influence in the rest of Germany.

And a new industrial age was beginning. Through the 19th century, the history of Berlin parallels those of other western industrial cities, with the introduction of gaslight, railroads, municipal water supply, and electricity; the difference is in the pace of Berlin's expansion—there was always room, and there was always money to invest. Huge numbers of people were needed to work in the new electrical, machine, and chemical industries, and some pretty good fortunes were made in putting up housing for them. The result was, among other things, a population of more than 650,000 by 1865.

All the while, Berlin had grown—8,000 by the 1300s, 12,000 by the middle of the 16th century, 60,000 at the beginning of Frederick the Great's reign and 150,000 when he died. Less than a century later, in 1877, it was a million.

German unification

While growing in size Berlin grew in power. After three wars against the Danes, the Austrians and the French, Otto von Bismarck's dream of a unified Germany was realized at Versailles in 1871 with the crowning of the King of Prussia, Wilhelm I, as Kaiser of the German Empire.

This unification powered another massive growth period in Berlin, with the population rising to four million during the next 50 years. Berlin also became one of the centers of Europe for education, the arts and literature. But militarism was still the linchpin of the government, and it proved the government's undoing as it dragged Germany into World War I, which according to German military experts, was to be a simple action, but which continued for four years.

World War I to Hitler

Berlin was not physically affected by World War I, but the Treaty of Versailles which the Germans were forced to swallow lead to the abdication of the royal family and the foundation of a republic (*see Weimar chapter*.)

Berlin was a focus for the chaotic social unrest that followed the First World War. This was no accident: it was expected by many that Germany would be the next country after Russia to fall to communism. The Soviet Union chose Berlin as its prime outpost for the subversion not only of Germany but also of all Europe.

Ironically, before and during World War I, Germany under Bismarck and his successsors had furnished a good deal of money and other clandestine support to Russian revolutionaries, such as smuggling Lenin into Russia; the feeling was that any action to weaken the Tsar was a good thing.

However, though the revolution succeeded in Russia, it failed in Germany partly owing to the Communists' inattention to the rise of Hitler's Nazis (the Communists were too busy fighting the Social Democrats). The strikes, riots, and other forms of social unrest that formed a background to the Golden Twenties in Berlin also provided a fine target for Hitler to attack in his speeches, and when he came to power in 1933, Communist headquarters for European operations had to be shifted to Copenhagen.

World War II is too well known to describe here, but Berlin in particular felt the brunt. During the final years of fighting Berlin was bombed day and night by British and American planes. The Battle of Berlin which was left to the approaching Soviet troops was a textbook execution of the Russian army's massive artillery bombardment followed by sweeping armor and infantry. The Soviet troops were not burdened by Geneva Convention morals and dealt with the German population with the same brutality they had faced while defending their country. Not much of Berlin remained unscathed after the final onslaught.

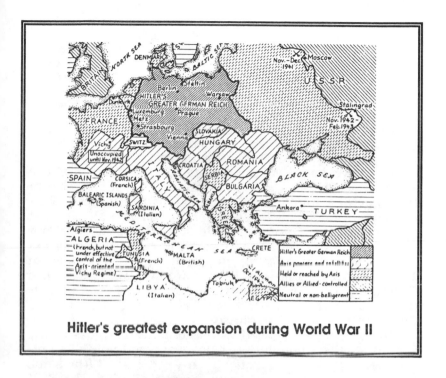

Hitler's greatest expansion during World War II

The Cold War, The Airlift, and The Wall

Berlin began its steady reconstruction under the rule of the Allied Powers who divided the city according to the Potsdam agreements (*see Potsdam chapter: Cecilienhof*). The growing distrust between Russia and the United States (with Britain and France) sealed the division of Berlin.

In 1948 the Soviets took their first action to cut off the city and force the retreat of U.S., British and French forces. Stalin was determined to starve them out, a modern seige on the capitalist island floating in a Communist sea. The British and U.S. resisted with the Berlin Airlift, which lasted almost a year until Stalin backed down. Rebecca West, in the aforementioned *A Train of Powder*, brilliantly described the Airlift:

There was so much traffic on the Berlin run that a plane which was seven minutes late at its journey's end had lost

its place in the queue at Gatow Airport and had to go back
to its starting point and try its luck the next day. . . . The
passengers were whisked off the ground, for each plane
had just fifty minutes at the Berlin airport to unload and
fuel. This athletic miracle was performed not only by the
slim and the straight and the young and the male, A great
many women worked on the loading and among them were
some of the lusty old girls who three years before had been
clearing up the rubble. Their eyes glittered among their
wrinkles as they cawed together like crows and hurled the
trolleys along. They had never missed a good fight in their
neighbourhood yet, and this was the best of all.

Only weeks after the lifting of the blockade the
Americans, British and French allowed the foundation of
the Federal Republic of Germany, also known as West
Germany. About half a year later the Soviets allowed the
creation of the German Democratic Republic or East
Germany. During these political maneuvers the border between the two new countries was fortified and sealed in
1952, but Germans could still freely circulate within
Berlin. Much of the circulation was one-way (and permanent) from East to West, which created problems for the
Communist workers' paradise.

In August 1961, faced with the continued loss of the
portion of their population who possessed youth, ambition, energy, skill, or practically any other asset (the same
sort of people who had always come to Berlin), the East
German government, with the connivance of the Russians,
erected the Berlin Wall, which would physically divide
Berlin for the next 28 years.

The Berlin Wall is, for the most part, gone. Sections
have been preserved, such as the part near Checkpoint
Charlie, to remind everyone of the 28-year period from
August 13, 1961 until November 9, 1989. Around the border between Berlin and the former DDR long tracts of
cleared "no-man's-land," guard towers, ditches, fence
posts without fencing, large reinforced concrete slabs of
dismantled wall, and felled lamp posts still serve in
isolated areas as crumbling reminders of a nation held
prisoner.

The end of the Communist era

East Germany, though it enjoyed the best lifestyle of Soviet client states, had been continually bombarded with TV and radio visions of the good life in the West. Young people had been clamoring for change for over a decade, and finally with the liberalization offered Eastern Europe by Gorbachev, the fortified borders of repression were torn down.

It all started in Hungary, which opened its borders with Austria, then Czechoslovakia opened its borders with West Germany and Austria. East Germans who could travel within the Eastern Bloc opted to leave in droves. Eventually protests grew in every major DDR city and the Communist government lost control.

Helmut Kohl, Chancellor of West Germany, decreed that if the East Germans would vote for it, he would move for immediate German unification. His Christian Democratic party won a landslide victory. He then convinced the Soviets, through massive payments, and the Americans, British and French through promises of non-aggression, that Germany should be allowed to re-unite. German reunification took place on October 3, 1990.

The Basics of Berlin

Arriving in Berlin
By air: The main airport in Berlin is Tegel. It was built in a few months during the Berlin Airlift, but has been considerably modernized in the past 40 years. There is also an airport at Tempelhof which is only used by a few charter flights and private planes. Schönefeld, the former airport for East Berlin, is used by more and more airlines.

By train: The main destination for those who want to get off near the hustle and bustle of the center of what was once West Berlin is Bahnhof Zoo. The next stop on the line is called Hauptbahnhof, but is in the middle of old East Berlin and not as convenient to hotels.

Getting around

From the airport
By bus: Bus #109 leave Tegel Airport for downtown Berlin and the Europa-Center every half hour, 6 a.m. to midnight. The ride takes 20-30 minutes and fare is DM3.

By taxi: The trip will take 20 minutes, except at rush hour when it can take as long as the bus. Fare is about DM35.

If you land at Schönefeld (once in East Germany) take the S-Bahn, which connects directly with the airport.

City transportation
Berlin's public transport network is a model system — clean, efficient and comparatively inexpensive. The entire system operates from 4 a.m. to 1 a.m. Night buses run 1-4 a.m. Berlin has a subway system (U-Bahn), a suburban rail system (S-Bahn) and a network of buses and trams. (The S-Bahn is considered part of the national rail system, so you can ride it with a valid Eurailpass, GermanRail pass or other passes for GermanRail.) With its great expanse of water, Berlin also has extensive boat services.

The entire system is integrated, which allows travel on all types of transport, including boats, using the same ticket as long as you are moving in the same direction.

Tickets may be purchased from automatic machines out-side stations and at some main tram stops.

A ticket for the shortest link between two points costs DM2; an hour ride costs DM3; a 24-hour ticket for subway and bus costs DM12; a 24-hour ticket, which also includes select boats, costs DM18.50.

A bird's-eye view

The Fernsehturm (television tower) rises 1,209 feet above the city. It is Europe's second tallest television tower. There is a revolving restaurant at the 655-foot level with a magnificent view of the city. It is next to Alexanderplatz and is open daily.

The top floor of the Europa Center with restaurants, cafés and a nightclub, offers a beautiful nighttime view of bright city lights of West Berlin and Kurfürstendamm.

Discovering Berlin

The Historic Center

The main avenue passing through the center of Berlin is the mile-long, tree-lined **Unter den Linden**, with its wide promenade down the middle. This avenue was originally laid out to connect the Royal Palace with the hunting pre-serve, the Tiergarten. It stretches from the Brandenburg Gate to the river Spree.

The monumental **Brandenburg Gate** is the very emblem and symbol of Berlin, perhaps of Germany itself; it stood for thirty years just out of reach beyond the Wall, horses and chariot facing off to the East. This was the site of one of the old gates of Berlin, which stood in the late 18th century at the end of Unter den Linden, planned by Frederick the Great as a splendid avenue. His nephew Friedrich Wilhelm II oversaw the construction of Carl Gotthard Langhans' design, a ceremonial entrance to the city not in the Baroque style of the previous century but in the newly rediscovered spirit of classical Greece.

And larger than life, the **Quadriga**—the four copper horses and chariot, driven by Eirene, the goddess of peace—was set above the central opening, which was reserved for the royal coach. Soon the Quadriga was in Paris, having been appropriated by Napoleon; a few years later it was back again, and Eirene had been transformed into Victory.

The Brandenburg Gate

Eventually, Unter der Linden became the venue of military processions. Hitler had the lindens chopped down to make more room for his tanks on parade. The oversized **statue of Frederick the Great**, who designed and conceived this avenue, was moved by the Soviets out to Sans Souci Palace and then moved back in the late 1980s. The pedestal of the statue depicts scenes from Frederick's life and his love of the arts.

Humboldt University was originally the palace of Prince Heinrich, brother of Frederick the Great. This university has an amazing number of famous names associated with it. For Californians and their neighbors it will

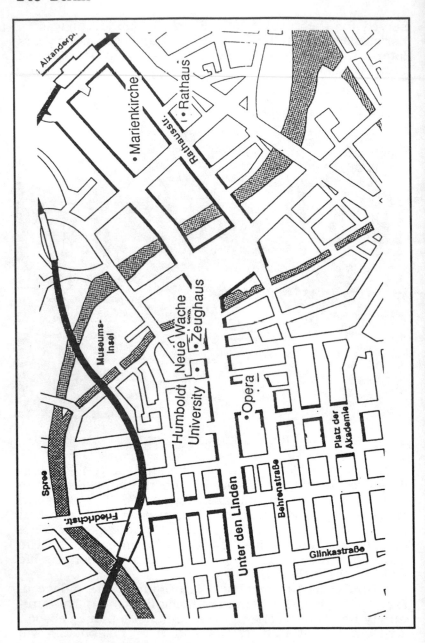

have a familiar ring: Alexander von Humboldt, one of the founding brothers, explored their coast early in the last century and his name is remembered with a county, a bay, a river, a town, and a Pacific Ocean current. One of the greatest travelers and naturalists of his or any era, he also made important explorations of South America and Central Asia in a day when these places were truly wild and unknown. His brother Wilhelm, an equally active philologist, diplomat, and public servant, presented his fellow linguistic scholars with the first description of the Basque language. The university they founded in 1810 was renamed for them in 1949, and has attracted 27 winners of the Nobel Prize. Hegel taught here, as did the brothers Grimm, Max Planck, and Einstein.

Just to the east of the Unversity is the neoclassical **Neue Wache**, which was the first building Schinkel designed in Berlin. He eventually placed his stamp on virtually every monumental building of his time. This small gray structure was Germany's tomb of the unknown soldier and then was turned into the monument for the victims of Fascism. Each day at 11 a.m. there used to be a goose-stepping changing of the guards quartered in the nearby Zeughaus. Today the tomb is quiet, with only flickering eternal flames.

The Baroque **Zeughaus (Arsenal)** built in the the late 1690's now houses changing exhibitions. A notable feature is the array of sculptures of dying warriors by Andreas Schluter on the outer façade.

Across Unter den Linden, the **Royal Library** was built during the 18th century. This is another gem of that period, with an outcurving Baroque façade based on the Hofburg in Vienna. It got the nickname "Die Kommode" (The Chest of Drawers) from its Berlin friends.

The **Staatsratgebäude**, which once housed the East German government, now stands empty, unusable thanks to asbestos polution. This building was built on the site of the former Kaiser's palace, which the Communist government dynamited. It may soon face a similar fate.

St. Hedwig's Cathedral stands behind the opera house. She was born in Bavaria in the 13th century and married Heinrich, Duke of Silesia. For a life of good works, especially the founding of monasteries, she was made a saint in 1267, and her cathedral is now the seat of the Berlin diocese. It was begun in the reign of Frederick the Great and based partly on his own designs, which had a strong feeling for the Pantheon in Rome. Owing to technical difficulties, the cathedral was completed 36 years later in 1773. It was the first Catholic cathedral in Berlin and remained the only one until the middle of the 19th century.

A short detour from Unter den Linden takes us to **Platz der Akademie**. Here the **Französischer Dom - Huguenot Museum** stands. Under the Potsdam Decree in the 17th century, the French Protestants were welcomed here and quickly became a vital part of Berlin's economic and social life, adding nearly a quarter to the population. In the tower of the Französischer Dom this relatively small archive and museum also has a library of Huguenot materials. Open Tues., Wed., Sat 10 a.m. - 5 p.m.; Thurs. 10 a.m. - 6 p.m. Admission: DM2.

The **Deutscher Dom** at the southern side of the square has no function as a house of worship and is still under renovation.

The **Schauspielhaus** (theater) stands in the center of Platz der Akademie. It has been rebuilt three times. This is where Leonard Bernstein conducted Beethoven's Ninth Symphony to mark the end of the Berlin Wall.

Across the Spree you'll reach **Museum Island**. Here on the main square stands the **Berlin Cathedral**, which is being sumptuously restored and can be visited Mon - Fri. 10 a.m. - 5 p.m., and on the north side of the former pleasure garden is the **Altes Museum**, described below.

If you cross Museum Island and then walk to the south along the Spree you will reach a reconstructed area, the **Nicolaiviertel** (St. Nicolas Quarter). This is a series of quaint streets created by the former regime to blend in with the older styles; it was to commemorate the 750th anniversary of Berlin in 1987. The only really antique building is the 13th-century Nikolaikirche (St. Nicolas Church). It has a small museum of city development and charges a modest entrance fee.

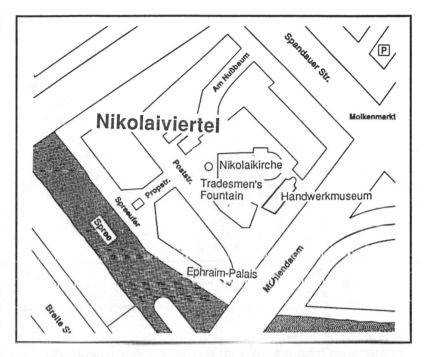

Behind the Nicolaiviertel is the **Rotes Rathaus**, built in 1859, which is again the seat of Berlin's city government.

Marienkirche stands on the other side of the massive square in front of the Rotes Palace in the shadow of the TV tower. This church is the second oldest in Berlin and is noted for its Dance of Death fresco from the 15th century—based on Berlin's suffering in the Plague and only discovered when paint was removed in the 1800s—and its pulpit, the work of Andreas Schluter. The earliest parts of the structure date from the late 13th century, the organ from the 18th century. Open Mon. - Thurs. 10 a.m. - 12, 1 p.m. - 5 p.m.; Sat. 12 - 5 p.m.

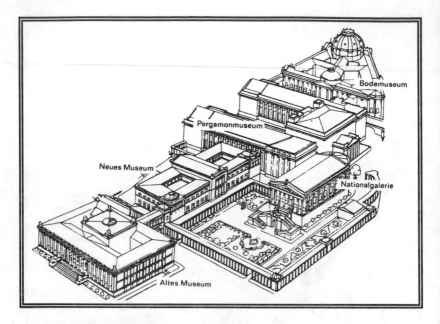

Museum Island

Museum Island was from the middle of the last century a major factor in making Berlin the undisputed museum center of Germany. For the last three decades and more, there was a dim awareness outside Germany that this was where you went to see the famed Pergamon Altar, but relatively few in the West had done so. The Pergamon, Bode, and Altes Museums, which include several other specialized museums described below, particularly reflect Germany's major 19th-century excavations and scholarship in the ancient Near East, which were rich and wideranging.

Pergamon Museum

Prepare yourself for wonder. This is one of the world's great archeological museums, perhaps the world's best. Give yourself time to wander slowly through the collection. The Pergamon Altar, the Roman Gate of Miletus, and the Ishtar Gate are the stars of this show, but around every corner another wonder seems to appear.

After purchasing your ticket, you will see a man handing out tape machines with guided tours of the three major exhibitions. Make sure to pick one up. I passed them by, thinking that it would be one more expense, but then returned when I saw that I needed whatever guidance I could get, and discovered that they were free. After starting the tape, turn the corner into the Pergamon Altar room and let the wonder begin.

The Pergamon Altar — In what is now western Turkey, close to the Aegean, the city-state of Pergamon flourished as part of the Greek Empire in the Second century B.C., the period following the death of Alexander the Great. Like Athens, it was built on an Acropolis, a natural stronghold.

Perhaps to commemorate a victory, the Pergamon Altar was built, probably dedicated to both Zeus and Athena. This however was an altar transformed and magnified: a wide set of marble steps, with piers projecting at each end and the entire structure surmounted by an Ionic-colonnaded walkway, was decorated all around its sides with a spectacular sculptured frieze, more than 300 feet long, the figures larger than life and standing out in three dimensions from the walls.

This frieze, a gem of the Hellenistic period, shows a moment from the battle between the gods and the giants, based on Homeric and later myth, and some local legend. Gods and goddesses of Olympus, the air, and the sea, with their auxiliary horses and chariots, dogs, lions, seahorses, serpents, nymphs and satyrs, fight the giants with sword and shield, arrows, spears, and their bare hands.

Every figure on the frieze is different and amazingly detailed. Muscles gracefully bulge and stretch, the folds of the clothing hang naturally, and the hair styles reflect the fashion of the time.

The genius of the sculptor has balanced violent action with dramatic tension—the gods fight with divine serenity, the giants writhe and struggle in agony. For the gods are about to triumph in this long-standing feud—it was known that they could win only if they were helped by a mortal, and Herakles (Hercules) has come to join them. As with many works of religious art, there was a political element here: Pergamon was in legend founded by the son of Herakles, Telephus, whose life and deeds are shown on a separate frieze, done in quieter style, that once decorated the upper courtyard of the altar.

The frieze is remarkably complete. Excavated from 1878 to the early 1880s—although digging in the rest of Pergamon continued to 1886—it would otherwise have almost certainly been lost to the active lime kilns in the area. Its completeness and its fine state of preservation are due to a happy accident—when the altar was broken up

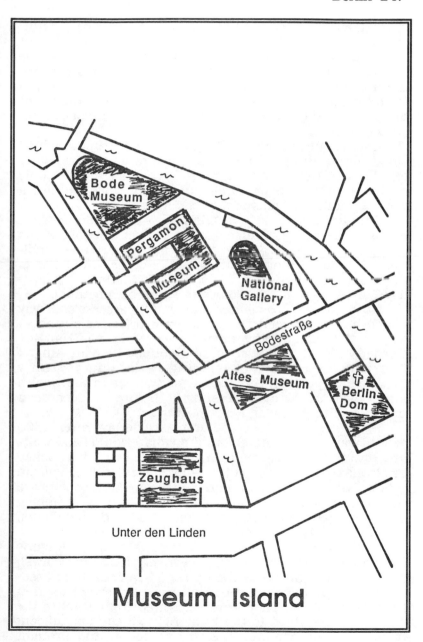

Museum Island

in the Byzantine period, it was used to build a new fortification and retaining wall, with many of the panels put face-down in the earth as a foundation, the best possible way of saving them. After a painstaking reconstruction, the frieze was moved from its earlier house on Museum Island (which had proved to be too small) to the present building, completed in 1930. This is *the* "must-see" of Museum Island.

Also from Pergamon is the **Temple of Athena,** which stood further up the Acropolis and into whose two-story façade, with Doric columns on the ground level and Ionic columns on the upper porch, the visitor may walk for a view of additional treasures in the interior.

Roman Market Gate of Miletus — From another Asia Minor excavation, the huge Roman Market Gate of Miletus occupies an entire wall and is likewise in very fine condition. This multi-storey entrance gate comes from one of the most important Roman ports in Asia Minor (modern-day Turkey) about 200 kilometers south of Pergamon.

Ishtar Gate — The Ishtar Gate and its processional way is another "must-see." This is believed to be the entrance-way to the legendary wonder of the world, the Hanging Gardens of Babylon. Erected by Nebuchadnezzar, King of Babylon, during several building periods in the early Sixth century B. C., this was a monument to the wealth and power of Babylonia shortly before it became a province of the growing Persian Empire.

What makes it spectacular to see today, after 2500 years, was the choice of building material. These walls and towers, some 30 feet high, were faced with kiln-baked brick glazed in bright colors—lapis lazuli blue, saffron yellow, light green, brown and white—and these colors are used to maximum effect in fields of deep blue, eye-grabbing geometric patterns, strings of daisy-colored medallions, and above all the pacing rows of snarling lions.

These low-relief lions and bulls, as well as dragons (which look rather like llamas with very long hind claws), march row on row above the viewer's head and were associated with Babylonian gods that were important for the New Year festival. They were excavated from 1898 to the 1920s, reassembled in Berlin along with the magnificent façade of Nebuchadnezzar's throne room, and brought here from their temporary quarters in the Bode Museum in the 1930s.

This reconstruction makes an interesting contrast with the Pergamon Altar—in Mesopotamia there was no marble, but only mud-brick, much like the adobe used in the American Southwest. However massive and heroic they built Babylon, it could not survive the centuries, nor could its Building Blocks: only these glazed and fired decorative bricks remain.

Near East Collection — Also part of the Pergamon Museum is the Near East Collection, with its magnificent assembly of Persian, Mesopotamian and Middle Eastern antiquities. There are fantasic stone reliefs from Firaktin in Asia Minor carved on a natural circle of rocks, friezes and figures from Sam'al in Syria, giant stone lions with eagle's heads, and other massive statues mixing elements of men and animals.

Around another corner are **the walls from Uruk**, a town south of Babylon. In the next room you may see mud figures creating a frieze or forming a glazed mosaic of color. There are also models of some of the largest Babylonian cities and temples. One room is filled with highly decorated Babylonian sarcophagi, another with precious ancient jewelry, yet another with glazed brick from the town of Susa in present-day Iran.

One of the most important pieces in the collection is the Persian counterpart of the Rosetta Stone, which allowed archeologists to translate the ancient Persian script into modern languages.

Islamic Collection and more—Also under this roof are the Islamic Museum, especially rich in domestic artifacts such as carpets and wood paneling, the **Museum of Ethnography**, and the **East Asian Collection**, which concentrates on China and Japan.

Open 10 a.m. - 6 p. m. daily, except for the Islamic, East Asian, and Ethnographic sections, which are closed Mon. and Tues. Admission DM2.

The Bode Museum

Also on Museum Island, the Bode Museum was originally called the Kaiser Friedrich Museum, but in 1956 was renamed in honor of its architect, Wilhelm von Bode. This is one of the museums whose collections and displays are expected to change dramatically as the contents of former eastern and western museums are reassembled and rearranged for advantageous display.

Just the entranceway into the Bode Museum is breathtaking. You walk through ancient sculpture which seems to dance. Pick up a map of the collection when you purchase your entrance ticket—it outlines the main collections in various parts of this massive building. The main doors open into a large bright hall. I suggest you turn hard to your right and start with the Egyptian and Papyrus collections.

The Egyptian Collection, one of the world's best introductions to ancient Egyptian religion and mythology: the burial displays, with sarcophagi, mummies, canopic jars, mummies of sacred animals, and votive objects, are specially notable. One room is filled with wall paintings from 2450 B.C., and you'll find stylized statues and carved stone Egyptian designs.

The **Papyrus Collection** includes writing not only in hieroglyphics on papyrus, but also in numerous other ancient languages—written, inked, painted, scratched, and otherwise inscribed on various media.

After you have walked the length of the Egyptian collection along the right-hand side of the building you arrive at a small rotunda at the rear, with a spiral staircase swirling upward.

Walk through this rotunda and enter the back room of the **Early Christian and Byzantine Art Collection**. Facing you is a beautiful altar retable from Antwerp depicting the life of Christ. Look into each carefully carved square and you'll see the Annunciation, the Shepherds Hearing Angels, Three Wise Men, the Birth of Jesus, the Murder of the Innocents, the Circumcision, the Flight to Egypt, Mary Magdalen washing Jesus' feet, the Arrest in the Garden, the crucifixion and the Resurrection. To its left is a beautiful wooden Pieta.

The beauty of this collection of Byzantine art is that works of art typically distant and poorly lighted when you see them in Cathedrals are here presented at eye level, sparkling clean and brilliantly lit. One mosaic in particular, taken from a cupola over an altar in the Church of

St. Michael in Ravenna, is a treat with its golden glass sparkling only an arm's length away. In Ravenna, this same wonderful mosaic was adorning a chapel thirty to forty feet above the congregation. You can also see in the main center hall several excellent Della Robia ceramics.

As you wander through the Early Christian and Byzantine Art Collection you will end up returning to the front of the building. Go back into the front entrance rotunda and walk up the stairs under the cupola. The upstairs galleries feature masters from the 13th to 18th centuries. Of special note are Breughel's *Feast of Bacchus*, Rubens' *Christ Giving the Keys of His Church to Peter*, Savery's *Paradiso*, Giordano's *Archimedes and Euclid*, and Caravaggio's powerful *Jesus Casting the Moneylenders Out of the Temple*. There is also an unusual Cranach painting mimicking the style of Bosch, with many of the elements found in the Garden of Earthly Delights triptych, and opposite is another triptych by Dellegambe showing Judgment Day with Heaven to God's right and Hell to His left. Make sure to search out a wonderful painting, *Adam and Eve* by Jan Gossaert.

Open Wed. - Sun., 10 a.m. - 6 p.m. Admission: DM2.

Altes Museum

As one might guess from the name, this was the first of the museums on the island. Indeed, it is the oldest museum in Germany. Today it is used for temporary exhibitions.

Designed by Karl Friedrich Schinkel, whose plans made Unter den Linden a world-class boulevard, the Altes Museum was opened in 1830. Wilhelm von Humboldt, who was also co-founder of Humboldt University, began the graphics collection, which includes Botticelli's engravings for *The Divine Comedy* .

Open Wed.-Sun. 10 a. m. - 6 p. m. Admission: DM2.

National Gallery

This museum also has a wonderful collection of paintings and sculpture. Upon entering the museum you pass several large pieces of sculpture. To me great sculpture is almost mystical. It almost seems to come to life—the twist of a back, the curve of a leg, a sideways glance, all from a block of solid material. This sculpture is art which can capture the spirit and transcend simple representation.

One of the first pieces you see is by Johann Schadaw, *Resting Woman* carved in 1826. More sculpture follows in a series of rooms before entering the picture galleries.

Paintings here feature works from the 19th and 20th centuries. In the first rooms you'll see Goya's *The Maypole*, and Tishbein's *The Lamplighter*. A smaller version of the *Coronation of Wilhelm I* found in the men's bedroom of the Neues Palais at Sans Souci is here. Then comes a collection of Menzel's works. A grand canvas, *Frederick the Great Speaking with his Generals Before the Battle* by Lenthen dominates one wall.

In the next series of rooms are more modern works such as Menzel's *Ironwork*, Fritz von Und's *Heidi Princess*, Max Liebermann's *Shoemakers*, Courbet's *The Mill*, and Cezanne's *The Mill*, as well as one of his famous still lifes. You also find more modern sculpture, including a Degas' dancer and a Rodin miniature of *The Thinker*.

Upstairs on the second floor landing there is a sculpture by Rodin, *Man in His Thoughts*, crafted in 1896, and the green marble statue of *Der Eherne Zeitalter*. When you walk into the display halls on the second floor you are greeted by four large scupltures by Degas—*Eve with Cain and Abel*, *Venus and Love*, *Pan Comoforts Psyche*, and *Youngster with Bacchus*. My favorite canvas on this level was Von Hoffmann's *Traumerei* (Dreamgirl).

Wind up the staircase to the top floor. At the top of the stairs is a roomful of frescoes recreating rooms from Casa Bartholdy in Rome. As you enter these rooms, set above the arches to the left and right are murals depicting the Seven Fat Years and the Seven Lean Years. The other frescoes trace the story of Joseph—Joseph telling his dream to the Pharoah, Joseph interpreting dreams with fellow prisoners, Joseph being sold by his brothers, Joseph's brothers taking his coat back to Jacob, and Joseph returning and revealing himself to his brothers.

The rest of the collection on the third floor is a mixed collection of relatively modern art.

Open Wed. - Sun. 10a.m. - 6 p.m. Admission: DM2.

Now we leave Museum Island and eastern Berlin and focus on the treasures in what was West Berlin.

Around Charlottenburg

Schloß Charlottenburg

Late in the 17th century this was the first major palace to be contructed in Berlin. It began as a summer residence and a series of gardens for philosophical discussions for Sophie Charlotte, wife of the Friedrich III, the misshappen lover of beauty. (*see Berlin history*) His massive equestrian statue stands in the Court of Honor. It once stood in East Berlin just off Unter den Linden, but sank in the Tegelersee when it was being returned to Berlin from Potsdam, where it was hidden during the war. It took seven years to retrieve the statue, and by that time the West Berlin authorities had decided to keep it themselves and placed it at Schloß Charlottenburg.

The original palace building comprised the central section (11 windows wide) of the palace as it now stands, with a small French garden stretching behind it. Additions were made over time—notably the long wings on either side that create the courtyard—and it soon became a palace in the Baroque style to rival other European pleasure domes. Napoleon is said to have considered it a rival to Versailles. It isn't quite on that foot-killing scale, but plan to spend plenty of time enjoying the interiors of the Prussian royal apartments, filled with art works by names already familiar: Schinkel, Schlüter, Knobelsdorff, Boucher, and Watteau. Several rooms are filled with tapestries on themes from classical antiquity. The oriental Porcelain Chamber is filled with colorful vases and other porcelains, multiplied by massive mirrors.

The New Wing features a masterpiece of Prussian Rococo, the sparsely furnished Golden Gallery, which on sunny days is filled with sunlight. The White Hall has a wonderful collection of Watteau paintings featuring the *Voyage à Cythère*. Downstairs, the Romantic Gallery is filled with German Romantic works such as paintings by Friedrich. (Recommendation: pick up an English-language description at the entrance to augment the guided tour.) Behind the palace is a French formal garden which stretches into a less structured English garden.

Open: Tues. - Sun. 9 a.m. - 5 p.m. Admission: DM3 for children under 14, DM6 for adults.

Egyptian Museum

Opposite the Charlottenburg Palace is Western Berlin's Egyptian Museum, not to be confused with the Egyptian Museum under the Bodemuseum roof. These collections also show numerous replicas of everyday objects needed for life in the next world and buried with mummies, as well as actual tools, jewelry, and other artifacts. There are also royal portrait sculptures, including the most famous of all: Queen Nefertiti (she made a cloak-and-dagger trip here from the other Egyptian Museum in 1945). Another notable display, from the period of Roman rule in Egypt, is the reconstructed Kalabsha Gateway, originally built for Roman Emperor Augustus in 20 B.C. The gateway is 80 percent complete and was removed from Egypt when its location was to be flooded by the Aswan Dam. (Note: This collection will probably be consolidated with the Egyptian Collection of the Bode sometime before the turn of the century.) Open Mon. - Thurs. 9 a.m. - 5 p.m., Sat. and Sun. 10 a.m. - 5 p.m. Admission: Free.

Antikenmuseum

Also at Charlottenburg, this museum of Greek and Roman antiquities presents a superb collection of ancient art covering half a millenium and all the Mediterranean. On view are decorative objects in all materials: fine glassware from Syria, the best in the Roman Empire; jewelry in gold, silver, and precious stones; bronzes; marble sculptures, including a portrait of Cleopatra; an outstanding collection of Greek red-and-black pottery; and countless other works of Greek, Etruscan, Egyptian, and Roman art.

Open Mon. - Thurs. 9 a.m. - 5 p.m., Sat and Sun. 10 a.m. - 5 p.m. Admission: Free.

Around the Tiergarten

These next museums and palaces are located around the Tiergarten in the center of Berlin. The best starting point is from Lützowerplatz. The Bauhaus Archive, National Gallery, Handicraft Museum, Musical Instrument Museum and Philharmonie are all within a few steps of each other on the southern side of the Tiergarten.

A walk to the northern edge of the Tiergarten takes you past the Reichstag, Congresshall, Scholß Bellevue and the Siegessäule victory column. The Zoo and the Aquarium are at the far western end of the Tiergarten.

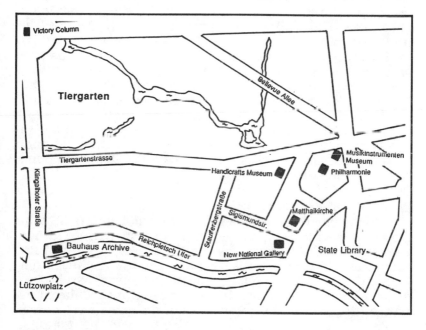

Bauhaus Archiv

This building, designed by Bauhaus founder Walter Gropius himself, was opened in 1979. For American visitors interested in the roots of much of our modern architecture, and particularly our steel-and-glass skyscrapers, this is where it began: Gropius and such alumni as Mies van der Rohe had an enormous influence on this side of the Atlantic even before they were forced to leave Germany. Going far beyond architecture, the Bauhaus, a school which was founded in Weimar in 1919 and later moved to Berlin, created a basis for teaching industrial design that was employed practically everywhere. These materials present a fascinating view of the complex, surprising ways in which modern industrial design touches so many other fields. Open daily except Tues. 11 a.m. - 5 p.m. Admission: DM3.

New National Gallery

Just down the road from the Bauhaus Archiv, this new building completed in 1969, done in the modern style by Mies van der Rohe, has an appropriately up-to-date collection, very strong in 19th and 20th century paintings by such German artists as Max Beckmann and Menzel as well as other Europeans—Klee, Munch, Ernst, Dufy, Picasso, and Bacon—with additions of works by current artists. Going back a bit earlier, the French Impressionists such as Monet and Renoir are also well represented.

Part of the collection comes from artwork hidden in the West which had long ago been part of the National Gallery on Museum Island. Open Tues. - Fri. 9 a.m. - 5 p.m., Sat. and Sun. 10 a.m. - 5 p.m.

Handicrafts Museum

Moved from Charlottenburg, this collection of religious and domestic art covers a thousand years and has numerous room interiors with all their furniture and fittings from all over Europe. Some of the finest church objects in existence, such as chalices, reliquaries, and monstrances in precious metals and crystal, are displayed as part of the medieval Guelph Treasure; more recent rooms show Bauhaus and other contemporary furnishings. Notable collections of Majolica, Venetian glass, porcelain, and fine gold work, as well as special exhibitions.

Open Tues. - Fri. 9 a.m. - 5 p.m., Sat. and Sun. 10 a.m. - 5 p.m. Admission: Free.

Museum of Musical Instruments

Next door to the Philharmonie, a fascinating collection of some 2000 instruments, some of which (beautiful examples) will be familiar to the modern audience, and others—dating from the 1500s—less so. In addition to seeing how the instruments of the present day developed from these Dudelsaks, Krummhorns, and Serpents, you may also view Edvard Grieg's piano and a flute played by Frederick the Great, not only a performer but also a good composer.

Open Tues. - Sat. 9 a.m. - 5 p.m., Sun. 10 a.m. - 5 p.m. Admission: Free.

Philharmonie

This concert hall has become famous for its excellent acoustics and innovative layout. The orchestra is encircled by the 2200-seat audience which rises to nine levels. Concert tickets are hard to come by, but tours are given every Sunday.

Reichstag

At the eastern end of the Tiergarten, close by the Brandenburg Gate, the famed Reichstag stands in open ground, its dome still to be replaced. Built in the 1880s after a design competition, this parliament building was a neo-Renaissance monument to the wealth and strength of the new German Empire. The mysterious Reichstag Fire in 1933 served as a pretext for laws allowing the Nazis unprecedented power, and the building suffered even greater destruction in World War II. Rebuilt after the war as a hopeful symbol of eventual reunification, it came into its destiny in 1990 as the site of the first parliamentary assembly with delegates from all of Germany, and it was here that Berlin was voted, once again, the German capital. There are historical exhibits and a restaurant.

Open (German history exhibit) Tues. - Sat. 10 a.m. - 5 p.m. Admission: Free.

The Kongresshall

This building was a gift from the people of America to Berliners. It was originally designed to echo the shapes of the carnival tents which had been set up in this area as far back as the 18th century. The design was only partially successful; it once collapsed, and its unusual shape has gotten it such names as "The Pregnant Oyster" and "Jimmy Carter's Smile."

Schloß Bellevue

This is home to the German President. It was built on the banks of the Spree in 1785 as a summer house for the brother of Frederick the Great, August Ferdinand. It is not open to the public.

Zoo

One of the oldest in Europe, the Zoologischer Garten has rebuilt from its terrible wartime losses to become one of the biggest, best and most innovative anywhere; it occupies a large quarter of the Tiergarten and uses its natural greenery to splendid effect in presenting its collection of more than 14,000 animals and birds, often in a nearly natural habitat. As in earlier days, many individuals are such public favorites that their nicknames are known to most Berliners, but today this zoo is also a major part of the worldwide effort to preserve species threatened with extinction. Modern methods of display give the visitor a chance to view hundreds of types of birds, a remarkable group of monkeys and larger anthropoids, and even nocturnal animals in a special environment that simulates the night hours.

Open 9 a.m.-7 p.m. daily. Admission: DM7.50 (See Aquarium for combined admission price).

Aquarium

Close by the Zoologischer Garten, this is a fitting partner for it. Not only are an amazing collection of more than 6000 species of fish from all the world's oceans, lakes and streams on show in their glass tanks, but also on other floors entire separate environments of snakes, crocodiles, monitor lizards, tortoises, amphibians of all types and insects.

Open 9 a.m.-6 p.m. daily. Admission: DM7 (Admission to both Zoo and Aquarium: DM11.50).

Dahlem Museums

Our last group of Berlin museums are in the western part, in the Dahlem area. These were all created after World War II, and it is expected that they will be incorporated in other collections around the city in the next decade. In the meantime, this massive building still houses a staggering wealth of collections, including paintings, sculpture, Indian art, Islamic art, Far Eastern art, and international culture.

These collections have quite a story, with much of the artwork having been "liberated" by the Americans in 1945 and brought back to the National Gallery in Washington. When West Germany was formed these museums were built and the artwork returned, to rival the collections in Eastern Berlin.

The Dahlem Museums complex, like the Bodemuseum, has several independent collections, and this, the **Gemäldegalerie** (Painting Gallery), is one of the best in Germany. Slated to move to more spacious quarters for display of all its important holdings, it is still not to be missed: here you can see religious works, principally from altarpieces, by German masters as early as the 1200s, and paintings by Dürer, Cranach, and Altdorfer; a fine selection from the Italian Renaissance, including Rapahel, Titian, Correggio, and Botticelli; Rembrandt's precursors, with van Eyck, Breughel, and Bosch represented; and an entire floor of Rembrandt and his Dutch and Flemish contemporaries. His *Man with Golden Helmet*, recently much discussed as to its true authorship, is here along with 20 other definite Rembrandts and nearly as many works by Rubens.

The **Skulpturengalerie** (Sculpture Gallery) houses more than 1,200 European pieces created by artists from the early Christians to the Renaissance. The two-storey gallery has ivory, wooden, marble and bronze sculptures.

The Ethnological Museum is one of the world's largest collections of antiquities from throughout the world—South Pacific, South America, China, and North America. The German Ethnological Museum focuses on rural German culture before the Industrial Revolution.

The **Indian Art Collection** is the most important in Germany and one of the best in the world, covering a period of over 4000 years of civilization. The Turfan Collection of frescoes depicting Buddist legends is fabulous. It also houses a wonderful collection of art from

Buddhist monasteries located along the Silk Road as well as an excellent collection of art from Nepal.

The Islamic Art Collection features a collection from the 8th to the 18th century. You will find parchment from a 9th-century Koran, as well as glassware and tapestries.

The Oriental Art Collection was established in 1906 and provides a good overview of Oriental decorative and fine arts. Some of the displays date from 3000 B.C. These displays are changed regularly to limit the exposure of the ancient artifacts to sunlight and changing climatic conditions.

Laanstraße 8. tel. 83011. Open Tues.-Fri. 9 a.m.-5 p.m., Sat. and Sun. 10 a.m.-5 p.m. Admission: Free.

Botanical Gardens

Close by the Dahlem Museum, this garden shows off its huge variety of trees and plants outdoors and in tropical greenhouses.

Open 9 a.m. - 8 p.m. daily. Admission: DM2.50.

Other museums and sights

Checkpoint Charlie & Museum

Few remember where Checkpoints Able and Baker were; now even Charlie, the principal and most famous border crossing point between East and West for four decades, is without its barricades. The Museum of the Wall has displays showing the background and construction of the Wall, and a good look at the parallel histories of both Berlins from 1945, but the central theme is escape to the West by every possible means, including false papers, aerial cables, balloons, boats and tunnels.

Admission: DM4.

Pfaueninsel

On the Wannsee, reached by ferry, this charming island has both history and atmosphere going for it. Friedrich Wilhelm II, successor to Frederick the Great, decided in 1794 that this was the perfect spot for a small palace for getting away from it all; later an English garden was added. Peace and quiet is still the form here, with smoking, dogs, and radios *verboten*, and a good thing too. The boat trip costs about DM4.

Spandau Citadel

The first records we have of Spandau date from 1197; it's older than Berlin and many who live here still feel a separateness from the capital, which they became part of— on paper—only in 1920. A garrison town from the 1500s, it was enclosed in an oval wall, which the shape of the old town preserves and which helped preserve the character of the old town. Here, where the Spree and Havel join, was a natural spot for a fortification, and there were wooden strongholds here to protect this river crossing for the trade routes even in Slavic times. The Citadel has the oldest surviving structure—the round Julius Tower, nearly a hundred feet high, built in the early 1200s and still giving the visitor a marvelous view. It was a refuge for the people in times of invasion as well as a vantage point, and its present turret, created by the architect Karl Friedrich Schinkel, was added in the 19th century. The rest of the Citadel as it now stands (one of the best-kept fortifications of this size anywhere) was designed and erected by Italian master builders in the 16th century. Its four great bastions point outward into a moat and the Havel, and it has been used as a fortress and a prison, among other things; it now includes a museum of its long and varied history. (This, by the way, was not the prison where Rudolf Hess spent 40 years after the Nuremberg trials and where Albert Speer wrote his secret diaries—they were incarcerated in another building in Spandau proper, now razed.)

Open Tues. - Fri. 9 a.m. - 6 p.m., Sat. and Sun. 10 a.m. - 6 p.m. Admission: DM6.

Kaiser Wilhelm Gedächtniskirche

One of the other major landmarks of West Berlin for the last 40 years, this church was built as a memorial to Kaiser Wilhelm I, father of the last Kaiser and final Hohenzollern ruler. Finished in 1895, in the great period of expansion of the German Empire, almost destroyed in World War II, enough of the original was left so that Berliners decided to keep it, calling it the "Hollow Tooth."

They built a high-rise, naturally lit adjunct which quickly got the pet name,"The Cosmetic Box." With its location on the Kurfürstendamm, it has been the scene of many a demonstration, rally, and speech over the years.
Open daily, 9 a.m. - 7:30 p.m.

Shopping

Berlin is not a shopper's paradise. Prices are just as high as they are at home. However, there are some shopping experiences you will enjoy and several street markets which shouldn't be missed.

Wilmersdorfer Straße, the pedestrian street in Charlottenburg, is the main street as far as department stores go. You'll find **Hertie**, **Karstadt** and **Quelle** one after the other.

The real shopping experience of Berlin is a trip through **KaDeWe** on Wittenburgplatz, short for *Kaufhaus des Westens*—department store of the West. This is the largest department store in Europe with a quarter of a million items. If you can think of it you can probably buy it here . . . and that includes wedding planning, travel, theater tickets, and food. The 6th floor is the top attraction with its food emporium: you can find a thousand kinds of sausages, more than 1,500 different cheeses, hundreds of breads, hundreds of different types of tea . . . You can also take a break and eat here. It is open during normal hours.

For the best street markets try one of these:

The Weekend Handicraft Market also known as the Market at Straße des 17 Juni or the *Trödelmarkt* just to the west of the Tiergarten S-Bahn station. Here you'll find everything from jewelry to clothing and sketches to barrettes. It is open from 10 a.m. - 5 p.m. on Saturday and Sunday. Get there early for the best bargains.

The Turkish Market along the bank of the Maybachufer in Kreuzberg is the biggest this side of Istanbul. There are plenty of vendors with oriental spices, food and clothing. The market is only a five-minute walk from the Kottbusser Tor U-Bahn stop. It is normally open from noon to 6:30 p.m. Tues. - Fri.

Berlin's largest weekly fruit, vegetable and flower market, **Winterfeldplatz Market**, takes place near Nollendorfplatz Wed. - Sat. from dawn to about noon.

Weinachtsmarkt (Christmas Market) radiating from Wittenbergplatz takes place every December. There are other Christmas markets in Spandau.

Dining

The choice of a dining spot in Berlin, at least in Western Berlin, is overwhelming—rumor has it that there are more than 6000 restaurants and *Schnell Imbisse*, serving every type of cuisine in the world. You'll find the best Turkish restaurants outside of Turkey serving great aubergine (eggplant), peppers and fresh figs along with spicy lamb kebabs slathered with yoghurt. There are also Chinese, French, Italian, Indian, Japanese, Greek, Thai, Mexican, Cambodian and of course a few German eating spots. Many gourmets compare Berlin's choice of international dining establishments with Paris and New York.

Not so in Eastern Berlin. That part of Berlin has even fewer restaurants than before, as many have closed, unable to cope with exploding capitalism. The restaurants that have remained open have not experimented with international fare, sticking to Berlin basics such as pea soup, lentils, pork, cabbage and potatoes. You may see *Bouletten* or Berlin meatballs on the menu or a variety of sausages—Bockwurst, Currywurst, Bratwurst. There are also plenty of salty things it seems such as pickles and herring.

Beer is the libation of choice in Berlin. They drink their own version of shooters, called a *Molle mit Korn*— beer with a schnapps chaser. The local brew is *Schultheiss*.

Some suggestions, by nationality of the cuisine:
For a taste of old Berlin head into the East. Try **The Last Instant**, Waisenstraße 14-18, tel. 2125528, which is where prisoners were allowed to stop to make their last wish in medieval days, and which claims to be the oldest restaurant in Berlin. It still serves Berlin specialties with a large tourist crowd. **Zum Paddenwirt**, Eiergasse, in the Nicolaiviertel, tel. 21713231, serves large portions of ba-

sic fare. **Die Moewe**, Hermann Matern Straße 118, is located in a series of century-old rooms which was once an actors' club. During the last regime it was a private club for party elite. **Bistro 1900**, Husemannstraße 1, tel. 4494052 is an art nouveau style restaurant. And finally, as in any good German city, head to the **Ratskeller**, Rathausstraße, tel. 2125301, for vaulted ceilings, beer and basic fare.

A "must" is a stop in the **Operncafe**, Unter den Linden 5, tel. 2000256, in a former palace originally built in 1733. A big breakfast will run around $10 and dinner should end up costing around $25-$30 without wine. Upstairs is a more elegant restaurant, **Königin Luise**, with more expensive food and a great view of the avenue. The fresh pastries and cakes are to die for.

For a medieval dining experience try either **Zitadelle**, Am Juliusturm, Spandau, tel. 3342106 or **Tafelrunde**, Nachodstraße 21, tel. 2112141. Both have simple long tables and allow you to eat only with a knife and your fingers. You'll be entertained by Prussian wenches and minstrels. Zitadelle is in an actual medieval castle and saves the banqueting until the weekends. The fixed-price meal runs about $50 per person.

The most expensive Italian food is found at **Ciao Ciao**, Ku'damm 156, tel. 8923612, serving Neapolitan cooking with plenty of red sauces and seafood. **San Marino**, Ku'damm88-9, tel. 3136086, serves inexpensive Italian fare. **Tucci** on Gromanstraße 52, tel. 3139335, is good down-home Italian with fresh pasta. In the Kreuzberg if you want a change from Turkish, try the Italian at **Osteria #1**, Kreuzbergerstraße 71, tel. 7869162. **Rococo**, Knesebeckstraße 92, also has great Italian food.

For French cooking try one of the East German spots **Rôti d'Or** in the Palast Hotel, tel. 2410, or the **Silhouette** in the Grand Hotel, tel. 20920, and bring your wallet. In the West try **Zum Hugenotten** in the Intercontinental Hotel, tel. 26020, or **Chez Moncef**, Budapester Straße 11, tel. 2625123—both are expensive. For cheaper French fare try **Ty Breizh**, Kantstraße 75, tel. 3239932, with cooking from northern France and Brittany, and where the dining experience will be agreeable, down to the bill. Another good French food value is **Cour Carré**, Savignyplatz 5.

The best Turkish cooking is arguably in Kreuzberg, but for those of you who are sticking to the traditional sections of town try **Istanbul**, Knesebeckstraße 77, tel. 3129255, which is between Ku'damm and Savignyplatz in the center of the action. You'll even get belly dancing on weekends. **Karavan** on the Ku'damm 11, serves cheap eats across from the Kaiser-Wilhelm Gedächtniskirche. In Kreuzberg stop at **Merhaba**, Hasenheide 39, tel. 692173, which is one of the best in this part of town. **Hasir**, Adalbertstraße 15, is one of the best values, with good basic food.

For Russian and Ukrainian dishes go to **Moskau** in the east, Karl-Marx-Alee 34, tel. 2792869, near the TV tower.

For Greek, try **Hyperion**, Yorckstraße 90, with real Greek food, not the German version of it, or go to **Taverna Plaka**, Joachimstaler Straße 14, tel. 8831557, **Karagiosi**, Klausenerplatz 5, tel. 7982379 is recommended by many. The cheap **Athener Grill**, Ku'damm 156, tel. 8921039, is open almost all night and serves cafeteria fare.

For Thai food try **Mahachai**, Schlüterstraße 60, tel. 310879, near the Ku'damm; or go to **Grung Thai**, Ku'damm 202, tel. 8815350, for good food with more than a hundred items on the menu but no big bargains.

Nightlife
Berlin has a great reputation for nightlife and the city's entertainment reservoir has a lot more going for it than simply wild discos and risqué cabarets. Berlin is also a world capital by virtue of its orchestras, theater, opera, dance and jazz.

Pick up a copy of *Tip* or *Zitty* for a listing of what's happening in Berlin. Each costs around DM3. *Zitty* is the more outrageous of the two magazines, but both do the job of letting you know what's up. A more mainstream program, with show dates and times as well as museum hours and tours, is called *Berlin Programm Magazin*; it comes out monthly and costs DM2.50.

If you want to head to the opera, theater or symphony concerts you'll have to make reservations in advance. For a commission you can probably pick up tickets at the KaDeWe department store, Wittenbergplatz (tel. 248036);

Centrum at Meinekestraße 25 (tel. 8827611); Europa-Center, (tel. 2617051); the Wertheim department store at Ku'damm 231 (tel. 8822500); Kant-Kasse, Kantstraße 54 (tel. 3134554); Theaterkasse im Palasthotel, Spandauer Straße (tel. (9) 2125258.

For opera check out the **Staatsoper**, Unter den Linden 7, tel. (9) 2054456 which is considered the best in Berlin. **The Deutsche Oper**, Bismarckstraße 34-37, tel. 34144449, is the best in western Berlin.

For classical music try to get tickets to the **Philharmonie**, Matthäikirchstraße 1, tel. 2614383, home of the Berlin Philharmonic Orchestra. The **Schauspielhaus** on Platz der Akademie, tel. (9) 2272129 is home to the East Berlin Symphony. The **Staatskapelle**, Unter den Linden 7, tel. (9) 2054456, associated with the Staatoper, also has excellent orchestral programs.

For jazz head to **Quasimodo**, Kantstraße 12a, in the basement, tel. 3128086. **Flöz** at Nassauische Straße 37, tel. 8611000 and **Eiershcale** at Rankstraße 1, tel. 8825305 also have good jazz, plus check to see if jazz is on tap at **Go-In**, Bleibtreustraße 17, tel. 8817218. In the East try **Haus der Jungen Talent**, Klosterstraße 68-70, tel. (9) 21030.

For disco try **Big Eden** on the Ku'damm 202, tel. 8826120; **Zanzibar**, Nurnbergerstraße 50, tel. 242447; **Metropol**, Nollendorfplatz 5, tel. 2164122; **Lipstick**, Richard-Wagner-Platz 5, is for women only.

The Prenzlauerberg area is the emerging new center of Berlin nightlife. The safe traditional spot is the **Altberliner Bierstuben** at Saarbrucker Straße 17 decorated in old Berlin style. Punk and New Wave rule at **Jugendklub**, and for a look at old East Berlin's only all-night disco head to **Café Nord**. But the best spots in this neighborhood are yet to be discovered.

In the Kreuzberg bars you'll find the greatest concentration of punkers and societal dropouts . . . all seeming to wear black. The section of Kreuzberg near Yorckstraße is a little less wild; you can check out bars such as **Riehmers** or **Café Wirtschaftswunder**. Deeper in Kreuzberg try **Madonna, F.S.K., Bronx, Casino** or **Wienerblut**, all on Wiener Straße.

Accommodations

There are so many places to stay in Berlin that your best bet is a travel agent or check in with tourist information when you arrive. But be advised that Berlin, even with hundreds of hotels, is usually packed. If you are planning on looking for a room when you arrive, get there early . . . no later than noon to insure that there will be space.

I found a small pension outside of the city in the dorf of Seeburg with shared bath through the Potsdam Tourist Office. Ask the Berlin Tourist Office about similar types of accommodations.

Tourist Information

The main tourist office for walk-up information is in the Europe-Center at the end of the Kurfürstendamm. It is open 8 a.m. - 10:30 p.m. daily. Telephone is 2626031.

Other smaller tourist offices are located at the Bahnhof Zoo, in Tegel Airport, in the TV tower at Alexanderplatz, and Dreilinden.

The administrative headquarters for the tourist information is at Martin-Luther-Straße 105. Telephone is 2123/4.

U.S. Embassy

The U.S. Embassy will probably move here from Bonn in the near future, but the current U.S. Consulate at press time is at 170 Clayallee, phone 832-4087.

Journey through the East
Part VIII

The morning came with brilliant sunshine. I wandered into the breakfast room and chatted with the American whom I had gone with to Potsdam and Frau Gerlitz came by beaming an ear-to-ear smile. "*Guten Morgen. Hast du gut geschlaffen.*"

"*Ja,*" I answered and smiled back. "It's going to be a great day to drive to the *Ostsee* (German for the Baltic)."

Her husband came out and we all smiled at each other. I settled my bill and after goodbyes, headed north to discover more of Eastern Germany. I decided to take a back road and zig-zag through the Mecklenburg Lakes District. The sun was shining, it was warm for mid-October, I wasn't in a hurry and no one else seemed to be.

Gransee's strange Cathedral

About 50 kilometers north of Berlin I noticed a walled city with an interesting cathedral sporting a mismatched pair of steeples. Never one to drive past a curiosity, I turned into the town. It was called Gransee. The town walls were virtually all intact and when I drove to the church, I met the pastor, who had been collecting food and clothing to send to Romania.

He was just closing up to go to a meeting, but reopened the church and gave me a tour of the interior which featured a 1744 Baroque organ. I asked about the unusual steeples. He smiled and rubbed his fingers together. "Money," he said, "It has always been a problem. This church was begun in the 1200s but it was not finished until the 1500s. The towers were not added until 1606 and 1711.

It was after a massive town fire that burned 300 houses as well as the church that the people decided to reerect the the church towers. The first to go up was the south tower with the clock. But we ran out of money and had to build the second tower out of wood." He points upward to the steeples. "There you have it. Two different steeples. All because of the same problem we all have today—not enough money."

We all smiled and shook hands. He hurried off to his meeting and I continued my drive to the north.

Winding through the Lakes District

Just to the south of Neustrelitz I turned to the west and headed into the Lakes District. The road on the map showed that it was relatively major, but reality proved that it was only a small two-lane country road. The road twisted along the edges of a dozen lakes. The towns were all tiny and picturesque and none of the lakesides had been developed. It looked as it must have looked centuries ago. I drove through the village of Mirow and crossed a small canal that connected that smaller lake with the larger Müritz See. When I reached the Müritz See I hugged the coastline, twisting along tiny roads to Röbel which is the main town on the Müritz, the largest lake in the region. Boats were cruising on the lake and one of the locals told me that I could take a two-hour tour of the lake by boat for DM10.

I only paused to admire the scenery and kept heading north. I needed to get to Stralsund before mid-afternoon. The countryside was relatively flat and the fields were empty. I passed a palace of sorts in a town called Kittendorf but couldn't find anyone to let me in, so I continued north to Demmin where I stopped in St. Bartholomew Church to see the organ, which had grown with the church. In 1705 it had 22 registers, in 1817 there were 40, and in 1868 it grew to have 50 registers. It is considered on of the best in North Germany. This is another church with a history linked with war and fire. It was first started in 1260 and was finished in 1422 with the completion of the south portal. It was destroyed during the Thirty Years War, rebuilt, then burned down again and rebuilt again. The pulpit is about 20 feet high and the steeple crowning the church rises almost 100 feet.

The next town I passed through, Grimmen, had a series of churches but everything was locked up tighter than a drum.

Searching for a room
in Stralsund and Rügen

Naturally, I managed to roll into Stralsund late. Too late to get to the tourist office. I knew this was going to be tough. I spoke with several people and they pointed out the hotels in town. I stopped in several but the reasonable hotel didn't have any singles and the owner didn't think it would be right to let me stay in a double when a couple would probably show up any minute to rent it . . . in fact a couple arrived as I was walking out. The other hotels in town cost more than I wanted spend (more than DM120). I decided to head out to the island of Rügen since I was planning to drive through there in the morning anyway.

I stopped in the town of Bergen in the center of the island. The only hotel in town, on the main town square, was cheap but abysmal. The serving girl who showed me the room could see that I wasn't too excited about staying there and suggested that I head to the town of Binz, where she assured me I could find a hotel. So, as the sun was setting, I realized that I was facing my Eastern German nightmare—no room at the inn.

I arrived in Binz and stopped at the first pension. "*Voll.*" I understood that to mean in English—full, it sounds the same in both languages. I asked one of the townsfolk where I should look for a place to sleep. He pointed me in the direction of the sea and told me that there were plenty of places.

I turned right, then left, then went across the next street, then left again trying to follow the directions he had given. When I saw some hotels, I parked and went in to ask about rooms for the night. Aha, look at all these hotels. I was certain that there would be a room. After asking at more than a dozen places, I wasn't so sure and was resigning myself to a night in the car or a drive back to Bergen, assuming that the room I had been shown earlier was still available. As I was getting ready to turn onto the highway I decided to try one last hotel. SUCCESS!! They had a room! They had a room for only DM45! I could have danced.

The gingerbread world of Binz

Binz, it turns out, is a beautiful resort. I took my bags up to my room and then walked down to the beach. The sky was moonless and the stars were brilliant. The waves rolled with a dull roar onto the sandy beach and I tiptoed along the edge of the water. Across the water, Danish or Swedish lights sparkled. Lining the beach were gingerbread houses which I planned to see in daylight. I found my first Italian restaurant in an Eastern German city. I kept on wandering down the promenade. I stopped in the Strand Buffet, which was really a local bar, and tried a local brew called Lübzer (maybe from Lübeck) and asked the bartender where he recommended I should eat.

"What do you want to eat?" he asked.

"I don't care, really." I answered. "I would like something good and local and inexpensive."

"Then go next door to Dünanhaus."

I did. It was filled with locals, but they placed me at a table alone. That didn't last long. A couple wandered in and sat with me. They were teenagers who had grown up on the island and were from Binz. They suggested that tomorrow I look for the old fishing villages on the island. They gave a list which I jotted down phonetically—Mittel Hagen, Loppe, Tisso, Alt Reddowitz.

After dinner I wandered through the town and then walked back to my hotel along the beach again playing dodge with the surf and running with the brisk ocean breeze past Binz's tripledecker gingerbread houses.

You could forget you were in Germany here.
This could be any resort town, anywhere in the
world.

The next morning I took an early walk on the beach and then headed to the building which had the breakfast room. It seems that I was in a hotel group which had a central breakfast dining room. I found it. It was filled with hundreds of Germans, all on group tours, all wolfing down brotchen, cooked eggs, and cold cuts. It was the ultimate mass breakfast frenzy.

Driving through old Rügen

I climbed into my car and struck out to see Rügen. I drove down to Sellin, then found some of the old fishing villages the couple at dinner told me to see. One of the old houses was having a new thatched roof constructed and the workers showed me how much effort went into the thatching. These thatched roofs are about three feet thick and very intricate.

I headed back to Stralsund from Rügen. Then when arriving, I decided to drive south to Greifswald which I had heard has a beautiful inner city thanks to the mayor surrendering to the Soviets before they had a chance to level it with an artillery barrage. Still your beating heart. This town is not really worth the effort. I know it was Sunday, but Greifswald was quiet even by Sunday standards, and I fail to see anything worth traveling to see. Sorry. I turned around and headed back to Stralsund.

Stralsund: A pristine gem

Stralsund, on the other hand, really is a beautiful city. The town walls are still standing and the churches were not destroyed during the war for some reason. The tourist office was closed, but I had a few brochures and papers I had picked up from hotels, so I was off on discovery. Stralsund is described in the next chapter.

After leaving Stralsund I took backroads to Rostock. I knew that it was Sunday and that I would have to deal with getting a place to stay once I arrived, but I figured something would work out. The roads along this northern section were lined with trees. I commented on this when I stopped for lunch. An old man at the restaurant chuckled and told me a story about the trees.

"Years ago, when Napoleon was marching across Europe and had conquered this area of Germany, he spoke to one of his engineer officers. 'I want you to plant trees along these roads to shade the troops when they march between the towns.' The engineer, a young captain, said 'But your excellency (or something like that) it will take thirty years for these trees to grow.' Napoleon answered, 'I know, don't you think you should start planting them immediately?' " The heavy-set man chuckled again to himself. "You've got to plan ahead."

Rostock and Warnemünde

The tree-lined roads eventually lead to Rostock. It was raining. I drove through the city, but didn't want to deal with this relatively large city and decided to head north to Warnemünde, the resort area of the town. After my experience with Binz on Rügen, I had learned that seaside resorts had plenty of hotel rooms.

The first hotel I stopped at in Warnemünde, very high rise, had rooms, but to the tune of DM300+. Ouch. I headed down the street and found the Strand Hotel with a room for DM55 with shared bath, and they took credit cards. I said "O.K." I wasn't interested in fighting the rain. After settling in I walked along the beach and then turned into the harbor. Warnemünde had proved to be a good idea. The old harbor was lined with cozy bars and during a break in the rain when I took a walk, I even found a cash machine which would take MasterCard and Visa for cash advances. Oh, wonder of wonders, in Eastern Germany!

The next morning the rain had stopped and Rostock awaited. I took a last walk along the old harbor and had breakfast, then drove into Rostock. I spent the morning there and then drove southward to Schwerin, the last town on my trip.

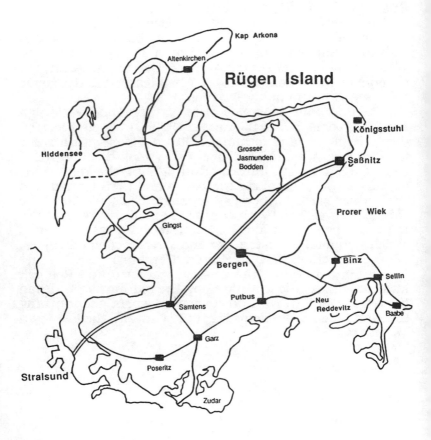

Rügen Island

A trip to Rügen, Germany's largest island, is a journey through natural beauty from the Königsstuhl chalk cliffs plunging a dramatic 380 feet into the Baltic Sea to the two-mile long white sand beach stretching beside the resort of Binz. The island also has fishing villages complete with thatched cottages, as well as prehistoric ruins and a game preserve. More important, if you get to one of Rügen's resorts in the near future you'll have a chance to step back into the vacation whirl of the Roaring 20s, with a walkway along the sea, afternoon tea dances at cafés, evening dancing at hotels, and gingerbread houses little changed since that time.

Rügen has both its remote natural side and its glitzy (compared to the rest of Eastern Germany) aspect. Nature more or less surrounds you everywhere on the island, but is most unblemished along the western and northern sections and on the long, narrow island of Hiddensee, which doesn't even allow motorized transport. Rugen's main port town, Saßnitz, is in the northeast, while the main tourist beach resorts—Binz, Sellin, Baabe and Göhren—are on the eastern peninsula.

The island provides a changing panorama of hills, cliffs, beaches, fields and forests. The twisting coastline is over 350 miles long, an amazing length when you consider that Rügen is only about 30 miles across at its widest point (from Cape Arkona, the northern tip, to Zudar, the southernmost peninsula).

The best way to get around the island is by car. Though there are buses and trains, they run infrequently and require several changes; they also connect only the major cities, and the real beauty of Rügen is in its more remote natural areas.

The major centers worth visiting from a normal tourist point of view are the seaside resorts located in the east-northeast section of the island—Binz and Sellin. If you plan to stay near or on the beach, go to tourist information early, very early. I suggest a room in a private house—it is your best bet, especially in summer. The hotels fill up througout the year with busloads of senior citizens vying for their last dance and vacationing families. Some of the high-rise hotels in Binz have enough rooms for you to catch one vacant in the morning, but bed & breakfast inns fill up almost immediately. Even though this stretch of beaches has more lodging than anywhere else in Eastern Germany other than downtown West Berlin, it is still tough to get a room. (You can camp almost everywhere, though.)

Binz is the first resort you reach after leaving the very forgettable main town of Bergen in the center of the island. It has also recently been connected to the InterCity rail lines, and this makes getting there much easier.

The old town section of Binz might remind a New Englander of Martha's Vineyard or Nantucket. Old three-storey wooden gingerbread houses line the roads and stand looking out over the sea and the three-mile beach. Sandpipers play tag with the surf and a seemingly constant breeze cools the air. At night the lights of Sweden, about 80 miles away, sparkle on the horizon. At the western end of the beach promenade a series of high-rise (six-storey) hotels have been built, but fortunately they do not interfere with the Old World ambiance. There is a youth hostel in Binz right on the beach at Strandpromenade #35 (tel. 2423). Binz-Information is in the middle of the small town tucked away of Heinrich-Heine-Straße (tel. 2215), open Mon. - Fri, 9-11 a.m. and 2-5 p.m., Sat. 9-11 a.m. and 3-5 p.m., closed Sun.

Sellin is only a short drive from Binz or a short narrow-gauge steam train ride on the *Rasender Roland* (Racing Roland), which chuffs along at about 30 miles an hour. You pay approximately $2.50 in each direction and can hop on and off at each station to explore the town. If you travel between Binz and Sellin by car, on the back road, you'll pass the castle-like **Jagdschloß Granitz**, a 19th-century hunting lodge built by one of the island princes. If you are chuffing (excuse me, racing) along on the Roland, alight with the rest of the crowd and hike up, following the signs, to *Tempelburg*. In summer the lodge is open, with wonderful views from the tower after a 154-step climb up a beautiful circular staircase.

Sellin is a more impressive town than Binz, with stately houses and trees lining the main road leading to the beach. This town has fewer hotels than Binz, but seems to have many more bed & breakfast inns. The beach is less convenient, however. You'll have to walk down about 50 stairs to reach the sand stretching below the town's cliffs. Tourist Information, Wilhelm-Pieck-Str. #40, can normally find rooms. Open Mon. - Fri, 9-11 a.m. and 2-5 p.m., Sat. 9-11 a.m. and 3-5 p.m., closed Sun.

A drive further south, or the Roland, takes you to another tourist town, Göhren, where there is a good local history museum and a display of old fishing and farm houses. The tourist office, Elisenstraße #5, can often find rooms when Binz and Sellin are full, and it has all the schedules for buses back to the mainland, as well as information on bicycle rental and boat tours of the island. It is open Mon. - Thurs. 9 a.m.-noon and 1-5 p.m., Fri. 9 a.m.-noon and 4-6 p.m., Sat. 4-6 p.m., Sun. 10 a.m.-noon.

You'll need a car to continue on to **Baabe,** which has a very wide beach and a group of bungalows and campsites but no hotels. The narrow roads then connect a series of old fishing villages such as **Alt-Reddevitz,** where houses all have thatched roofs. These picturesque towns all have many private rooms (*Zimmer Fwrei*) available all year long, but hard to find empty in summer.

Just 8 km. to the south of Bergen is the former royal seat of **Potbus** founded in 1810. Only the terrace remains since the "decadent" palace was demolished by the socialist government in the early 60s, but there are several 19th-century classical buildings looking very neat and white. Locals refer to Potbus as *Weisdorf* or White Town.

The far north of the island is **Kap Arkona**. Bus tours reach here from Saßnitz or drive along the narrow Schaabe, which connects the peninsula to the mainland. Once at the cape, climb the old lighthouse for a great view. Most bus tours to Kap Arkona from Saßnitz will take you via the **Königstuhl**, which is at the top of the chalk cliffs dropping into the Baltic. In this part of the island, don't plan on splendid isolation—be ready for crowds of pushy tourists armed with cameras, especially on weekends.

Stralsund

Stralsund is the northernmost large city in Eastern Germany. The old town center is almost completely surrounded by water, making it seem like an island. We're on the Baltic, which the Germans call the Ostsee. The town is filled with Gothic, Renaissance and Baroque buildings which have been carefully restored to look as they did centuries ago. Stralsund also serves as the gateway to Rügen Island, an unspoiled area with many seaside resorts. The island has only been connected with the mainland by a causeway since 1936; before this the only access was by ferry from Stralsund.

This city, originally founded in 1209, was a leading member of the powerful Hanseatic League, which enjoyed its peak of power in the late 1500s. The Treaty of Denmark between the Hanseatic League and the Danish kingdom was signed here in 1370. But Stralsund's strategic position made it a major chip on the political bargaining table for the next half century. The city remained virtually independent for almost 200 years starting from 1234. During the Thirty Years War it was under seige by Albrecht von Wallenstein's Catholic Army in 1628 but was not conquered. With the Peace of Westphalia in 1648, it was ceded to Sweden. About 160 years later, in 1807 it was taken by Napoleon's troops, then passed to Denmark in 1814 under the Treaty of Kiel, only to be dealt off to Prussia the following year at the Congress of Vienna.

Fortunately, Stralsund's inner city has not been marred by the socialist structuralism which has blighted virtually all the surrounding modern city. We can thank the gods of economics that there was no driving necessity for redeveloping the old town within the medieval walls.

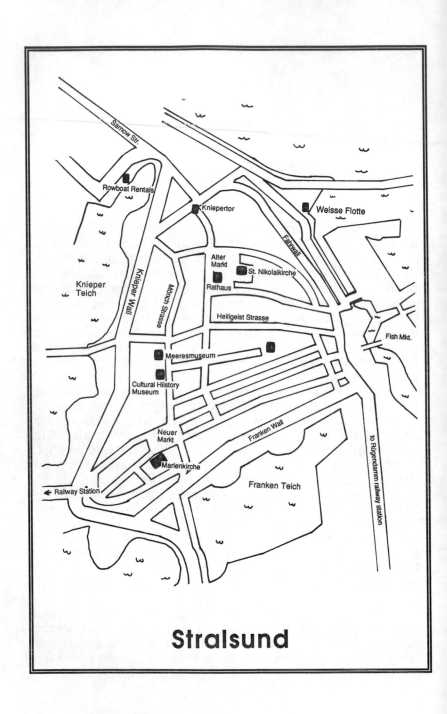

Sarnow Str.

Rowboat Rentals

Kniepertor

Weisse Flotte

Fahrwall

Alter Markt

St. Nikolaikirche

Rathaus

Kniep er Teich

Kniep er Wall

Mönch Strasse

Heiligeist Strasse

Fish Mkt.

Meeresmuseum

Cultural Hiistory Museum

Neuer Markt

Franken Wall

to Rügendamm railway station

Marienkirche

Railway Station

Franken Teich

Stralsund

Nicolaikirche (Church of St. Nicholas)

This huge Gothic brick edifice was built from 1270 to 1350. With no ready source of the limestone we're used to seeing in the great French cathedrals of this period, but with a fine supply of clay for brick, this was the material for interpretation of the Gothic school of church architecture in this part of Germany. It stands almost adjacent to the Rathaus but the entrance is near the rear of the town hall. The interior will be breathtaking and colorful when the renovations are complete. Even now, the arches adorned in bright blues, reds, and greens painted above a sea of soaring white Gothic columns with golden highlights are beautiful.

An ornate 14th-century crucifix, more than 15 feet tall, hangs over a beautiful seven-panel altarpiece and Baroque altar. In the rear of the church a massive organ dramatically rises to the rafters. The 17th-century pulpit is intricately carved and most of the pews were hand-carved in the 1500s.

One section of the the church used to be reserved for merchants. At the entrance a sign in North German dialect reads, *"Dat ken Krämer is de blief da Buten, oder ick schla em up de Schnuten"* which roughly translated means, "If he's not a merchant he'd best keep out, or I'll punch him in the snout."

Marienkirche (Church of Our Lady)

This is the largest church in Stralsund and considered by many to represent the highest achievement in Gothic brick cathedrals. It was built from 1360 to 1380. This church became a center for the Reformation in 1525.

The interior is relatively plain but the organ built in the rear of the church in 1659 by the organmaster Stellwagen of Hamburg is enormous and beautifully carved, with the pipes set in a series of angel-topped columns. Organ concerts are held in summer on special weekends and every other Wednesday evening.

The church tower is 338 feet high and has a viewing platform 293 feet above the square. It is open for those with the stamina to climb the 226 steps of a circular staircase and then 119 more, very steep ones up something very much like ladders between the bells. (If you have any nervousness about heights, don't bother with this climb—the scary part isn't the top of the tower, but those last 119 open stairs . . . and going back down is worse.) From the top the views on a clear day, over the town and across the sound to Rügen Island, are magnificent

Marienkirche is open Mon. - Fri 10 a.m.-5 p.m., Sat. 10 a.m.-12:30 p.m. and 2:30 p.m.-5 p.m., Sun. 2:30 p.m.-5 p.m. Admission to the tower is DM1 for adults and 50 pfennigs for children.

The Alter Markt and Rathaus

This square was once the center of both commerce and politics in the town. The buildings surrounding the Alter Markt (Old Market) all have stories to tell.

The most impressive building, certainly the most impressive front, is the Rathaus (Town Hall) built in the 13th and 14th centuries. The airy façade, rumored to have been built with ransom money collected for kidnapped 14th-century noblemen, is considered one of the high points of Gothic brick architecture in Northern Germany. The upper four storeys, with their arched and round windows leading to six gables, are purely ornamental—the building behind is only two storeys high. Inside the Rathaus a glass-covered two-level gallery lined with columns leads through the building. The city tourist office is located here. Opposite the town hall, an ornate gabled house that belonged to the former mayor, Bertram Wulflum, stands at Alter Markt #5. This red brick merchant's house built in the 1300s features a four-step gable decorated with eight delicate copper turrets. To the left of this building stands another merchant's house with a double Baroque gable. Many other merchants' houses, constructed with warehouse space behind ornate fronts, frame this beautiful square.

Kulturhistorischesmuseum (Cultural History Museum)

This museum is built into the Dominican cloister portion of the St. Katharinen monastery on Mönchstrasse about two blocks north of Marienkirche. It is attached to the church which was turned into the Oceanographic Museum. It traces the history of Stralsund and then some. Exhibits annotated only in German with no English language guide available outline the history of the area from prehistoric times, through the Stone, Bronze, and Iron ages, with tools, combs, needles, jewelry, stirrups, swords and other weapons found in this region. Maps show the trade routes that made Stralsund such a major trading power during the 1500s, and models of the town show its growth from the Middle Ages to the great days as a trading center. The second floor of the museum displays furniture, porcelain art, portraits, pianos, harpsichords and ceramic stoves from patrician houses built in the town's Golden Age. The top floor includes an extensive collection of wonderfully furnished large and small doll houses and dolls, as well as an entire gallery of toys.

Admission: DM3; students,children and seniors, DM1. Open Tues. - Sun. 10 a.m.-5 p.m.

Meeresmuseum (Oceanographic Museum and Aquarium)

This museum is cleverly built into a Gothic church on Mönchstrasse. This church, part of the former St. Katherinen Monastery, was abandoned during the Reformation, turned into a storage house and then into a stable, and eventually taken over by the State during the Communist regime and turned into a museum.

The maritime displays showing the development of the fishing industry and explaining the world beneath the sea are built on three floors under the soaring Gothic arches of this church. In the chancel the skeleton of a giant finback whale hangs where a crucifix once was suspended over the altar. The ground floor displays show the formation of the oceans in one area while elsewhere turtles glide in tanks and octopi frolic to the merriment of school kids. The second floor is dedicated to the fishing industry, with tackle, nets, hooks and displays demonstrating how everything works. The top floor shows life-size models of what many men considered sea monsters—king crabs, giant squid, and massive lobsters.

A hallway takes visitors through several more displays and a small gift shop (check for English-language guides of Rügen and the surrounding area) then steps lead underground to a small aquarium with a fine collection of sea critters. You'll find starfish, sea scorpions, sole, flounder, eels, hermit crabs, sand sharks, Norwegian lobsters, tiny sea ants seen under a magnifying glass, doctorfish, sea perch, and many more, as well as a tank full of playing seahorses.

Admission: DM3 (students,children and seniors, DM1). May through October Open Mon. - Thurs. 9 a.m.-4 p.m., Fri. - Sun. 9 a.m.-5 p.m. November through April Wed. - Sun. 10 a.m.-5 p.m.

Getting around

Stralsund can easily be managed on foot. It takes less than ten minutes to walk from Marienkirche in the south to the Alter Markt in the north. The train station is only across a causeway from the old town. There is an information desk there (little English spoken) which hands out bus information.

Ferry tours of the harbor leave from the pier at Seestraße and cost around $4 for adults and $3 for children. The Weisse Flotte boats, at Fahrstraße #16 (tel. 6020), connect Stralsund with Hiddensee and several Rügen harbors.

Tourist information

The Tourist Information Office is located in the gallery of the Town Hall on Alter Markt (tel. 2439). As I recommend everywhere, get to the tourist office in the early afternoon (2-3 p.m.) for room reservations. Note: Don't plan to arrive on the weekend unless you are arriving quite early Saturday or already have a reservation; the tourist office closes at 11 a.m. on Saturday and doesn't re-open until 2 p.m. Monday, and the other private reservation offices are also closed. Open Mon. 2-5 p.m, Tues. 9 a.m.-12:30 p.m. and 2-6 p.m., Wed. and Thurs. 9 a.m.-12:30 p.m. and 2-5 p.m., Fri. 9 a.m.-12:30 p.m. and 2-4 p.m., Sat. 8-11 a.m.; closed Sat. Nov.-May; closed Sundays.

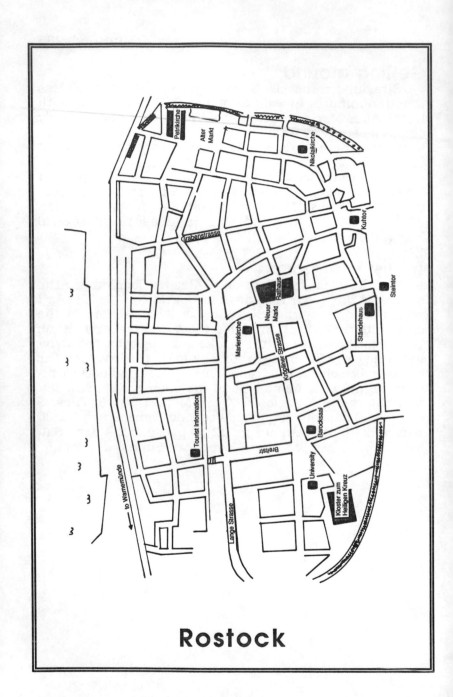

Rostock

Rostock

One of the powerful merchant city-states that formed the medieval Hanseatic League, growing in strength and prosperity as the League grew, this is the largest city on Germany's Baltic coast. A port about five miles inland on the Warnow River afforded good protection as well as access to important continental transportation. In 1419 Rostock began the first university in northern Europe, and the noted astronomer Johann Kepler was a professor here in the 17th century. Rostock suffered through fires and invasions in the Thirty Years War, and was later occupied by Swedes, Prussians, Russians and Napoleon's troops. It wasn't until the development of the local fleet in the mid-19th century that Rostock began to re-emerge economically. After World War I the development of the industrial base of refining, aircraft building and shipyards propelled Rostock again to relatively important economic power in the region. Unfortunately, these very industries made this port a frequent target of British and American bombers during World War II, resulting in the destruction of much of the old town.

Not much of the medieval and Renaissance city remains, but the street plan still bears the clear imprint of the old town walls. Many of the original city gates still stand, and Rostock retains several impressive churches which have been adequately maintained and are now undergoing restoration. And along the inner-city streets many of the gabled façades still grace buildings adding a Renaissance flair to otherwise square Socialist architecture.

About 5 miles downriver where the Warnow empties into the Baltic is the resort and port town of Warnemünde which adds nearby beaches, cozy pubs and much more lodging to what is basically an industrial town.

A walk through the old town

Much of Rostock can be enjoyed from its streets. The *Marienkirche* (Church of Our Lady) and the *Kloster zum Heiligen Kreuz* (Monastery of the Holy Cross), which has been turned into a museum, are the only sights where you have to pay attention to opening times.

Start your walk at the **Tourist Office** at Schnickmannstraße #13/14. It is built in a restored 1795 half-timbered five-storey grain storage building with a brick façade. This street is just off Lange Straße down several steps toward the river. Continue your walk past the brick buildings in the Harbor neighborhood. You'll arrive at a good river vantage point after only two blocks. Turn left, take the next left, and head back toward the town center on **Wokrenterstraße,** which is lined with many reconstructed Rostock-gable houses including the **Hausbaumhaus** built in 1490. It is one of the oldest Gothic merchant houses in Rostock.

Cross Lange Straße and walk down to **Marienkirche** (see Marienkirche section for details) which will be towering to your left. After leaving the church take the walkway to your left, which opens onto *Neuer Markt* (New Market). This square, normally filled with parked cars, is lined with a good collection of colorful gabled houses dating from the end of the 1400s. Opposite stands the **Rathaus** (Town Hall) with its 13th-century Gothic brick superstructure with seven towers topping off an otherwise 18th-century Baroque look.

If you have time, I feel a walk into the section of town behind the Rathaus is well worth the stroll. This is the oldest section of the town, enclosed by walls before the area west of the Rathaus was even conceived. The entire area has fallen into disrepair but much is being fixed up at a feverish pace. Walk down the short Weißgerberstraße across Grubenstraße then up Molkenstraße, cross Wollenweberstraße and continue walking up the same street (the name changes to Am Bliesathsberg). You'll come to a "T" on **Altschmiederstraße**; turn left. This street is a prime example of the recent reconstruction and renovation. In 1989 these houses were only shells, and today they are filled with German yuppies recapturing the past. Altschmiederstraße runs into the Alter Markt (Old Market) dominated by the **Petrikirche** built in the 1252 with a 380-foot tower which for many years served as the main landmark for ships. The church was destroyed during World War II and reconstructed, but without the tower. Behind the church a monument is dedicated to Slüter, one of the leaders of the Reformation, who like Luther, preached in Low German to the working people. From this memorial you get an excellent view of the old town wall.

Leave the Alter Markt and walk down Lohgerberstraße paralleling the town wall. This street used to house the most important craftsmen of the city. At #11 is a typical leatherworker's warehouse built in the 1700s. This street leads to the **Nikolaikirche** (Church of St. Nicholas), not only the oldest church in Rostock, but also the oldest hall church in the region. Just as you arrive at the church you will see an unusual underpass which allows a town street to pass under the altar. The church was originally built in 1250 and has been restored since World War II with the part under the high roof being turned into three storeys of apartments and offices. The interior of the church is also currently under resotration—from the inside and from the outside, you'd never know there were 20 apartments tucked into the church attic.

Walk down the street directly in front of Nikolaikirche to Grubenstraßse (there will be tram tracks in the street here). Walk to your left and you will see the **Kuhtor** (Cow Tower), so called because this was the gate through which the herd were brought back into the town after grazing. This tower is the oldest town wall tower in the northern Germany, built in 1262. A walk around the section of wall here takes you past the **Lagebuschturm**, once a powderhouse, to the **Steintor** here since 1270.

Next to the Steintor is the **Ständehaus** or Registry. This four-storey brick building was constructed in the 19th century and served as the center of the government for mostof this whole region until 1918. The four statues high above the entrance are of dukes from the region of Mecklenburg—from left to right, Johann Albrecht (ruled 1547-1576), Friedrich Franz II (ruled 1842-83); George (ruled 1816-60); and Christian Ludwig (ruled 1747-56).

Near the Steintor you will also find the **Schiffahrtsmuseum** (Ship Museum), August-Bebel-Str. #1, which is filled with models of ships used in the Baltic. Open May to Sept. daily 9:30 a.m.-4:30 p.m; Oct. to April Tues. - Fri. 9:30 a.m.-4:30 p.m. Admission: DM3.

Walk up the main street paralleling the tram tracks back to the Rathaus at Neuer Markt and turn left walking down the pedestrian street, Kröpeliner Straße, lined with many gabled houses. **House #82**, once a rectory, provides Rostock's best example of a late-Gothic gable. You then reach Universitätsplatz which is fronted by the bright yellow **Barocksaal** (Baroque Hall) built in 1750, restored and today still one of the most beautiful reception halls in Northern Germany. It is used as a concert hall and is normally open to the public during weekends. Opposite the Baroque Hall stands an uninspired modern version of a five-gabled house and along the western side of Universitätsplatz is the main building of the University which was built in a neo-Renaissance style in 1870. The original **University** was founded here in 1419 and its alumni include Albert Einstein, Fritz Reuter and Heinrich Schliemann.

Just to the left of the main university building is the attractive *Klosterhof* (cloister entranceway) leading to the **Kloster zum Heiligen Kreuz.** This convent, built in 1270 by the Danish Queen Margarete, was restored and turned into a cultural history museum. Open Tues. - Sun. 10 a.m.-6 p.m. Admission DM3.

Kröpeliner Straße continues to the west ending at the 175-foot high **Kröpeliner Tor** built as an entrance to the city in the 13th century. Today the tower is used for changing art diplays.

Marienkirche (Church of Our Lady)

A church on this spot has been mentioned since 1232, but it was only after one of the support arches collapsed in 1398 that the massive brick church we see today was begun. It was completed in 1440 in a square shape with two crossing naves, each almost 200 feet long and soaring to a height of 100 feet.

The most impressive sights upon entering are a towering Baroque organ, a Renaissance pulpit from 1574, a bronze baptismal font from 1290, and the oak high altar with three paintings—the Last Supper, the Resurrection, and the Coming of the Holy Spirit.

Walk around behind the altar to find one of Europe's true curiosities—a 40-foot-high clock built in 1472 by Hans Düringer and reconstructed in 1643, new technology added. This is not your normal church timepiece. Yes, the Apostles parade at noon and midnight, and there is music on the hour as with many other Glockenspiels, but there's more, lots more. This clock tells not only the time, but also tells a dozen other types of time.

The upper, more ornate clock face is set within intricately carved wood, the symbols of the four Evangelists at the corners. It includes phases of the moon, months, current zodiac sign, and the hour—all very interesting and relatively obvious. But below this clock, requiring a closer look, is a series of ivory etched rings operating in conjunction with the upper clock face. Working from the outside inward to the hub, each ring has a different function. They tell: the day upon which the next Easter will fall, the number of weeks from now to Christmas and until lent, Roman tax time, date of next Sunday, the year, Golden Time (who knows what that is), time of sunrise, the name of the current Saint's day, day of the week, date, name of the month, and finally the current astrological sign of the zodiac. Hold onto your hat—it's all accurate to the year 2017, with no adjustments.

The church tower is open to those willing to brave 300+ steps for a great view of the town and harbor. Admission to the tower is DM1.

The church is open Mon. - Fri. 10 a.m.-4 p.m., Sat. 10 a.m.-2 p.m., Sun. 11 a.m.-noon.

Rostock Zoo

If you like polar bears a visit to the zoo might be worth your while. The collection of these massive white bears at this zoo is one of the best in the world, with many of them bred here. Open May to Sept. daily 8 a.m.-8 p.m; Oct. to April 8 a.m.-5 p.m. Admission: DM3, children and seniors DM2.

Warnemünde

This resort, shipbuilding town and port is only a few miles north of Rostock. If I had my druthers, I'd spend the nights and evenings out here in Warnemünde and take the 25-minute ride on the S-Bahn into Rostock for sightseeing. The old harbor is picturesque and packed with fishing boats, the sandy beach with its two-mile promenade is perfect for walking, there are more hotel rooms here than in Rostock, you have more restaurants from which to choose, and the sailor bars and tourist pubs along Alter Strom (Old River) are lively. And even on days with bad weather there is a heated pool with giant waves to keep smiles on faces of those who came to swim.

Accommodations

Here are the main hotels in descending order of comfort and cost. The **Hotel Warnow** is uninspired but centrally located on Lange Straße; tel. 37381. **Hotel Congress** is geared to business travellers with spartan rooms at St.-Petersburg-Straße 45; tel. 7030. **Hotel Nordland,** Steinstraße 7, in the center of town, may be your best bet, having just been renovated in early 1992; tel. 23706. **Promenadenhotel** on the beach of Warnemünde is better on the inside than it appears on the outside; Seestraße 5, tel. 52782. The **Strandhotel** is, well, old fashioned with most rooms sharing bath and in need of restoration, but rooms are the best value on the beach and they take credit cards; Seestraße 12, tel. 5335.

Getting around

Rostock has an excellent tram and S-Bahn system which connects the railway station with the center of the city as well as connecting service between Rostock center and Warnemünde. A 24-hour tourist card costs DM4. One way tickets range from DM1 to DM2.

Tourist information

The tourist office hands out maps of the town and if you haven't already found a place to stay, it makes lodging reservations at hotels and private homes. Open Mon. - Fri. 9 a.m.-6 p.m., Sat. 10 a.m.-4 p.m., Sun. (May - Sept only) 10 a.m.-4 p.m.

If you arrive at the train station, a new information office offering the most important basics of maps, pamphlets and room reservations will be open Mon. - Sat. 9 a.m.-8 p.m.; closed Sun.

Güstrow

This small low-lying town was once the residence of many of the princes and dukes of Mecklenburg. The Renaissance palace in Fritz-Parr-Platz with its gardens is considered one of the most beautiful in Germany, and the town, which has been very well restored, is also one of Germany's gems.

Güstrow was founded in 1228 on a small tributary of the Warnow, the Nebel River, named for the fog which hangs over the riverbanks for much of the year. It is only about 30 feet above sea level, in the midst of the Mecklenburg lake district; we're directly south of Rostock here, and about 30 miles inland from Warnemünde.

This town prospered by its location on north-south (connecting Rostock and Wismar with Berlin) and east-west (Hamburg to Warsaw) trade routes. The goods traded included herring, salt, grain, fabrics, and a potent "knee-knocking" beer.

Güstrow also sat more or less at the center of the region of Mecklenburg, and the merchants, with their growing prosperity, lobbied the church hierarchy so that this became a cathedral town. It grew as an administrative center from the 13th to the 17th century around the court of regional princes and the dukes of Mecklenburg.

During the Thirty Years War Güstrow sided with the Danish King Christian IV, who was routed in a major battle. Wallenstein conquered the town and took over the castle as a spoil of war. After the Peace of Westphalia Güstrow came under Swedish domination.

The town center is a mixture of neo-Classic, Gothic, Renaissance and Baroque buildings. Besides the Renaissance palace, you'll find a beautiful Gothic church and a collection of small museums.

The town is known among art aficionados as the home town of Ernst Barlach, one of the best known German sculptors, graphic artists and poets, active early in this century. During World War II the Nazis melted down one of Barlach's most famous bronze works, *Der schwebende Engel* (The Silent Angel), to make bullets. The residents have since recreated it from a plaster cast of the original and it hangs in the cathedral.

Dom (The cathedral)

This Gothic Dom is dedicated to Our Lady, John the Baptist and St. Cecilia. It is not the church you see in the center of the town next to the Town Hall; the Dom is located on the town walls at the southwest corner of the old town. (The church in the center of the town is the Pfarrkirche, open daily 10 a.m.-noon and 2-4 p.m.)

Construction of the Dom was started in 1226 and completed over two hundred years later. The Gothic altar is graced by a 1500 painting of The Passion. To the left of the pews is the famous recreated Barlach statue noted above. Make sure to see the *Güstrower Domaposter* (Güstrow Cathedral Apostle), a statue created in 1530.

The cathedral is open daily, 10 a.m.-noon and 2-4 p.m.

Güstrow Schloß

This palace was originally built from 1559 to 1598 as the residence of the Dukes of Mecklenburg and had a colorful history in the Thirty Years War. Rumor has it that Wallenstein, when he resided here with his troops from 1628 to 1630, rode up and down the stairs of the palace on horseback.

The palace went through an additional building phase from 1670 to 1695 under the Swedish king Gustavus Adolphus who built the entrance tower and the stone entry bridge. It is a gorgeous building surrounded by a relatively small but very well-kept garden.

After Gustavus Adolphus's death the palace fell into disrepair. In the 1800s it was turned into a regional work house and eventually became a barracks for those displaced by World War II. Not until 1964 was restoration work begun on the building. The interior was turned into a

Renaissance showpiece by Polish craftsmen who carefully painted and carved architectural details until 1980.

Today, the palace houses the town's art museum featuring 16th century European masters, the ceramic collections, tapestries, concert hall and the town library. In the basement is a restaurant open daily 11:30 a.m.-11 p.m. Open Tues.- Sun. 9 a.m.-12:30 p.m. and 1-5 p.m.

If you arrive in Güstrow on a Monday and the palace is closed, take a walk into the library (open 10 a.m.-6 p.m., closed Thurs., Sat., Sun.) and have a look at the beautiful arches and ceilings which have also been repainted in their original glistening gold and lily white.

Gertrudenkapelle

A small museum dedicated to Barlach's works is in this chapel located at Gertrudenplatz #1. The pieces on display include *Wanderer im Wind* (Wanderer in the Wind), *Mutter Erde* (Mother Earth), *Der Zweifler* (the Sceptic) and the *Gefesselte Hexe* (The Chained Witch). This chapel is located a bit outside of the city walls across the moat only a five-minute walk away. Open Tues.-Sun. 10 a.m.-5 p.m.

Burlach's workshop with over 100 pieces of sculpture and many of his drawings and sketches, is located outside of town on the Inselsee, am Heidberg #15. Open Tues.- Sun. 9 a.m.-noon and 1-5 p.m. (open at 10 a.m. on Wed.)

Museum der Stadt Güstrow (Town Museum)

This small museum is located on Franz-Parr-Platz #7 within sight of the palace. On the ground floor changing exhibits. The second floor is a recreation of what life in the 1700s, with a kitchen, sitting room and other rooms all with original furniture and period paintings.

Open Mon. - Fri. 9 a.m.-noon and 12:30-5 p.m., Sun. 10 a.m.-noon and 2-4 p.m., closed Sat. Admission: DM1.50; 50 pfennigs for children, seniors and students.

Tourist information

The Tourist Information Office is at Gleviner Straße #33 (tel. 61023). Here you can make private room reservations and pick up brochures (in German) and maps. Open Mon. - Fri. 9 a.m.-5 p.m., closed Sat. and Sun.

Schwerin

This picturesque town seems almost an island, surrounded by the water of the Mecklenburg Lake District, about 50 miles south of the Baltic Sea. It is nestled on a narrow section of lowland where ten lakes meet, resulting in a water-surrounded location. The beauty of the setting is matched by a well-preserved *Altstadt* (Old Town) and a palace set on an island, connected with a royal garden.

Schwerin was the last home of the Mecklenburg royal family, who resided in the massive palace until 1918. It has recently become the capital of Mecklenburg-Pomerania, and this has increased the pace of reconstruction and heightened cultural activities.

This city's history started more than 800 years ago, making it the oldest in Mecklenburg. It was founded in the 12th century by Henry the Lion. The Slavic tribe that had occupied the region called it "Zuarin," meaning "animal land." The name more or less stuck through the centuries.

During the Thirty Years War, the entire Mecklenburg region was devastated. Wallenstein stormed Schwerin, then left to take up residence in nearby Güstrow, and eventually the Swedes took over this city as they did most of Mecklenburg. The disaster of losing the war was followed twenty years later by a devastating fire that destroyed almost all the dwellings in town. It wasn't until the early 1700s that Schwerin began to come back to life, but strong growth didn't begin until the mid-1800s when the city and palace took on their current appearance.

Today the town allows visitors to combine history, natural beauty, and relaxation. Wander through the *Altstadt* streets, tour the *Schloß*, wander through the gardens or take a boat ride (motor or rowboat) on the surrounding lakes.

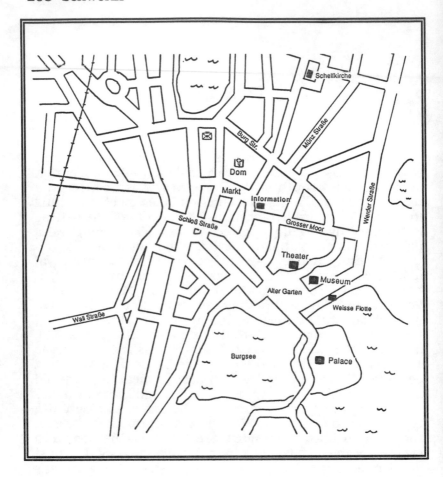

Markt (Market) and the Altstadt (Old Town)

Markt, the old center of the town, offers a pleasing splash of pastel Renaissance houses and the unusual town hall, consisting of four connected timber-framed houses with a neo-Gothic façade constructed in stages from 1351 through 1835, and the nearby **Neuen Gebäude** (New Building) built in 1783 and fronted by 14 Doric columns. A section of the **Historical Museum**, depicting the history of the city, is located in the Neuen Gebäude (open Tues. - Fri. 10 a.m.-5 p.m., Sat. and Sun. 2-5 p.m.).

Most of Old Town Schwerin has been turned into a pedestrian zone. Broad Mecklenburgstraße and narrow Buschstraße, Schmiedestraße and Schusterstraße are all filled with old houses and tiny boutiques and shops. Just to the north of the pedestrian zone on what once was, and might still be, Pushkinstraße, is the Baroque **Schelfkirche**, whose ornate beauty is well worth the walk.

Dom (Cathedral)

The cathedral, located just off the Markt, is an excellent example of Northern German brick Gothic. Originally there was another church here, erected as early as 1171. This church dates from 1270, most of it built during the 14th and 15th centuries, and it is the oldest edifice in town.

Inside, the unusual stripe painting decorating the ceiling and columns adds a different dimension. The very size of the cathedral adds to its magnificence—it is over a football field long, with a width of 94 feet. Make sure to examine the 14th-century bronze baptismal font, the intricate altar painting created by Gaston Lenthe in the 19th century, the altar triptych donated by the bishop in 1495, the ornate organ built in 1871 and, in a small chapel (*Marienkapelle*), what remains of the original paintings that adorned the walls in the Middle Ages.

The 380-foot high tower, added to the cathedral only in the last century, offers a panoramic view of the town and the surrounding lakes. Entrance is DM1 for adults and 25 pfennigs for children for the more than 200-step climb to the viewing platform at 320 feet.

On Wednesdays in summer there are organ concerts at 8 p.m.

Alter Garten (Old Garden)
with Staatliches Museum (State Museum)
and Theater

This art museum, located in a grand neo-Classical building, stands on the Alter Garten (Old Garden) across from the massive ornate palace. This square with its surrounding buildings, created where royal gardens once grew, has been used for years as the venue of important town gatherings and military parades.

The museum has an excellent collection of Dutch and Flemish masters from the 17th century, thanks to the wild passion for Dutch art of Duke Christian Ludwig II. Upon entering the gallery you walk into five Gerard Dou paintings, then an alcove filled with still lifes, then a parade of masterpieces by Rembrandt, Rubens, Bols, Hals and others. There is a grouping of paintings by Brueghel which is worth an extended pause, including *Nymphs with Satyrs* and *John the Baptist Preaching*. Downstairs, the museum displays porcelains, glasswork, jewelry, furniture, and woodcarvings, and has rooms for changing displays of contemporary art.

Open Tues.- Sun. 10 a.m.-5 p.m. Admission charged. Next door, to the right on the Alter Garten, is the Theater. Tickets are available through the tourist office for many of the performances. The theater itself is wonderful, with three levels of white balconies undulating above the orchestra, all set beneath a white and gold ceiling. Even if you are only there for the day and haven't time for a musical or theatrical performance, be sure to look into the foyer to see the splendid, ornate decor.

Schloß Schwerin (Schwerin Palace)

This majestic palace has the perfect setting on its own tiny island where two lakes meet. During the summer ducks and swans swim across the placid lake and drooping weeping willows line the shores, making for plenty of pleasant spots for a picnic.

From the town a bridge leads to the monumental entrance dominated by a massive statue of Niklot (the last pagan prince before Henry the Lion) on horseback, which faced the Alter Garten. The actual entrance to the interior and museum is through the Garten portal, around the palace to the right.

Palaces and castles have been built on this spot for almost a thousand years. Arab traders mentioned the island in their writings and the king of the original Slavic tribe that settled here built his castle on this spot, which was eventually beseiged and taken by Henry the Lion.

When the Mecklenburg line came to power they took up residence here in the mid-1300s.

Much of the palace as it stands today was built between 1843 and 1857, after it had fallen into disrepair. The new palace was inspired in many ways by the famous châteaux of the Loire Valley in France, especially Chambord near Orléans. But Schwerin Palace has many more towers and is much more ornate. The plans for the new palace were created by an auspicious group of architects: Semper, of Dresden fame, made some original sketches which were then modified by Demmler, the court architect, and the final building phase was directed by yet another architect, Stüler, after Demmler made some politically incorrect remarks favoring democracy.

Only four historical parts from the 16th and 17th centuries remained a part of the palace—the rooms above the kitchen, the Bishop's house, the New Long House, and the Chapel. But these old sections, combined in the varying designs of different architects, create a pastiche of architectural styles that blends effortlessly.

In all, fifteen turrets, both large and small, and at differing heights, crown this 80-room building. The monumental entrance under the aforementioned statue of Niklot is actually a massive archway. Behind it towers the main cupola topped by a statue of Michael the Archangel. The main tower, facing the palace gardens, is 227 feet high and was one of Semper's original ideas.

You enter the palace through terra cotta pillars emblazoned with medallions depicting the muses and the seasons. A wide, marble circular staircase sweeps you up to the *bel étage*, the living and social quarters of the Mecklenburg princes. Before getting to that floor, though, you might take a few minutes to explore the Archeological Museum on the floor just below the royal apartments.

Upon entering the restored royal apartment sections of the palace you wander through the **Silvester Gallery** with its ersatz marble walls, stucco pilasters, ornate fireplace and six frescoes of allegorical scenes of the seasons and the times of the day. Throughout the palace the highly polished inlaid wooden floors and wall panels are of special interest.

The next room is the **Woodpaneled Room** with beautiful carvings and a stained glass window depicting the legend of St. Catherine. The **Red Audience Room** with its timbered ceiling was one of the primary living rooms. It opens into the circular and sunny **Tea Room** or **Winter Room** with wonderful views into the palace gardens. The **Flower Room** in the tower with deep mirrored window recesses has direct access to the gardens. Above the windows are medallions of women holding flowers.

One floor above is the festive level and state rooms. Here, depending on how the palace tour is organized during your visit you'll probably first enter the **Library** with its floor-to-ceiling shelves and busts of Schiller and Goethe. The **Billiard Room** has a model of the old castle and pictures of the new palace. The **Ancestors Gallery** is filled with massive paintings of the dukes of Mecklenburg displayed across from large windows opening on the garden below. Many of the more recent paintings are originals. However, some are reproductions.

The **Throne Room** is spectacular with Carrara marble columns, guilded stucco, massive ceiling frescoes, ornate cast-iron doors, red silk wall coverings and fine decorated wooden floors. The throne itself dates from 1750.

On your way out of the castle you'll probably pass through the **Gallery of Castles** with frescoes depicting various castles of the royal family, all painted in 1857.

After visiting the palace walk across the bridge to enjoy a stroll through the 18th-century Palace Gardens with its cross-shaped canal and pools.

In the basement, or Grotto, of the palace is the regional **Technical Museum** (open Mon. - Fri. 10 a.m.-4 p.m., Sat. Sun. and holidays noon-4 p.m.)

The palace and Archeological Museum are open Tues. - Sun. 10 a.m.-5 p.m. Admission: DM3 adults; DM1.50 children, students and seniors.

Mecklenburg Folk Museum

For those who want to get a taste of the Mecklenburg farmer's lifestyle, this museum just outside of town offers such an opportunity. It provides thatched-roof farmhouses furnished much as they were in the past and still are in many areas today. Open Tues. - Sun. 9 a.m.-5 p.m. Admission: DM1 adults; 50 pfennigs children and seniors.

Getting around

Schwerin has a good tram and bus system that loops around the Altstadt without ever disturbing the old streets. The railway station is a bit out of the old town, but within walking distance of Markt and the tourist office.

You can rent rowboats for about DM4 an hour to the right side of the bridge (heading to the palace), or take a short walk to the left to the Weisse Flotte dock for a cruise of the surrounding lakes; these leave throughout the day.

Tourist information

The Schwerin information office is located at Markt #11 (tel. 812314) where you can buy maps and make private room reservations. Open Mon. - Fri. 10 a.m.-6 p.m., Sat. 10 a.m.-3 p.m., closed Sun.

Head down to Körnerstraße #18 and follow the signs upstairs to a tiny room. Here a wizened woman opens a rental agency at 4 p.m. and often has rooms when the tourist office has filled everything they have, or has already closed.

Journey through the East
Epilogue

When I had arrived in Schwerin, I was stuck in the mother of all traffic jams. I parked my car and walked rather than sit in traffic. A local directed me to the tourist office where I learned that they had no more rooms. The lady in the office directed me to a private *Zimmervermittler* who fixed me up with a room at the edge of town.

I drove to the apartment and met my hosts, a couple about 50 years old. They had been part of East German society for almost their entire life. We spoke briefly, they gave me tram tickets, explained the tram schedule and carefully told me which number to catch and where to get off; then I struck out for the town and dinner. I had an uneventful night, simply wandering through the town. When I got home everyone was sleeping. I wrote for a while and then looked around the living room, in which I was staying. I noticed the family's bookshelf. There were dozens of books extolling communism.

I counted 36 volumes of the works of Marx and Engels, 40 volumes of the works of Lenin, and other books such as the Soviet October Revolution, a biography of Ernst Thälmann, The Russian Wonder, Clarification of Fascism and a couple of dozen other books. These had been True Believers.

The next morning the husband was off at the dentist, but his wife was ready with an excellent breakfast and had put bread, cheese and cold cuts aside for me to make a sandwich to take along with me on my drive to Hamburg. I asked her what her husband had done in the old regime.

Eastern Germany's middle class

"He was a policeman," she answered, "But he's not working now. They don't want any old police now." I ate my rolls and sipped my coffee while she told me about what life had been like before the unification.

"My husband and I were comfortably existing in the old system. There was not much we could buy, but we didn't need much. We own our home. My husband had a good job and my children were in the university." She looked at me as if to ask, "Can anyone want anything more?"

"You are the first American I have had a chance to speak with, the first I've met who speaks German. Life here was not all that bad. From reading the papers it seems that everyone in the West thought we were suffering here. We didn't have the things you had but our life was not so bad." She went over to get me another cup of coffee.

"We had good kindergarten programs. When my children were younger I could take them to day care for DM25 a month while they were younger than three. When they were older the cost was less, only DM14 a month. That way I could work and help to support the family."

She pointed out the window and said, "Out there today there is nothing like that anymore. I can't imagine how women will be able to work."

"I wanted to go somewhere in the car the other day. I can't afford gas any more. Before, at least I could afford gas to go where I needed to go. Before we could go on vacation for DM140 for two full weeks. We would stay at our union hotel on a lake and have a chance to relax. That's impossible now."

She takes the cold cuts that I left on my plate and puts them between a couple of slices of bread. "Do you want any mustard? This will be good on your trip. I know you have to go, but my husband will be back any moment and he wants to say goodbye."

We moved to the living room and she pointed to several pictures of her with a group of nurses. "I've been working at a nursing home. They've cut the staff by 50 percent. I'm lucky I still have my job. My husband has been a policeman all his life, but now he's 57 and has no job. Now we don't know whats going to happen. Will he have a pension? Will I have a pension? We don't know. We have worked hard within one system and now it has been ripped out from under us. It makes everyone very nervous."

"Losing your job is bad enough, but to lose your pension and to have nothing with which to live when you grow old is even more difficult."

She walked across the room and picked up another photo. "This is my daughter. She just graduated from the university with a degree in in philosophy. She was ready to take a position teaching in the high schools. Now there is nothing. Her career basically has been eliminated by the new government."

We heard fumbling at the door latch. "Ah, my husband is coming home." He walked in and extended his hand. "Good morning. I trust my wife took good care of you."

"Yes," I replied.

His wife quickly said, "He has leave. He's going to Hamburg today then flying to Amsterdam. He waited to say goodbye."

Herr Braun nodded and smiled. "Yes, have a good trip. It was very interesting for me to meet you and to speak with you. I have many people come, but you seemed interested in us. I hope you have learned something about what life was like for us before and what it is like now."

". . . the hardest part for me? . . . I didn't see."

"Thank you, I really enjoyed the short time we had together. Thank you for showing me how to get around the town and for the hospitality." I had already put my bags in the car and was heading out the door when I decided to ask Frau Braun one last question. "I know that you lived within the Communist system and you have many good things to say about life then and you have problems with life now, but what was the worst thing about living under the DDR government in those years?"

She answered me slowly. "I want you to know that many of us believed in what we were doing. We knew that we were not living the good life that we saw in the West, but we were told that we were sacrificing so that everyone could live better. We recognized that. The biggest disappointment to me and to my husband was that our leaders betrayed us. *We* sacrificed and *they* lived the good life. We thought we were working to build a better life and they were destroying the country and destroying our industry instead of building it. Many people were just like us, who believed in the ideal of the system and were betrayed by our leaders."

She took my hand and looked directly at me and said clearly, "I remember when I was a little girl after the war when the country was in ruins and Hitler had been defeated. I remember asking my mother, 'Didn't you see that Hitler was leading the country to ruin?' I remember her answer—'No, I really thought we were doing the right thing.' Now, today I have to answer the same question from my children, and I find it hard to believe, but my answer has to be the same to them as my mother's was to me." She squeezes my hand and says, "That's the hardest part for me. I didn't see."

We looked at each other for a few seconds. She broke the silence. "Go, you'll miss your flight."

I said goodbye again and walked to my car. I'm lucky, I can drive away. The people of Eastern Germany have to restart their lives and learn to wrestle with a new system.

Tourist Information Offices and Phone Numbers

These phone numbers have been gleaned from scores of magazines, faxes from regional tourist offices, the German National Tourist Office, and other guidebooks.

Nothing in this list is cast in stone:

The number in parenthesis is the city code. (NOTE: these are changing rapidly, and change within Eastern Germany depending from where you are calling.)

The offices addresses, where the street refers to a Communist hero, will also probably change. Where the term "Reisebüro" is noted, you can also expect changes since those numbers belong to the state-run tourist offices which formerly were in each town.

Where fax numbers are noted, do not assume dedicated fax lines. Often you will have to call during business hours and ask someone in the office to switch you to fax. (The word FAX seems to be universal.)

Altenberg Tourist Office
Hauptstraße 24
8242 Altenberg
tel. (52696) 5852

Bad Berka Information
Markt 10
5302 Bad Berka
tel. (6218) 22012

Bad Doberan Information
tel. (8203) 2154

Bad Frankenhausen-Info
Anger 14
4732 Bad Frankenhausen
tel. (4568) 233

Barth-Information
Lange Straße 51
2380 Barth
tel. (8281) 2464

Bautzen Information
Hauptmarkt 5
8600 Bautzen
tel. (54)534242, 42016

Berlin Information
Martin Luther Straße 105
tel. (30) 2123
fax (30) 21232520

Berlin Information
at Europa Center
tel. (30) 2626031

Cottbus Information
Altmarkt 4
7500
tel. (59)24254

Demmin Information
tel. (990) 56321

Dessau Information
Friedrich Naumann Str. 12
4500 Dessau
tel. (47) 4661

Dresden Information
Prager Straße 10/11
8010 Dresden
tel. (51) 4955025
     (51) 4841990
fax (51) 4952264
     (51) 4841991

Eisleben Information
Hallesche Straße 6
4250 Eisleben
tel. (443) 2124

Eisenach Information
Bahhofstraße 37
5900 Eisenach
tel. (632) 76161/2

Erfurt Information
Krämerbrücke &
Bahnhofstr.
5010 Erfurt
tel. (61) 23436 Krämerbr.
     (61) 26267 at
     Bahnhof

Greifswald Information
tel. (834) 3460

Grimmen Information
tel. (827) 21129

Güstrow Information
Gleviner Str. 33
2600 Güstrow
tel. (851) 61023

Halberstadt Information
Spiegelstr. 12
3600 Halberstadt
tel. (926) 21803

Halle Information
Kleinschmieden 6
4020 Halle
tel. (46) 23340

Hohnstein Tourist Office
Rathausstr. 10
8352 Hohnstein
tel. (52895) 228

Jena Information
tel. (78) 24671

Leipzig Information
Sachsenplatz 1
7010 Leipzig
tel. (41) 79590
fax (41) 281854

Lübben, Tourist Office
Lindenstraße14
7550 Lübben
tel. (586/584) 2181, 3090

Magdeburg Information
Alter Markt 9
3010 Magdeburg
tel. (91) 31667

Meiningen Reisebüro
Gerogstraße 27
6100 Meiningen
tel. (676) 2173

Meissen Information
Am Frauenkirche 3
8250 Meissen
tel. (53) 4470

Moritzburg Tourist Office
at the palace, am Schloß
8105 Moritzburg
tel. (5197) 356, 441, 494

Mühlhausen Information
Görmarstr. 57
5700 Mühlhausen
tel. (625) 2912

Naumberg Information
Lindenring 38
4800 Naumberg
tel. (454) 2514

Neubrandenburg Info
Pfaffenstraße 11
2000 Neubrandenburg
tel. (90) 2267, 6187

Neustrelitz Reisebüro
Am Markt 7
2080
tel. (991)3050

Nordhausen Information
Rautenstr. 2
5500 Nordhausen
tel. (?) 4938

Pirna Sächsische-
Schweiz-Information
tel. (56) 85235

Potsdam Information
Friedrich Ebert Straße 5
1501 Potsdam
tel. (33) 21100, 23385
fax (33) 23012

Rudolstadt Reisebüro
Am Günterbrunnen 1
6820 Rudolstadt
tel. (7926) 22150

Rostock Information
Schnickmannstr. 13/14
2500 Rostock
tel. (81) 25260
fax (81) 34602

Rügen Information
Binz: (82791) 291
Baabe: .(82793) 218
Bergen: (827) 21129
Göhren: (8303) 306
Putbus: (82791) 271
Saßnitz: (?) 22382
Sellin: (82793) 293

Schwerin Information
Markt 11
2750 Schwerin
tel. (84) 812314, 864509

Stralsund Information
Alter Markt 15
2300 Stralsund
tel. (821) 252251

Suhl Information
Steinweg 1
6000 Suhl
tel. (667)20052

Torgau Reisebüro
tel. (407)2433

Weimar Information
Marktstraße 4
5300 Weimar
tel. (621) 2173

Wernigerode Information
Breit Straße 12
3700 Wernigerode
tel. (927)3035

Wismar-Service
Stadthaus am Markt
2400 Wismar
tel. (824) 2958

Wolgast Information
tel. (836) 5256

Wustrow Information
Strandstraße 11
2598 Ostseebad Wustrow
tel. (8258) 557

Wittenberg Information
Collegienstr. 8
4600 Wittenberg
tel. (451) 2239, 2537

Zittau Information
Rathausplatz 6
8800 Zittau
tel. (522)3986

Zwickau Information
Hauptstraße 46
9540 Zwickau
tel. (?) 5433

**German National
Tourist Offices**
• **New York:**
122 E. 42nd St.
New York, NY 10168
tel. (212) 661-7200
• **Los Angeles:**
11766 Wilshire Blvd
Suite 750
Los Angeles, CA 90025
tel. (310) 575-9799

GermanRail
(see page 19)

International Road Signs

 Men at Work

 Narrowing Road

 Traffic Light Ahead

 Curves

 Crossroads

 Rough Road

 Offset Crossroads

 School Crossing

 Road Junction

 Pedestrian Crossing

 Railroad Crossing

 Falling Rocks

 No U Turn

 Do Not Enter

 No Passing

 Road Closed

 Quiet Zone

 No Cars Allowed

 Speed Limit

 No Left Turn

Metric Conversion Table

1 inch	= 25 millimeters	1 once	= 28 grams
1 foot	= 0.3 meter	1 pound	= 0.45 kilos
1 yard	= 0.9 meter	1 kilogram	= 2.2 pounds
1 mile	= 1.6 kilometers	1 kilometer	= .62 miles
1 sq. yd.	= 0.8 sq. meter	1 centimeter	= 0.4 inch
1 acre	= 0.4 hectars	1 hectar	= 2.5 acres
1 quart	= 0.95 liters	1 meter	= 39.4 inches
50 kpm	= 31 mph	100 kph	= 62 mph

Temperature Conversion Table

°Centigrade	°Fahrenheit
0° C	32° F
10° C	50° F
15° C	59° F
20° C	68° F
25° C	77° F
30° C	86° F
35° C	95° F

To convert from Fahrenheit to Celsius (Centigrade), subtract 32 and multiply by 5/9.

To convert from Celsius (Centigrade) to Fahrenheit, multiply by 5/9 then add 32.

Help us do
a better job

The research for this book is an ongoing process. In a part of the world like Eastern Germany everything is changing in quick time. By the time you take your trip, phone numbers will be different, street names are changing, there will be scores of new restaurants, and dozens of new hotels, pensions and bed & breakfasts .

If you find a hidden sight, small town, exceptional restaurant or hotel, which you feel should included, please let me know. Your input will help me keep abreast of the changes and make the next edition that much better.

If there is anything within these pages which is misleading or has changed let us know that as well.

Send your suggestions and comments to:

Charlie Leocha
Eastern Germany Guidebook
World Leisure Corporation
P.O. Box 160
Hampstead, NH 03841

JOURNEY NOTES & DOODLES